THE PERCEPTION OF WORK IN TOKUGAWA JAPAN

A Study of Ishida Baigan and Ninomiya Sontoku

Eiji Takemura

University Press of America,® Inc.
Lanham • New York • Oxford

Copyright © 1997 by
University Press of America,® Inc.
4720 Boston Way
Lanham, Maryland 20706

12 Hid's Copse Rd.
Cummor Hill, Oxford OX2 9JJ

All rights reserved
Printed in the United States of America
British Library Cataloguing in Publication Information Available

Library of Congress Cataloging-in-Publication Data

Takemura, Eiji.
The perception of work in Tokugawa Japan : a study of Ishida
Baigan and Ninomiya Sontoku / Eiji Takemura.
p. cm.
Includes bibliographical references and index.
1. Ishida, Baigan, 1685-1744--Contributions philosophy of work. 2.
Ninomiya, Sontoku, 1787-1856--Contributions in philosophy of
work. 3. Work--Japan--Philosophy--History. 4. Shingaku--History.
I. Title.
BJ971.S5T34 1997 306.3'6'0952--dc21 97-33154 CIP

ISBN 0-7618-0886-8 (cloth: alk. ppr.)

∞™ The paper used in this publication meets the minimum
requirements of American National Standard for information
Sciences—Permanence of Paper for Printed Library Materials,
ANSI Z39.48—1984

For N.T.

Contents

Preface   vii

Acknowledgements   ix

Special notes   xi

Part I   Work in Tokugawa Japan: An overview

Chapter 1   Introduction   3

Chapter 2   The concept of 'work' in Tokugawa Japan   23

Part II   Ishida Baigan

Chapter 3   Ishida's thought on work and the economy   49

Chapter 4   Skill, management, and workers' initiatives in Ishida's thought   75

Chapter 5	The spread of Ishida's thought on work	93

Part III Ninomiya Sontoku

Chapter 6	The idea of work in the thought of Ninomiya Sontoku	109
Chapter 7	The *shiho* programme	137
Chapter 8	Ninomiya's work thought and the peasants' perception of work: An analysis	181

Conclusion	193
Bibliography	209
Index	227

Preface

The study of work in the Tokugawa period by intellectual historians has revealed the linguistic and ritual ways in which work was ideologically represented during that time. Work, however, is not an activity which belongs only to the realm of ideology; the actual 'form' of work is dictated by economic and technological factors. This study focuses on Ishida Baigan and Ninomiya Sontoku, who both acted as key channels through which ideology and economy were amalgamated, the meaning of work identified and intellectual expression given to it.

Ishida and Ninomiya are often cited as role models used by the late-Meiji and prewar governments to impose self-sacrifice and blind submission onto the people, rather than as media for the social construction of work in the Tokugawa years. Few Japanese scholars specialising in Ishida and Ninomiya are familiar with the theoretical, empirical and anthropological studies of work developing in Western scholarship; attempts have yet to be made to approach the thought of Ishida and Ninomiya from such perspectives, and, as a result, their importance in the social construction of work in the Tokugawa era has not been fully acknowledged.

Neither of the two thinkers advocated passive adaptation to a portional role in society, nor submission to a particular role given by a superior: Ishida argued for a worker's active participation in decision-making in business affairs and for skills to maintain efficiency in the implementation of collective tasks (inter-personal and managerial skills). Ninomiya advocated the management of time, technology and the labour force in pursuing agricultural work. Ishida spoke of work for the benefit of the long-term prosperity of the household; Ninomiya viewed work not only as the means to secure the material prosperity of an individual but as a 'cumulative agency' for the successive betterment of the household for generations to come. In contrast to the accepted view of them as thinkers exclusively in favour of submission and hard labour, they acted as intermediaries through which elements of management and long-term vision were incorporated into the concept of work.

Acknowledgements

This book grew out of the thesis which I presented to the University of London. During the years spent researching and writing this book, I have run up a long list of debts, intellectual and otherwise, to many scholars and friends both in England and in Japan. At the School of Oriental and African Studies, London, Professors Timothy Barrett and Martina Deuchler, and Drs. Sugihara Kaoru and John Breen were kind enough to read and comment on various parts of the manuscript in different stages of completion. I benefited also from the comments of numerous scholars at various seminars and conferences at which parts of this thesis were aired. Professors Nakaoka Tetsuro and Nagano Hiroko, and Dr. Frank Dikottor have made invaluable comments at postgraduate seminars held at SOAS. Professors Sugihara Shiro and Fujita Teiichiro have kindly read and commented on my early Japanese scripts. I should also mention the participants in the Centre Seminar of Japan Research Centre (SOAS) in December, 1993, and in the *Nihon Keizai Shisoshi Kenkyukai* Seminar held at Rikkyo University in Tokyo in March of 1993 and 1997, for their useful comments.

I benefited from Professor Saito Osamu's wise counsel, as well as from consultations with Professors Odaka Konosuke, Yasumaru Yoshio, Wakita Osamu, Oto Osamu, Denda Isao, Minamoto Ryoen, Sawai Toru and Komuro Masamichi, all of whom gave me opportunities for fruitful discussions.

I must also record my gratitude to another group of people, without whose varied assistance this book would never have been published. Sanwa Bank Foundation offered research grant at the early stage of this project. Enduring financial support from Takemura Ken'ichi, my father, is very much appreciated. Finally, the most profound thanks go to my wife, Nobuko, for her support particularly in moments of great crisis.

Special notes

Japanese names are listed in native order; surname first, given name second (with the exception of the author's name on the title page). Japanese names and places are written in roman letters (except 'Ishida Baigan' and 'Ninomiya Sontoku' at their very first appearance). Apart from names and places, Japanese words are written in *italics*; but the terms in familiar use in this field of study are written in *italics* only at their first appearance in each chapter. Japanese words are transcribed according to the standard modified Hepburn romanisation.

Square brackets are used in quoted extracts to denote comments and interjections which do not appear in the original text, and also surround original Japanese words in the quotations. Square brackets are also used to surround reference numbers where these cannot be placed within the text.

Publication dates for the series volumes; the publication date of the particular volume(s) used is listed, except *Ninomiya Sontoku Zenshu*, which started publication in 1927 and culminated in 1932, and series volume dictionaries and encyclopedias such as *Nihon Kokugo Daijiten* (Shogakukan, 1972-1976) and *Nihonshi Daijiten* (Heibonsha, 1992-1994).

PART I WORK IN TOKUGAWA JAPAN: AN OVERVIEW

Chapter 1

Introduction

Objectives
Recent studies on work in industrial societies have shown that economic activity - even 'work' itself - is not just a matter of the objective character of jobs, pay, market forces or security, but is fundamentally related to people's *perception* of them. Influential factors here are the values placed on work by society and the identity which people hold in relation to them.[1] These values are, in Patrick Joyce's words, often socially *constructed* through their intercourse with such elements of society as politics, kinship, and religion, the development of which started well before the industrialising process itself.[2] Such 'cultural values' form shared conceptions about work beliefs and behaviour that are considered desirable within a group or society. Members aspire to these beliefs, and their behaviour at work is influenced by them. This fact directs our attention to the origins of worker's attitude in the industrial age, or, more specifically, to the ways in which the perception of work

developed in pre-industrial times.

To understand how people respond to industrial change, it is important to examine what kind of people they were at the beginning of the process, and to take account of continuities as well as new ways of thinking. It is the subtle interplay between culture and society, between the social and institutional factors that existed during the pre-industrial period and those that predominated during the industrialising process that decisively affect the way industrial work emerges.[3] Of the former factors, the politico-administerial framework and ethical teachings at the popular level contribute considerably to the construction of work as a concept. While the actual 'form' of work (how people pursue productive and other economic activities) is dictated by the technological changes the production process necessitated, political and ethical frameworks determine the way work comes to be perceived. Because these perceptions are important in determining the standard of discipline and incentive in an industrialising society, they also affect actual economic performance.

This study is concerned with this process of the development of work as a social construct with particular reference to pre-industrial Japan. It explores how work was perceived, conceptualised and diffused in the mid-to-late Edo period (1600-1868), through the examination of the thought of *Ishida Baigan* (1685-1744) and *Ninomiya Sontoku* (1787-1856), two of the preeminent thinkers of that era. Both men are worthy of investigation, for they acted as a medium for the social construction of work at that time: neither being alienated from the Tokugawa commoners and their form of economic activities. The two thinkers interwove the prevalent ideology and the 'form' of work in the economic reality of Tokugawa society, and identified the 'meaning' of work.[4] Their thought was not confined to the realm of 'intellectual discourse' but was applied to the daily activities of the populace, and had important practical influences on their

Introduction

economic activities.

Ishida was a thinker of agrarian origin who served two merchant houses in Kyoto for nearly three decades. His thought not only expressed the popular ethic in a language originally derived from Neo-Confucianism but also clearly reflected the predominant mode of task implementation, or 'way' of working, in the trading houses of Kyoto. The theoretical importance of his thought lies in its synthesis of Neo-Confucian beliefs and the economic values of thrift, diligence, and frugality. At a more specific level, it amalgamates a crucial element of Confucian teaching - coming to know one's nature (*sei*) through cultivation - and the everyday work of the populace in the secular world. The idea of viewing work as a process of cultivation was thus conceived, and an ideological foundation established. He was the founder of *Sekimon Shingaku*, or 'Ishida's school for the learning of the heart', a movement that emerged in 1729 and flourished during the second half of the eighteenth and the early nineteenth centuries. The movement prevailed through the establishment of organisational centres called *bosha* throughout Japan, as well as through its involvement in the foundation of the family precepts (*kakun*) of trading houses. Shingaku attracted a considerable popular attendance, and became the largest single ideological group of the time, in terms of practical influence.

Ninomiya's thought reflects the popular ethic in the late Edo period, which emphasised self-development and self-reflection through diligence, economy, and piety.[5] Although he was not affiliated with the Shingaku movement, his philosophy shared its tenor; he argued that work was not just a materialwise activity of production, but an act through which one's spiritual self would be cultivated. *Shinden kaihatsu*, which he advocated, literally meant the 'development and cultivation of one's heart'. The term suggests a conscious projection of the image of agricultural cultivation into the inner-cultivation of self. Unlike Ishida and other successive Shingaku teachers, Ninomiya did not hold frequent lecture sessions to teach his work thought; nor did he run schools. Instead, he put his thought into practice through '*shiho*', the village rehabilitation programme. Shiho comprises economic measures designed to fully activate labour, land, and capital resources in order to realise radical development projects. More importantly, the programme incentivised idling peasant producers, and nurtured them as entities capable of work process management and long-term production planning. Elements of management were incorporated into Ninomiya's concept of work, behind which was the idea that such productive activity was not an end in itself but an instrument for one's *shinden kaihatsu*. Ninomiya's philosophical discourse was thus interwoven with practical advice on village rehabilitation. The Bakumatsu (1854-1867) and the early Meiji (1868-1911) periods saw a rapid spread of Ninomiya's thought in the form of the *Hotoku* movement.[6] In short, Ishida and Ninomiya were the channel through which the predominant ideological constructs and forms of work came together, and their views were accepted by people, not merely as an 'ethic' to be observed but as an 'idea of work' that would activate and intensify economic activities, and serve as a means of self-cultivation and fulfilment.

Historiography

Much research had already been done on both Ishida and Ninomiya by the 1930s, most of which was published in Japanese. In postwar scholarship, however, both thinkers appear as negligible at best, and, at worst, denounceable, for they quickly bring to mind the governmental admonition of hard work in the late Meiji and the prewar periods. The Meiji leaders, realising the need for civic edification in their pursuit of modernisation, sought to construct an ideology which compelled people to serve the national cause.[7] Ninomiya, a common man who started out penniless and established himself as an agrarian leader, was a familiar figure to the populace, and thus was ideal for the government to put forward as a paragon of hard work. He featured in elementary school textbooks from 1893, and a stone statue of him appeared in every elementary school playground. The concept of work expressed in the thought of Ninomiya, and in that of Ishida, was integrated into government ideology where it tended to be degraded into a mere admonitory discourse which functioned as internal psychological constriction for diligence and loyalty.

The increasingly repressive prewar military government of the 1930s set out media restrictions that extended to academic works, but, on the other hand, vigorously encouraged the publication of works on such subjects as loyalty and submission. Ninomiya and Ishida appeared as role models in these prewar academic works where their thought on diligence translating into selfless devotion, on thrift into self-sacrifice, and piety into blind submission.[8] Such misapplications helped dogmatise their thought and form a one-sided image of them as thinkers advocating sacrifice and submission virtually exclusively; an image that this study will prove to be highly misleading.

Despite these biased depictions and the subsequent disregard of the two thinkers, reliable research works do exist, including some published in the restrictive prewar period. Among the most important on Ishida are Ishikawa Ken's *Sekimon Shingakushi no Kenkyu* or 'A Study of the History of *Sekimon* Heart-Learning', and the works of Shibata Minoru, including his edition of *Ishida Baigan Zenshu* or 'The Complete Works of Ishida Baigan'.[9] A chapter by R.N. Bellah, 'Shingaku and its founder, Ishida Baigan' in his *Tokugawa Religion* (first published in 1957), has been the most influential work in English to date.[10] Bellah attempted to show the ways in which the rationalising tendencies in Japanese religion contributed to economic and political rationalisation in Japan. In a sense it represented the antithesis of Weber's view of the role and position of Japanese religion and its rationalising process, which assumed that religion neither played a vital role in forming people's values and behaviour, nor underwent a rationalisation process, which was crucial for the formation of an ethic of economic rationalism.[11] At the same time, Bellah conformed to the Weberian model, in that he saw religious rationalisation as contributing to economic rationalisation. Bellah argued that 'generalised' particularism serves as a functional equivalent for universalism. Japan's primacy of political values, of which collective goals and loyalty form a central concern, and thus normally prioritise ascription, reveals its strong association with performance values.[12] In a society where the polity takes precedence over the economy, 'work itself is not a value, but rather work as an expression of selfless devotion to the collective goal is valued', and this value system has brought about a strong motivation for work.[13] In Bellah's view, this mechanism generated an achievement orientation similar to the one advocated in the Weberian thesis.

Bellah's thesis on the development of a work ethic certainly deserves credence since it highlighted economic development of a non-Western kind, a kind which till then had been dismissed as merely 'feudal' or 'backward' (as in the Weberian thesis of 'Asiatic society'). However, its overemphasis on vertical relations and the selfless submission of retainers to lord needs serious qualification. As will be discussed in Chapter 4, it was expected that the retainers of a merchant household would participate in business decisions, not just submit to the top-down orientations of the leader. They were even entitled to terminate the headship of a household. Managerial involvement and initiative were at the heart of the work norm shared by the Japanese retainers (commoners). Bellah seems to have overlooked these "followers' stake" possessed by the Tokugawa retainers. To do so is to downgrade them to the level of mere submissive

Introduction

entities.

The monumental *Ninomiya Sontoku Zenshu* (The Complete Works of Ninomiya Sontoku), which brings together Ninomiya's philosophical writings, memoirs, details of the shiho programme in all the villages where it was implemented, and correspondence during its implementation was edited by Sasai Shintaro.[14] With his immense empirical knowledge of Ninomiya, Sasai published a substantial essay in 1935 in which he reconstructed Ninomiya's life and experiences, and explored his philosophical discourse on the universe and man's everyday life and work.[15] But Sasai was a leading member of the Hotoku movement in the prewar period, and thus his writings on Ninomiya are preoccupied with his discourse on diligence and loyalty. However, his editorial works - including *Ninomiya Sontoku Zenshu* - do not manifest this tendency, and provide a solid basis for the study of Ninomiya.

It was not until 1959 when Naramoto Tatsuya published his study on Ninomiya that the prewar image of him was ameliorated at least in part. His study focuses on the centrality of the concept of planning in Ninomiya's thought on the economy. Naramoto paid special attention to the credit system in the shiho programme, and noted that the programme was designed to loan capital, unused or reserved, in accordance with the different needs of individual households and included long-term plans for accumulation.[16] In the meantime, economic historians such as Oto, Fukaya and Otsuka studied specific shiho programmes with the knowledge of local history. Unpublished materials related to the shiho programme have been collected in Hotoku Museum in Odawara, although the cataloging of these materials is still in progress.

So far, few Japanese research works on Ishida and Ninomiya have made their way into English. Works with important historiographical contributions exist in Japanese literature, but they have been made largely inaccessible to non-Japanese speakers. On the other hand, few Japanese scholars specialising in Ishida and Ninomiya, even present day ones, are sensitive to the theoretical, empirical, and anthropological studies of work that have recently developed in Western scholarship; no attempt has been made so far to approach the thought of Ishida and Ninomiya in the light of these recent methodological development, and the importance of the two thinkers in the social construction of work in the Edo period has not been fully acknowledged for this reason.

Furthermore, most of the studies on the two thinkers, including the ones mentioned above, presuppose that the concept of hard work and its justification are central to their thought, as well as to the Japanese concept of work generally. This study will show, instead, that the essence of the thought of Ishida and Ninomiya was to regard work as a process of self-refinement, or, as a means for the cultivation of the worker. Although this has been referred to in the works of Ishikawa Ken, Sakasai Takahito, and in a comment on Ninomiya by Yasumaru Yoshio in their respective studies, it has not been considered as fundamental to the emergence of the Japanese perception of work.[17] Hard work alone would not necessarily lead to self-cultivation. In the thought of Ishida and Ninomiya, a wider range of ideas and economic forms was identified as relevant to the meaning of work, including the practice of inter-personal and managerial skills. Self-cultivation acted as a central concept which would motivate workers to enrich the meaning of their work, and would enhance their capacity to handle their social relations.

Significantly, this last point implies the fundamental importance of social relations in the meaning of work. In existing scholarship, work has been understood in terms of an individual worker's action towards a physical object, and cultivation has been assumed to be sought through the interaction between the worker and the object. Work,

Introduction

however, is not merely an act of individuals; nor is it a unitary act. Typically it is an aspect of social relations which involves a division of labour of some kind. As such, it calls for the serious consideration of the effects of the social relations of the Edo period on the development of the perception of work at the most fundamental level of conceptualisation. Ishida was concerned with this aspect of work, and argued for the importance of inter-personal as well as managerial skills in striving for the maximum activation of human resources. Co-ordination and management of labour were complementary elements in Ninomiya's organisation of work in his shiho programme. Moreover, human resource management was not his sole concern; the management of such resources as capital, technology, time, and land was emphasised and identified as an intrinsic element of work.

Equally important was Ishida and Ninomiya's valuation of work in relation to the household (*ie*); the corporate transgenerational entity, seat of the highest moral values in Tokugawa Japan. Ishida was concerned with smooth communication and consensus formation between household members, for these were vital in maintaining the stability of and succession in the trading houses. Skills in consolidating personnel affairs and facilitating information exchange between workers were valued even more than highly specialised individual skills in trading. Ninomiya for his part viewed work not only as the means to secure the material prosperity of an individual but also as a 'cumulative agency' for the successive betterment of the household for generations to come. In his thought, the prosperity of the present members of a household was directly brought about by the industry of their ancestors. Similarly, the descendants' quality of life depended on the work of the present members. Effort was accumulated over generations in order to improve the prosperity of the household. In the thought of Ishida and Ninomiya, work was not an individual's act for the benefit of that individual, but an act which upheld the transgenerational merit of the household. In turn, the household members' valuation of work stemmed from this aspiration. Both thinkers regarded work as a process of cultivation, not, however, as a process of attaining individualistic aspirations and goals set by the worker himself; rather, it served to fulfil a 'role' in social and diachronic contexts that cultivated people.

Moreover, virtually no study has taken on board the task of relating the notional construction of work to socio-economic development in the Edo period, and of exploring how the work thought of Ishida and Ninomiya merged with the prevalent form of work. Both the narrow focus on 'hard work' and the understanding of work as an individual's act made it difficult for scholars to relate the thought of Ishida and Ninomiya to the economic and social realities of Tokugawa Japan. This study attempts to fill this gap by relating the thought of Ishida and Ninomiya to the then predominant form of work on the one hand, and by tracing the process of the diffusion of their thought through the populace on the other.

It may be helpful, at this juncture, to comment on the two existing academic approaches related to the study of work in Tokugawa Japan - intellectual history and people's history (*minshushi*) respectively - in order to locate our approach and level of analysis within the general context of Japanese historiography.

Intellectual historians have largely focused on the development of the most sublime discourses of intellectual elites. For them, Ishida and Ninomiya may not be the figures of prime importance. However, they assimilated, interpreted and amplified the work consciousness of the people; as thinkers with 'active experience' of work in real life, they represented popular work culture, which was deeply embedded in language, consciousness, and behaviour, and

Introduction

gave an intellectual expression to it. In this regard, they are even more important than the great figures of the Tokugawa intelligentsia. In the words of Nakai Nobuhiko, a social and economic historian profoundly versed in popular thought in the Tokugawa period, there are certain 'strata' (*sōi*) in thought; there is 'intellectual thought', which is by nature highly abstract, and there is also thought that is more akin to a representation of popular consciousness. The latter may be alien to sublime discourses of intellectualism, but is of prime importance if one wishes to understand the substructive consciousness of the common people[18], including its implications for work. The thought of Ishida and Ninomiya is, as we shall see in this study, preeminently representative of this type of thought.

H.D. Harootunian's work on *kokugaku* (the nativist school) has dealt extensively with the notion of work (and/or labour) developed within this school. Harootunian argues that the collective pursuit of agricultural cultivation, coupled with practices of economy and thrift, were viewed in *kokugaku* as a primal act through which the 'founding fathers' of the nation were worshipped and the principle of creation continuously reproduced.[19] While Harootunian's study has made an important contribution to the assessment of *kokugaku*'s ideological origins and its essence, and discusses how the valuation of work as an expression of worship is developed in that context, it views work as an ideological construct, not as the product of an interplay between social, politico-administerial, and economic factors in Tokugawa society. Najita Tetsuo's *Visions of Virtue in Tokugawa Japan* explores the thought of the *Kaitokudo* scholars. The *Kaitokudō*, a merchant academy in Osaka established by wealthy merchants of the city, consisted of scholars of *chonin* origin, and stood as the medium through which their 'virtuous' thought and morality were expressed. Najita discusses the attempts by the *Kaitokudo* scholars to formulate an ideological justification of trading and of the merchants' 'public' role as economic management specialists. The focus of his study, however, lies in the merchants' ability to grasp the form and substance of moral and political norms, which was, in Najita's view, on a par with that of the ruling class (*samurai*).[20] The core of Najita's discussion is 'morality' and the capacity of the merchants to understand and manoeuvre the political economy of Tokugawa society. On the other hand, the prevalent form of work in economic reality was not primarily his concern.

Both Harootunian and Najita deal with thought that developed close to the people, but they deal with it as sublime 'intellectual thought' of a highly abstract kind, rather than as thought developed through an interactive process between commoners and popular thinkers, or as the representation of a socially constructed popular consciousness and an expression of the popular attitude towards work.

The term 'popular consciousness' might remind readers of the literature on peasant uprisings and disputes in Tokugawa Japan, and of the people's history (*minshushi*) approach, which gained currency in the discussion of the history of socio-political consciousness during the Bakumatsu and Meiji periods. Indeed, *minshushi* studies have provided us with significant insights into the customs and mores of the populace.[21] Some researchers were concerned with the emergence of political consciousness among the common people, and traced their socio-political interactions with other people in different status groups. Most of the *minshūshi* studies of the Edo period concentrate on this element, and are based primarily upon records and manuscripts dealing with village turmoil (*murakata sōdō*), legal action against domains (*kokuso*), and peasant uprisings (*hyakushō ikki*).[22] The primary focus of these studies has been the fusion of popular consciousness and political action at the level of specific events. However, one cannot construct an idea of work prevalent in the everyday life of the people using as a

Introduction

basis particular political steps taken by them on extreme occasions. Studies on customs and mores inform us about the life of the people, but it is necessary to adopt a different approach if one's primary interest is in their thoughts and attitudes towards work. This study will attempt to identify these very thoughts and attitudes, in the hope of widening the horizon of the history of popular consciousness.

Structure

This book is divided into four parts. Part I (the first two chapters) provides an overview of the Tokugawa concept of work which serves as a general background of the subsequent studies; Part II (Chapters 3 to 5) deals with Ishida, and Part III (Chapters 6 to 8) deals with Ninomiya. These are followed by a conclusion. Altogether this thesis consists of a group of historical studies related to a single topic - work - rather than a genuinely historiographical, consecutive narrative.

Chapter 2 discusses the main intellectual and economic apparatus within which work developed as a conceptual construct. It suggests that work in Tokugawa Japan was perceived in terms of 'role-play' within a particular collective entity such as the household, the village, or the state. It was not an individual activity based on a single skill speciality. With the exception of a few highly specialised artisanal tasks, work was seen as an activity that involved plural tasks.

Part II is a study of Ishida Baigan. Chapter 3 describes the ideological background of Ishida's thought, and discusses his idea of cultivation and the means of attaining it. A distinct feature of the 'method' of cultivation in Ishida's thought lies in his emphasis on commitment to or 'immersion' in work, rather than in the pursuit of sublime Neo-Confucian practices for attainment. One's intensive pursuit of a daily task, rather than investigation or meditation, constituted the main means of cultivation.

The perception of work in Tokugawa Japan

Chapter 4 explores particular elements of Ishida's discourse as economic thought. Referring to such economic concepts as 'skill', 'management', and 'work initiative', it clarifies the sort of skill referred to in his thought, and the way in which this affected the concept of work. Ishida did not perceive work merely as an act of the individual but as an act which involved social relations, and he argued for the indispensability of managerial and inter-personal skills in the carrying out of collective work in merchant household businesses. Individuals in the household were not only to supply labour but to join in the managerial and business decision-making processes. Accordingly, 'cultivation' in his thought was not to be sought only through individual labour - the interactive process between worker and object - but also through one's participation in business management, and the practice of skills which could enhance the performance of other workers.

As stated earlier, Ishida's students set up Shingaku academic centres throughout Japan. They were also involved in the formation of family precepts of trading houses. Shingaku did not remain in the realm of intellectual discourse but spread through the actual work processes of the populace. Chapter 5 examines the process of diffusion of Ishida's thought and the extent of its practical influence.

Part III is a study of Ninomiya Sontoku. After a brief introduction sketching his background, Chapter 6 investigates the idea of work expressed in his philosophical writings. Ninomiya viewed agricultural work as a means through which a peasant could contribute to the succession of his household, and cumulatively raise this ideological entity to the highest moral and economic level. Moreover, one's intensive involvement in agricultural activities was directly related to the cultivation of humanity: the cultivation of land brought about the cultivation of the human heart, and vice versa. It was, however, not merely the investment of manpower that cultivated human beings. Ninomiya was

Introduction

concerned with management of time, labour, and other resources. Cultivation was sought through work, but this was accompanied by careful planning and management.

The study of work thought expressed in practical work programme may sometimes enhance a fuller understanding of the idea of work. The shiho programme was a comprehensive package of economic measures for village rehabilitation, designed and organised by Ninomiya. It contained measures which provided peasants with a specific framework of economic activities which had the effect of reshaping and institutionalising the structure of peasant work.

Chapter 8 consolidates the main elements found in the studies of both Ninomiya's thought and his shiho programme. Resource management and planning were integral parts of Ninomiya's idea of work. The notion of a continuous and cumulative amelioration through future generations was also vigorously encouraged. The idea of the stable succession of the household and the village was at the core of his thought.

Collective efficiency was of great importance to Ninomiya, but he encouraged neither a 'selfless devotion' to collectivity nor an individualistic approach to work. Rather, he nurtured the idea of individual initiative within the framework of the household or cooperative entity (i.e., the village), and this initiative was to involve those qualities of planning and coordination by which he set such store. Ninomiya's thought should be seen as evidence of the growing recognition in Tokugawa Japan of the importance of individual drive of the promotion of efficient coordination and production management.

The conclusion brings together the main findings of the thought of Ishida and Ninomiya, and locates them in the general context of the development of the Japanese perception of work. Both thinkers succeeded in gathering the undercurrents of the attitude to work of a largely inarticulate populace in the mid-to-late Edo period, cross-fertilising them with the prevalent ideology, and passing a concrete idea of work back to that populace. In other words, they acted as key channels of interaction between ideology and society.

Neither thinker solely advocated hard work; nor did they simply teach moral and ethical virtues. Commoners were nurtured by them as able entities in efficiently managing the economic activities of their own, perceiving the long-term benefits for the individual, the household, and society, and identifying the meaning of work for the enrichment of their social and economic life. The two thinkers widened the people's perception of work, and, at the same time, cultivated their attitude towards and capacity for work. The impact made by Ishida and Ninomiya, and the responses engendered by their thinking, on socio-economic change in Tokugawa Japan can thus scarcely be overestimated.

Notes
1. Roberts, B., R. Finnegan, and D. Gallie, 'The Meaning of Work: Value and Identity', B. Roberts, R. Finnegan, and D. Gallie (eds.), *New Approaches to Economic Life*, Manchester University Press, Manchester, 1985, p. 459.
2. Joyce, P., 'The Historical Meanings of Work: An Introduction', P. Joyce (ed.), *The Historical Meanings of Work*, Cambridge University Press, Cambridge, 1987, pp. 1-3.
3. Briggs, A., 'Review of Thompson, *The Making of the English Working Class*', *Labor History*, 6 (Winter, 1965), pp. 84-91. H.G. Gutman, 'Work, Culture and Society in Industrializing America, 1815-1919', R.E. Pahl (ed.), *On Work: Historical, Comparative & Theoretical Approaches*, Basil Blackwell, Oxford, 1988, pp. 125-37.
4. Work does not develop independently of technological and other economic factors. It is thus necessary to look at the 'form' of work constructed by 'economic' factors, in addition to work as a conceptual construct, if one is

Introduction

concerned with work as a social construct.
5. Yasumaru Yoshio, *Nihon no Kindaika to Minshu Shiso*, Aoki Shoten, Tokyo, 1974, pp. 9-10.
6. The word '*hotoku*' literally means the 'repayment of virtue'. Ninomiya advocated that human beings received such 'virtuous gifts' as soil, seed, and water from nature, and with these man's life was made possible. Man has to pay for these received virtues in the form of agricultural work. This was the basic ideological pillar of Ninomiya's work thought, and the movement started by him was named after this. Ninomiya's thought will be dealt with in some depth in Chapter 6.
7. Gluck, C., *Japan's Modern Myths - Ideology in the Late Meiji Period*, Princeton University Press, Princeton, 1985.
8. See, for instance, Takahashi Tansui, *Shingaku Shuyo Monogatari*, Daibunkan Shoten, Osaka, 1933, a research work on Ishida. For Ninomiya, see Mizumachi Kiyoshi, *Ninomiya Sontoku-O no Dotoku Keizai Shiso*, Meirosha, Tokyo, 1937.
9. Ishikawa Ken, *Sekimon Shingakushi no Kenkyū*, Iwanami Shoten, Tokyo, 1938. This large volume by Ishikawa, a specialist in the history of education in pre-modern and modern Japan, includes intellectual analysis of Ishida's thought and its ideological origins, detailed historiographical research on the diffusion of his thought, and its impact on society from the perspective of popular education in Tokugawa Japan. Ishikawa's another work, *Shingaku Kyoka no Honshitsu narabi ni Hattatsu*, Seishisha, Tokyo, 1982 (first published in 1931 by Shokasha, Tokyo) consists mainly of statistical analysis of the spread of Ishida's thought in the second half of the eighteenth and the early nineteenth centuries. Shibata Minoru (ed.), *Ishida Baigan Zenshu*, Sekimon Shingakukai, Tokyo, 1955. Abbreviated to '*IBZ*' hereafter. Shibata is a descendant of a Sekimon Shingaku disciple, Shibata Kyuo, and was the head of Meirinsha, a leading Shingaku academic centre which still exists in Kyoto. His works include *Baigan to sono Monryu*, Mineruva Shobo, Kyoto, 1977, and *Shingaku* (Nihon Rekishi Shinsho), Shibundo,

Tokyo, 1967, a concise introduction to Ishida and the Sekimon Shingaku. Works by both scholars eclipsed, though not completely, the earlier image of Ishida and his thought. Their works provide solid empirical foundations, but fall short of generating an intellectual debate on the nature and significance of Ishida's thought on work.
10. Bellah, R.N., *Tokugawa Religion*, The Free Press, New York, 1985 (first published in 1957), chapter 6.
11. Weber's discussion of the role of religion in Japan remained more or less marginal in his study of the sociology of religion, due largely to the limited availability of materials in his time. He nonetheless referred to the issue, stating that religion remained 'rigidly ceremonial and directed towards purely inner-worldly concerns'. See M. Weber, 'The Religions of Asia' in W.G. Runciman (ed.), *Weber: Selections in translation*, Cambridge University Press, Cambridge, 1978, pp. 196-97. The article was translated from *Gesammelte Aufsatze zur Religionssoziologie*, 2nd edn, Tubingen, 1923, II, s. 363-78. The original edition was published in 1917.
12. Bellah, *Tokugawa Religion*, pp. 5, 14.
13. *Ibid.*, p. 5, 15.
14. Sasai Shintaro (ed.), *Ninomiya Sontoku Zenshu*, Ninomiya Sontoku Igyo Senyokai, Shizuoka, 1927-1932. Abbreviated to '*NSZ*' hereafter.
15. Sasai Shintaro, *Ninomiya Sontokuden*, Nihon Hyoronsha, Tokyo, 1935.
16. Naramoto Tatsuya, *Ninomiya Sontoku*, Iwanami Shoten, Tokyo, 1959.
17. Ishikawa, *Sekimon Shingakushi*. Sakasai Takahito, 'Sekimon Shingaku ni okeru Jissen Tetsugaku no Tenkai - Ishida Baigan to Teshima Toan', *Rikkyo Keizaigaku Kenkyu*, 34-3 (December, 1980). Yasumaru, *Nihon no Kindaika to Minshu Shiso*.
18. Nakai Nobuhiko, 'Kaidai', Nakai Nobuhiko and Naramoto Tatsuya (eds.), *Iwanami Nihon Shiso Taikei, vol. 52: Ninomiya Sontoku, Ohara Yugaku*, Iwanami Shoten, Tokyo, 1973, p. 483.
19. Harootunian, H.D., *Things Seen and Unseen: Discourse*

Introduction

and Ideology in Tokugawa Nativism, University of Chicago Press, Chicago, 1988.
20. Najita, T., *Visions of Virtue in Tokugawa Japan*, University of Chicago Press, Chicago, 1987.
21. The scope and method of *minshushi* study, and the achievements of the scholars involved in the subject are concisely presented in C. Gluck, 'The People in History: Recent Trends in Japanese Historiography', *Journal of Asian Studies*, 38-4 (November, 1978). A select bibliography is also attached.
22. See Walthall, A. (ed. & tr.), *Peasant Uprisings in Japan*, University of Chicago Press, Chicago, 1991, for examples of the sources.

Chapter 2

The concept of 'work' in Tokugawa Japan

Recent historiographical and quantitative studies of the Tokugawa economy have revealed the centrality of market forces in society, the growth of market-oriented institutions in urban areas, and their penetration into the rural economy in the second half of the Tokugawa period. The growth of the market in cities and the flourishing of proto-industry in rural areas made economic factors, as distinct from political, social, and cultural ones, a dominant element of Tokugawa society. By this time, society had become a predominantly 'economic' one, where most members of society behaved largely in accordance with economic rationale.[1] Such pre-industrial economic development that occurred in this era helped Japan's relatively smooth industrial transformation in the subsequent period of economic modernisation.

Surprisingly little, however, has so far been done on the understanding of work in pre-industrial Japan, in spite of the existence of a sizeable amount of literature on the labour history of modern Japan.[2] Several studies by intellectual historians have revealed the linguistic and ritual ways in which work was represented at the time[3], but few have been successful in accounting for how the intellectual notion of work was developed in relation to the actual form that work took (how people pursued work) in Tokugawa society.

What was actually considered 'work', conceptually or otherwise, in Tokugawa Japan? This chapter seeks to provide a general picture of the concept of work in this period, by looking at linguistic representations of work, and by examining relevant secondary literature on linguistic, economic and social history. In the next section we examine the impact of political and institutional foundations and the dominant social relations within Tokugawa society on the construction of work as a concept; each status group - samurai, peasants, artisans, and merchants - had a certain assigned role, which was largely responsible for defining the nature and scope of the perception of work. This will be followed by a discussion of the influence of the strengthening of household ties - which took place in this period - on work, and argues that the household and the village further strengthened the importance of role assignment. The third section argues that this role assignment was reinforced, rather than checked, by economic development. It discusses the relationships between the system of role-playing and economic development in more general terms, and suggests that the concept of role-playing acted as a powerful tool which shaped the perception of work under economic change.

Occupational division and role assignment

Social anthropology of work reminds us that work takes its organisation and meaning from other non-economic social institutions, and its meanings vary according to the predominant societal values, beliefs, and institutions of the time.[4] Patrick Joyce, the author of *The Historical Meanings of Work*, argues that work is a 'cultural' activity, in the social construction of which 'non-economic' elements play a critical rôle. In contrast to the development of the idea of 'work in general' in the late nineteenth century which constituted a clear demarcation of work from other social activities and institutions, recent studies of work have helped reveal the links between productive activity and other social spheres (social structures) such as kinship, religion, and the politics, in the context of Western historical experience.[5] How does work in Tokugawa Japan look in this light?

In the contemporary Japanese language, the term *shigoto* (仕事) is generally used to translate the English term 'work', while *rodo* (労働) corresponds to 'labour'. Work and labour were both translated as *shigoto* for a noun, and *hataraku* (働く) for a verb in Hepburn's Japanese-English and English-Japanese dictionaries of 1867 and 1872.[6] Neither of these translations, however, satisfactorily represents the concept of work in the Edo period. In fact, work was conveyed by such words as *shokubun* (職分), *tenshoku* (天職), and *kagyo* (家業). *Sugiwai* (すぎわひ、生業), and *nariwai* (なりわひ、産業) were also in frequent use. Among the second group of words, *sugiwai* appears in the Japanese-Portuguese dictionary of 1603, and translated into Portuguese as the word representing productive and other activities to gain the means of living.[7] The word seems to have been used without major change in its meaning during the early part of the Tokugawa period.[8] From the second-half of the seventeenth century onwards, however, the word also began to represent also the activities not directly linked with the economy, such as priestly orders.[9] The word *nariwai* appeared at a much earlier time than *sugiwai* and was already in use in the eighth century, mainly representing agricultural production as well as the crops produced.[10] In the Edo period, however, *nariwai* began to represent the various activities carried out to gain a living, and was often used almost synonymously with the word *sugiwai*. In fact, the distinction between these two words became obscure, and they were used interchangeably; in *Hodo Tsūkan*, a series volume of popular literature (*dangibon*) in the mid-Edo period, for instance, 産業 was read as *nariwai*, while the same word was read as *sugiwai* in a "learning text" compiled by the Sugawara family, a *Joruri* school. "生活" was read as *nariwai* in *Nanso Satomi Hakkenden*, a work written by Takizawa Bakin in the late Edo period.[11] 産業 - read as *sangyo* - became a word in common use in contemporary Japan, usually referring to industry as, for example, the automobile industry (*jidosha sangyo*) or the distribution industry (*ryutsu sangyo*).[12]

The words examined above represent work as the means through which the individual or the household to which that individual belongs gains economic benefit. On the other hand, the first group of words introduced earlier were far less clearly 'economic' than those in the second group, and were closely related to the politico-administerial and institutional frameworks and the ethical teachings prevalent in the Tokugawa period. Words such as *shokubun* and *tenshoku*, for instance, were sanctioned in part by *shi no ko sho*, the Tokugawa social status groupings stratified according to the nature of the occupations of samurai, peasants, artisans, and merchants. *Shokubun* was the term in frequent use in the Edo period, literally meaning one's occupation or trade (*shoku*) fulfilling an allotted part (*bun*) in society.[13] According to Kaibara Gakken (1625-1702), the pursuit of '*shokubun* means, for instance, a bow craftsman crafting bow and arrow, . . . an artist painting pictures, . . . (and) an emperor as a deligate of Heaven blessing people, administering justice, and offering comfort to people . . . Samurai, peasants, artisans, and merchants shall be concerned with this principle, and be diligent in fulfilling one's own *shokubun*'.[14] *Shokubun* meant, in other words, a portion of social role assigned to each.[15] In the words of Muro Kyuso (1658-1734), a Neo-Confucian thinker, the pursuit of the occupational assignments of *no ko sho* (peasants, artisans, and merchants) was to meet the necessities and shortcomings of society (*tenka no fusoku o oginai, tenka no yo o totonou*).[16] Miyauchi Yoshinaga (1798-1843), a pupil of Hirata *kokugaku* in the late Edo period, compares the status groups and the occupations assigned to each of them to the parts of the body and their functions. The ideological springboards of individual thinkers varied, but they share a similar view of the functional indispensability of work to each status group.[17] Samurai, peasants, artisans, and merchants were ranked in this order in Tokugawa society, but the assigned work of each was considered as important a role to each other.

Tenshoku also referred to a role in society, but one that was laid down and guided by *tendo* (天道), the Heavenly Way. All tasks were sanctioned in Heaven to be fulfilled by people in each status group, in order that social relations should be formed according to 'Heaven's intention'.[18] Thus, work in Tokugawa Japan constituted a role assigned to a particular status group in a varied social context; the constituent parts of this role, or the tasks actually involved, were not specific.

Although this discussion has only referred to linguistic representations of work in the Edo period, it nevertheless gives an idea of how work as a conceptual construct existed in Tokugawa Japan. Work was seen not only as productive action, but as an act whereby workers formed social relations. An important linguistic feature of work in the Edo period lies - as represented in the second group of words - in the obscure distinction between the productive activity of the individual and the notion of 'role-playing'. Both *shokubun* and *tenshoku* assumed that all existing occupations were complementary activities in the formation of social relations, and were, at least in theory, activities of equal importance.

Arguably, the demarcation of *shi no ko sho* has contributed to the development of the notion of work as 'social role'. But this broad definition of role assignment was refined and further strengthened by the prevalence of the concept of *yaku* (役), as demonstrated by, among others, Bito Masahide, an historian specialising in the politico-intellectual history of Tokugawa Japan.[19] The term *yaku* originally referred to the use of a person's labour, although it began to be used to mean various forms of 'service' to the domainal lord by the sixteenth century.[20] Bito argues that in the Edo period it came to represent one's 'role' in society and the assumption of responsibility attached to that role; its meaning was no longer confined to the taking on of a particular task or labour.[21] A samurai's *yaku* was not confined to his commitment to possible military service. As Ogyu Sorai points out, '[a samurai's] nature is a military man, but he must be a master of people to rule the state; to be an administrative officer means to be a man of court rank [who is entitled to rule]'.[22] The samurai's *yaku* included, in other words, various political and administrative duties. A samurai's service to his lord was called *hoko*, and he received a salary (*go'on*) in return; the feudal lord-vassal relationship of the medieval age remained in Tokugawa Japan, but service was pursued as a national 'public' duty rather than as a service in a private lord-vassal context.[23] Peasants' *yaku* often included various types of labour needed for the development of infrastructures such as roads and river banks, and their maintenance and improvement. The direct contribution of a labour force was regarded as corresponding to the payment of annual dues (*nengu*), usually in the form of rice, and such a contribution was often rewarded by a reduction in these dues.[24] In other words, peasants' *yaku* could be met through various means (tasks); it was not an activity specific to a particular task or skill. The transformation in the use of the term *yaku*, as pointed out by Bito, was a product of the nature of Tokugawa work as described above, in which the tasks involved were plural; in turn, this transformation was propitious for accommodating and further legitimising work as role-play in its own line of conception. *Shi no ko sho*, the status groupings - stratified according to the nature of the occupation of each - would not have sufficiently justified work which was multi-task in nature. The concept of *yaku* could justify work as role-play without task specificity, as a 'unit of responsibility' which included varied tasks.

Asao Naohiro, an intellectual historian of Tokugawa Japan, criticised Bito's definition of *yaku* for regarding it as a social role nonetheless considering that role as the one to be fulfilled by *individual* members of society; *yaku* was, in Asao's view, the public role to be pursued by the people in each status group *collectively*; *yaku* existed as a public or social role, running through the entire spectrum of social relations, and that the individual workers (or 'labouring subjects') did not exist in the theory of *yaku*.[25] Whichever stance one takes, this debate on *yaku* defines work not as a particular task but as a social responsibility. The strong socio-political formation of collective social entities (which effectively corresponded to the Edo status groups of *shi no ko sho*) ensured that each group would meet that responsibility.[26]

Mizumoto Kunihiko reveals that the concept of *yaku* was 'transplanted' into village work; the term for 'public responsibility' (*kogi no yaku*) was used almost synonymously with the term for 'tasks and duties of the village' (*mura yaku kinshi*), which suggests the merging of the social (or public) responsibility of *yaku* with village tasks.[27] Furthermore, this study provides us with historiographical evidence of the prevalence of the *yaku* concept and the notion of role-play in Tokugawa villages; which also gives authenticity to conceptual studies of *yaku* by Bito, Asao, and other intellectual historians.

What happened to the concept of *yaku* in the eighteenth and nineteenth centuries when the household (*ie*) became the dominant unit of agricultural production as well as socio-political organisation? No study has explicitly pointed out the possibility that the concept of *yaku* was transplanted into *ie*, but there are works which effectively suggest this. Oto Osamu's argument on the Tokugawa social strata and the concept of *ie*, for instance, actually shows that the concept of social role was injected into the concept of *ie*; the role was, in his words, institutionally 'attached' to the household. From the late seventeenth century on, this amalgamated concept spread within the emerging small-scale peasant economy.[28]

The household and role assignment

The household and the village both acted as the basic economic, social and administrative units of the Tokugawa social order. The notion of role assignment was further strengthened also by these two key social institutions of the Tokugawa period; the household in particular was responsible for linking the idea of role assignment to actual tasks.

Nakane Chie's classic study on the Japanese household concisely describes that entity and the concept attached to it. The Japanese household was a social institution which aimed at its own successive continuation. Economically, the household formed the productive and managerial unit for agricultural and other activities in the eighteenth and nineteenth centuries. Conceptually, it was recognised as the perpetual entity of lineal continuity from the ancestors to the unborn members of the household. It was the medium through which the household members identified themselves with this lineage. The succession of the household was often more important than the welfare maximisation of the present members of the entity. Evidence suggests that the household was a social institution capable of picking a talented heir. Adoption was commonly practised to find the best successor; and a close kinship tie could be dissolved if one's performance of duties and obligations were found to be unsatisfactory.[29]

Nakane perceives the Japanese household as an entity embracing families even outside the kinship relations, a large family system that includes "quasi-kin" families within certain territorial boundaries, namely, the villages. Recent socio-economic historiography, however, shows that each family unit possessed a clearer demarcation within the context of the household than Nakane had suggested. Saito Osamu, for instance, argues that the Japanese household followed neither the simple household system nor the joint household system. It may best be termed a "stem" system in which the constituent families and their members joined and parted elastically according to, for instance, changes in economic demand.[30] An important feature of the Japanese household has been brought to light here through economic historiographical and demographic research work; it was the smaller-scale family units, not the joint families, that emerged in Tokugawa villages as 'households'.

The meaning of *kagyo*, another key word which represented work in Tokugawa Japan, needs to be examined here. It literally means 'household work', but it originally referred to speciality occupations pursued by families in possession of a particular skill, i.e., medical and legal skills, in the eighth and ninth centuries.[31] The word also represented the 'property of the household' in the era of Heian, as it appears in *Shoku Nihongi* of 967.[32] In the Kamakura (1185 or 1192-1333) and Muromachi (1338-1568) eras, *kagyo* began to represent specific skills to be inherited by the members of the household, particularly the skills and techniques inherent in artistic, artisanal, and samurai professions.[33] In the Edo period, however, the use of *kagyo* was no longer confined to the description of a certain skill or profession; work of the household in any occupational group, including agriculture and trading, had come to be identified as *kagyo*. Hiraishi Naoaki argues that the concept of *kagyo* developed in Tokugawa society was a product of the 'interpermeation' of the concepts of *sugiwai* and *shokubun*. As we saw, *sugiwai* meant economic activity, while *shokubun* referred to an assigned role. According to Hiraishi, these two notions were incorporated into the context of *ie* (the household), and formed the concept of *kagyo*, in that work was recognised as role-play as well as economic production for the sake of the prosperity of the household.[34]

Further examination is necessary to ascertain whether the two concepts have in fact 'permeated' to each other. Evidence shows, however, that the word *kagyo* was used almost synonymously with such words as *shokubun* and *tenshoku*, as is apparent in the following words from Ishida Baigan:

> Hasn't one's stable life been actualised by one's own diligence in pursuing *kagyo*? Those who are not aware of their own *shokubun* are inferior even to beasts . . . Merchants not being aware of their own *shokubun* will ruin the household which they are delegated by their ancestors to succeed.[35]

The use of the word *kagyo* is interchangeable here with *shokubun*, and demonstrates the equal importance of role-play designed to preserve the well-being of the household to *shokubun* which constitutes the social process. One could assert that this was due to the influence of the ideology developed in the early Edo period, the ideology - as manifested in such words as *shokubun* and *tenshoku* - that recognised the work of each status group as complementary to one another in constituting the social process; the contribution of each member of the household was viewed as being just as indispensable in preserving and continuing the household as was the pursuit of *shokubun* in fulfilling the necessities of social welfare. The use of the word *kagyo* was 'universalised' for this reason, regardless of the type of skill or skill-level inherent in household work. The concept of *ie* suited this notional development of role-play.

The 'core' of the household consisted of *kacho* (the household head) and his wife. It would be wrong to assume that

The concept of 'work' in Tokugawa Japan

kacho, as the leader of the household, was a patriarchal, omnipotent figure:

> Succession of the headship of the household means that he is entitled to pursue a care-taking duty of the ancestral paddies and fields, household belongings, and mountains. He shall invest every effort to maintain these ancestral holdings, shall always be keen to care . . .[36]

Here he is recognised as 'delegated personnel' with responsibility for the successive continuation of the household. He was a person who 'temporarily occupied' the position or role of leading the household's lineal continuation. If he was found to be incompetent in that role, he was often pressed to resign by the village *yoriai* (the highest decision-making body of a village), kin group, and the main house (*honke*).[37] Thus, the headship was more a household role than one of patriarchal leadership. The village social order monitored the efficiency of the household head in carrying out household duties, and saw that appropriate practical considerations were taken into account.

In other societies, also, the household was often the basic economic unit within which work was carried out in the pre-industrial era. Studies on the English rural economy in the sixteenth and seventeenth centuries, for instance, suggest that most of the tasks - including wage-earning activities - were organised and carried out by individual households. Members of the household were allocated various tasks from garden digging, hoeing, harvesting to so-called domestic work.[38] However, such economic activities do not appear to have helped develop the notion of an assigned role. The household does not appear to have played a critical role in the conceptual construction of work in English society of the pre-industrial period.

The perception of work in Tokugawa Japan

Economic background to the multi-task concept of work

One of the most important factors which gave rise to this emphasis on role-playing in Tokugawa Japan was in fact an economic one. In Tokugawa society, the agricultural household was supposed to be primarily concerned with rice production. In reality, however, the household often could not maintain its subsistence through rice production alone. Its involvement in additional activities such as cotton and tobacco growing, charcoal and paper making was indispensable.[39] The pursuit of these extra tasks (*yogyo*) began to appear in the seventeenth century, and became widespread in the eighteenth century.[40] One of the Bakufu surveys, conducted in 1819 in a village of the Province of Shimotsuke, shows that only fourteen households out of eighty-six were not involved in any *yogyo*; that is to say, 84 per cent of households were engaged in non-rice production.[41] Both central and domainal governments attempted to restrict extra activities through written orders. But, at the same time, they often gave tacit approval of them. Eventually, domainal governments came to encourage these activities in the name of *tokusan* (special local production), for both revenue and 'foreign' exchange earning purposes.[42] Peasants thus became officially involved in various economic activities, and this situation was responsible, in Fukaya's view, for the multi-task nature of work in rural households in the mid- to-late Edo period.[43]

Japanese farming methods and technology continued to develop within the framework of the peasant household economy. The household mainly used family labour, and retained its dependence on the less task-specific, labour-intensive form of work with an emphasis on coordination and management, even in the nineteenth century. There was little evidence of proletarianisation, hence the dependence on skill-specific day labourers.

The development of these additional activities (*yogyo*) in rural settings increasingly encouraged the development of

The concept of 'work' in Tokugawa Japan

cottage industry, or proto-industry, in the second half of the eighteenth century. Unlike pre-industrial England, the Japanese economy did not become rapidly urbanised. Instead, it went through a transformation from urban-based to rural-based industrial development.⁴⁴ While the urban population declined, some rural areas developed into centres of handicraft production. Industries ranged from cotton spinning and weaving to *sake* brewing and paper making, although only a few regions were engaged in such skilled crafts as silk production. The Japanese case was clearly different from that of the English; while rural industries grew, this did not involve a departure from agricultural - more particularly, rice - production. Instead, industrial work was carried out in the form of by-employment by the members of the agricultural household, as part of the pursuit of *yogyo*. Thus the distinction between agricultural work and industrial work became blurred.⁴⁵ Such commercialised agriculture as cocoon production was closely linked to silk-reeling, and both of these were classified as 'extra-agricultural work pursued during slack seasons' (*nokan yogyo*). Some commercial and transport activities were also classified as *nokan yogyo*, and it was this type of proto-industrial work, rather than the work by skilled artisans, that supported Japan's proto-industrialisation in the second half of the eighteenth and the first half of the nineteenth centuries.⁴⁶

Of course, much of these proto-industrial developments were initially dependent on the superior technology and artisanal skill available in large cities such as Osaka and Edo. From the second half of the eighteenth century on, however, traditional centres of production and commerce, particularly the Kinai region (centred around Kyoto and Osaka), lost their competitiveness due largely to the wage increases of urban skilled workers. As a result, merchants and artisans went back to rural areas to build their businesses, taking advantage of the availability of cheap labour and the more reliable food supply. These rural areas gradually accumulated capital as well as technology, and formed proto-industrial areas.[47] Agricultural and proto-industrial tasks thus co-existed in one production unit (the household).

The implications of this kind of economic development are obvious. First, the rural household took on various types of work. Members of the household were engaged in more than one line of business, and often each member was involved in plural tasks. In this work environment, it was not appropriate to attribute the essential constituent of work to one line of business or its specificity. A concept of work which could accommodate the diversity of tasks - similar to *kagyo* (household business) - was needed. Second, once the conceptualisation of work of this nature emerged, it necessarily affected the perception of work; the activity had come to be perceived as multi-task, rather than as single-task. Whether or not workers with multi-tasks could perform better than those with a single-task would depend on specific economic circumstances. In the case of Tokugawa economic development, a multi-task pattern of work was better suited to the prevailing economic conditions. Third, the multi-task pattern of work helped emphasise the point of role-playing; without task specificity, emphasis on role was an effective way of making the members of the household understand what was expected when work was required. They simply had to identify and play a role, taking into account both the assigned role and the specific economic circumstances. Finally, this requirement implied that the *content* of the role in question was actually not assigned. Rather, it varied according to demand, which differed from one season to another; it also varied according to the type of extra tasks pursued. It was expected that the role would be 'played', regardless of the content of it. Role-playing without task specificity characterised the nature of work in Tokugawa Japan, and also formed the basis for the conceptual development of work.

Work as role-play in Tokugawa Japan

The lack of specificity in task and function is, according to Herbert Applebaum, one of the features of work in non-market societies. He argues that the presence of division of labour based on the breakdown of tasks and functions is the characteristic of industrial and market societies, whereas there is only a simple division of labour in non-market societies, involving basic cooperation and obligations of family units.[48] Work is intimately linked to all other social institutions such as kinship, politics, and religion in non-market societies, and is thoroughly embedded in the total cultural fabric. Work is directed to fulfil subsistence requirements, and is carried out for the sole purpose of meeting the needs of one's family or kinship group. A sense of competition in work is rare. Work relations are based on kinship, and the exchange of work or goods is based on reciprocity. There is little evidence of the existence of a distinct linguistic representation of work, because the productive activity is not separated from, or a dominant phase of, the social process.[49]

Work in Tokugawa Japan appears to correspond to Applebaum's description of work in a non-market society in at least two respects. First, task specificity has often been blurred by the multi-task nature of work, which may allude to the lack of task specificity. Second, the concept of role-playing rejects the clear-cut separation of economic activities from social relations; instead, it incorporates them into social relations.

There are, however, good grounds for arguing that the case of Tokugawa Japan does not fit into Applebaum's scheme. First, there is no doubt that task specificity was well recognised, notwithstanding the fact that people were engaged in plural tasks. Commodity production was widespread, and competition was present. Economic activities were integrated into the national, or at least provincial, economic fabric. Family labour was allocated in response to market demand, and additional labour, often from outside the kin-relation, was hired whenever necessary.[50]

But, in spite of these market developments, it was often advantageous in the Tokugawa economic environment to possess plural skills and take on plural tasks to produce economic results, as the peasants have demonstrated through the pursuit of extra tasks (*yogyo*). The nature of work in Tokugawa Japan, and the concept which developed concurrently with it, was a product of the presence of a combination of various tasks, not of the lack of task specificity.

Second, economic activities were clearly separated from activities in other spheres of society. Although festivals affiliated with religion were linked with seasonal regularities in the agricultural cycle, and agricultural work was interspersed with religious breaks[51], this does not imply that work was inseparable from them. Moreover, work was conceptually discernible, as was shown through linguistic representation, and was not embedded in the total social and institutional fabric, unlike productive activity in most of non-market cultures.

Third, the concept of role-play should be seen as an attempt to promote, rather than to hinder, the understanding of the importance of economic rationale for the meaning of work. Under the framework of the Tokugawa social order, considerations of economic rationale had to be incorporated into the more general and strongly sociopolitical terms of role-playing. But this concept allowed the members of the peasant (or merchant) household to identify their economic activities with their role in society. The clear-cut separation of economic activities from social relations would have denied them this opportunity: and it would have limited the range of incentives and justifications of work to a narrowly defined economic gain. Instead, the concept of role-play underpinned the idea that the greater

The concept of 'work' in Tokugawa Japan

one's economic performance, the greater role one was considered to have played in society.

It is possible to view society in the second half of the Edo period as a 'transitional' or 'mixed' one, as moving from a non-market to a market society. Applebaum employs such terms to define the nature of the closing stage of pre-industrial society, in order to understand the nature of work in such a society. The 'mixed' society typifies, in his view, an uneven and discontinuous social process which is frequently accompanied by resistance to changes affecting the social relations of non-market societies; it is often a painful adjustment and adaptation to a new way. Workers feel that they have no control over the tools and technology needed to perform work, and find that the only way to participate in the production process is to earn the means of living through selling their ability to others as a commodity.[52]

This was hardly the case in Tokugawa Japan. While Tokugawa society did go through "a painful adjustment and adaptation to a new way", particularly in the years of Bakumatsu, peasants were by and large willing to accept changes in their lines of business, their tasks and the technology of a specific task. They were far more concerned about the growing socio-economic stratification within the village, and, to some extent, the apparent inability of the Tokugawa regime to cope with forces of economic change.[53] Although people in Tokugawa society knew little about the impact of mechanisation, the society in which the concept of work was developed was undoubtedly the one where economic competition and market-orientation were prevailing.

An inquiry has been made in this chapter into linguistic representations of work, and the social, politico-administerial, and economic factors which contributed to the conceptualisation of work as it appeared in linguistic representations. It may be argued that work was constructed in the mid-to-late Edo period as a role to be played by individuals in such contexts as the household, the village, and society, where the tasks involved were variable. Work takes its meaning from economic as well as non-economic factors, but it clearly was a separate activity, discernible from other spheres of society.

Such findings are intended to serve as a general background for the more detailed study of work to be conducted in the following chapters. The thought of Ishida Baigan and Ninomiya Sontoku, which, arguably, was influential in shaping and institutionalising the idea of work of the populace in the mid-to-late Edo period, was in part a product of the socially constructed concept of work; they turned to the social and ideological teachings of the day to identify the meaning of work, and their ideas were expressed in a language derived from the religious teachings of the time, particularly Confucianism. In turn, their thought was not preoccupied with ethical and religious teachings but involved profound consideration of the elements of economics.

The thought of Ishida, as a representative of the eighteenth century Tokugawa merchants in the Kinai region, will be examined in the next three chapters. The thought of Ninomiya will be studied as an example of the agrarian work thought that had developed in the Kanto region by the first half of the nineteenth century; thought which not only reflected the prevailing form of agrarian work but intensified and conceptualised it.

Notes
1. Hayami Akira and Miyamoto Matao (eds.), *Iwanami Nihon Keizaishi, vol.1 (Keizai Shakai no Seiritsu)*, Iwanami Shoten, Tokyo, 1988. Shinbo Hiroshi and Saito Osamu (eds.), *Iwanami Nihon Keizaishi, vol. 2 (Kindai Seicho no Taido)*, Iwanami Shoten, Tokyo, 1989.

2. See works by Hazama Hiroshi, a leading scholar on labour history of modern Japan, including his *Nihon Romu Kanrishi Kenkyu*, Ochanomizu Shobo, Tokyo, 1978 (first published in 1964), and *Roshi Kyocho no Teiryu*, Waseda Daigaku Shuppankai, Tokyo, 1978, portions of which have been translated as "Japanese Labor-Management Relations and Uno Riemon", *Journal of Japanese Studies*, 5-1 (Winter, 1979). Reliable English sources on modern Japanese labour history include A. Gordon, *The Evolution of Labor Relations in Japan: Heavy Industry, 1853-1955*, Council on East Asian Studies/Harvard University Press, Cambridge (Massachusetts), 1985, and S. Garon, *The State and Labor in Modern Japan*, University of California Press, Berkeley, 1987.

3. Hiraishi Naoaki, 'Kinsei Nihon no "Shokugyo"kan', Tōkyō Daigaku Shakai Kagaku Kenkyusho (ed.), *Gendai Nihon Shakai*, vol. 4 *(Rekishiteki Zentei)*, Tokyo Daigaku Shuppankai, Tokyo, 1991. Harootunian, *Things Seen and Unseen*.

4. Applebaum, H. (ed.), *Work in Non-market and Transitional Societies*, SUNY (State University of New York) Press, Buffalo, 1984, introduction.

5. Joyce (ed.), *The Historical Meanings of Work*, introduction.

6. Hepburn, J.C., *Waei Gorin Shusei*, American Presbyterian Mission Press, Shanghai, 1867, pp. 95, 400 (J-E), 57, 131 (E-J). In a "Pocket Dictionary" compiled by Hori Tatsunoskay and published in 1862, 'work' was translated as *shigoto*, as was the term 'labour'. The Japanese term *saikumonogyō*, which literally means handicraft work, was also used as a translation of 'work'. Hori Tatsunoskay (Tatsunosuke), 'A Pocket Dictionary of the English and Japanese Language', Yedo (Tōkyō), 1862. Reprinted in Sugimoto Tsutomu (ed.), *Edojidai Hon'yaku Nihongo Jiten*, Waseda Daigaku Shuppanbu, Tokyo, 1981, pp. 835, 961.

7. Tsuchiya Tadao, *et. al.* (eds.), *Nippo Jisho* (Japanese-Portuguese Dictionary - translated into contemporary Japanese language from Vocabvlario Da Lingoa De Iapam: com a declaracao em Portugues of 1603), Iwanami Shoten, Tokyo, 1980, p. 583.

8. Kindaichi Kyosuke, et. al. (eds.), *Nihon Kokugo Daijiten*, Shogakukan, Tokyo, 1972-1976, vol. 11, p. 376. Hiraishi, 'Kinsei Nihon no "Shokugyō"kan', p. 47.
9. Hiraishi, 'Kinsei Nihon no "Shokugyō"kan', pp. 47-8.
10. Kindaichi, et. al. (eds.), *Nihon Kokugo Daijiten*, vol. 15, p. 357.
11. *Ibid.*, vol. 11, p. 376. *Ibid.*, vol. 15, p. 357.
12. Niimura Izuru (ed.), *Kojien* (third and revised edition), Iwanami Shoten, Tokyo, 1983, p. 992.
13. Kindaichi, et. al. (eds.), *Nihon Kokugo Daijiten*, vol. 10, p. 672 (*shoku*). In the Muromachi era, 職 read as *shiki* referred to revenue rights assumed usually by *shugo* and other administrators of similar ranks. In the Edo period, however, the term referred to one's occupation in general terms. *Ibid.*, vol. 9, p. 416 (*shiki*). *Ibid.*, vol. 17, p. 551 (*bun*).
14. Kaibara Gakken's 'Supplement' to Miyazaki Yasusada's *Nogyo Zensho*, published in 1696. *Nogyo Zensho* was edited by Tsuchiya Takao and published in 1936 from Iwanami Shoten, Tokyo. The quoted passage is from p. 348 of this Iwanami edition.
15. For more details regarding the use of the word *shokubun*, see Hiraishi, 'Kinsei Nihon no "Shokugyo"kan', pp. 48-50.
16. Muro Kyuso, No ko sho no Koto in 'Fubosho', Takimoto Seiichi (ed.), *Nihon Keizai Taiten, vol. 6*, Keimeisha, Tokyo, 1928, pp. 70-71.
17. Harootunian, *Things Seen and Unseen*, p. 249.
18. Hiraishi, 'Kinsei Nihon no "Shokugyo"kan', pp. 50-51.
19. Bito Masahide, 'Tokugawa Jidai no Shakai to Seiji Shiso no Tokushitu', *Shiso,* 685 (July, 1981). Also, *Nihonshi Kenkyu,* 324 (August, 1989).
20. Asao Naohiro, 'The Sixteenth-Century Unification', J.W. Hall, et. al. (eds.), *The Cambridge History of Japan,* vol. 4, Cambridge University Press, Cambridge, 1991, p. 52.
21. Bito, 'Tokugawa Jidai no Shakai', p. 5.
22. Ogyu Sorai, 'Taiheisaku', Nishida Taichiro, Maruyama Masao, et. al. (eds.), *Iwanami Nihon Shiso Taikei, vol. 36:*

Ogyu Sorai, Iwanami Shoten, Tokyo, 1973, p. 453.
23. Bito, 'Tokugawa Jidai no Shakai', pp. 5-6.
24. *Ibid.*, pp. 5, 10-12. Iwashiro Takuji's research on Ota village in the Province of Kawachi reveals the picture of peasants' involvement in *corvee*, and the ingredient of *buyaku* and *fusei* in some detail. Iwashiro Takuji, 'Kinsei Sonraku to Murayaku Rodo', *Nihonshi Kenkyu*, 324 (August, 1989).
25. Asao Naohiro, 'Kogi to Bakuhan Ryoshusei', Rekishigaku Kenkyukai and Nihonshi Kenkyukai (eds.), *Koza Nihon Rekishi, vol. 5 (Kinsei 1)*, Tokyo Daigaku Shuppankai, Tokyo, 1985, p. 49.
26. In addition to these arguments and intellectual debates on the concept of *yaku* by Bito and Asao, Takagi Shosaku's research on the legal aspect of the economic system of villages in 1976 suggests *yaku*'s 'multi-tasked' nature. Takagi Shosaku, 'Bakuhan Shoki no Mibun to Kuniyaku', *Rekishigaku Kenkyu*, special edition (November, 1976).
27. Mizumoto Kunihiko, 'Kogi to Mura, Hyakusho', *Koza Nihon Rekishi, vol. 5 (Kinsei 1)*, pp. 136-45.
28. Oto Osamu, 'Mibun to Ie', Fukaya Katsumi and Matsumoto Shiro (eds.), *Koza Nihon Kinseishi, vol. 3*, Yuhikaku, Tokyo, 1980, pp. 148-69. Oto specialises in economic historiographical research on Tokugawa villages, and also conducted studies on Ninomiya, which will be examined in Chapter 7 below. In this particular study, Oto simply intended to reveal the evolutionary process of the small peasant household towards becoming an independent production unit. It is not intended to be an investigation into the nature of the *yaku* concept itself.
29. Nakane Chie, *Kinship and Economic Organisation in Rural Japan*, London School of Economics/Athlone Press, London, 1967, Chapter 1.
30. Saito Osamu, 'Marriage, Family Labour and the Stem - family Household: Traditional Japan in a Comparative Perspective', R. Wall and Saito Osamu (eds.), *The Economic and Social Aspects of the Family Life-cycle: Europe and Japan, Traditional and Modern*, Cambridge University

Press, Cambridge, forthcoming, pp. 11-33.
31. Aoki Kazuo, et. al. (eds.), *Nihonshi Daijiten*, Heibonsha, Tokyo, 1992-1994, vol. 2, pp. 125-26.
32. Kindaichi, et. al. (eds.), *Nihon Kokugo Daijiten*, vol. 4, p. 400.
33. *Ibid.*, p. 400.
34. Hiraishi, 'Kinsei Nihon no "Shokugyo"kan', pp. 41, 54.
35. *IBZ*, vol. 1, p. 61.
36. Tamura (Jinzaemon) Yoshishige, 'Yoshishige Ikun', Iinuma Jiro, et. al. (eds.), *Nihon Nosho Zenshu*, vol. 21, Nosangyoson Bunka Kyokai, Tokyo, 1981, p. 224. Yoshishige Ikun is one of the examples of the family precepts of peasant households in the Tokugawa and the early Meiji periods which includes farming methods, family regulations and admonitions. Tamura is also the author of *Nogyo Jie*, which deals extensively with agricultural technology and its management. *Ibid.*, pp. 3-96.
37. Fukaya Katsumi, *Hyakusho Naritachi*, Hanawa Shobo, Tokyo, 1993, pp. 118-19.
38. R.W. Malcolmson, 'Ways of Getting a Living in Eighteenth-Century England', and M. Berg, 'Women's Work, Mechanization and the Early Phases of Industrialization in England'. Articles are in Pahl (ed.), *On Work*. Also, see Pahl, 'Introduction: Work in Context', *Ibid.*, esp. pp. 10-12.
39. Fukaya, *Hyakusho Naritachi*, pp. 159-84.
40. *Ibid.*, pp. 166-67.
41. *Ibid.*, p. 164.
42. *Ibid.*, pp. 173-74.
43. *Ibid.*, p. 178.
44. Smith, T.C., *Native Sources of Japanese Industrialization, 1750-1920*, University of California Press, Berkeley, 1988, Chapter 1.
45. Saito Osamu, *Puroto Kogyoka no Jidai*, Nihon Hyoronsha, Tokyo, 1985, p. 173.
46. *Ibid.*, Chapter 2.
47. *Ibid.*
48. Applebaum (ed.), *Work in Non-market*, p. 4.
49. *Ibid.*, pp. 1-3. In some non-market societies, however, a term representing 'work' exists, if not a rigid concept of

it; in traditional Tikopia society, for instance, the term *fekau* indicated 'expenditure of energy for accomplishment of ends, at some sacrifice of comfort or leisure'. R. Firth, 'Work and Value: Reflections on Ideas of Karl Marx', S. Wallman (ed.), *Social Anthropology of Work*, Academic Press, London, 1979, pp. 191-92. Exchange of goods between non-relatives with a certain 'exchange value' based on the amount of labour investment both in terms of time and skill also existed in Tikopia. *Ibid.*, pp. 193-95. Applebaum's assertion thus needs to be qualified.
50. Saito Osamu, *Puroto Kogyoka*, pp.183-84.
51. See, for instance, Fukuda Ajio, *Kanousei to shite no Mura Shakai: Rodo to Joho no Minzokugaku*, Seikyusha, Tokyo, 1990, pp. 36-50.
52. Applebaum (ed.), *Work in Non-market*, pp. 1-2.
53. Vlastos, S., *Peasant Protests and Uprisings in Tokugawa Japan*, University of California Press, Berkeley, 1986, especially, conclusion.

PART II ISHIDA BAIGAN

Chapter 3

Ishida's thought on work and the economy

Ishida Baigan
Ishida Baigan was born in a small farming village in the Province of Tanba, north of Kyoto. He was the second son of the Ishida family, a peasant household in the village of Higashi Agata, and spent most of his childhood, up to the age of eleven, in a rural environment. He was in no way highborn or rich, and, as is quite usual for a man of low birth, very little is known about his youth. Yet the outline of his early days and subsequent life course can be traced from retrospective accounts made by Ishida himself in his *Tohi-Mondo* ('City and Country Dialogue'), the master account, and the memoirs later compiled by his pupil. Ishida was the son of a farming family, but he spent most of his lifetime in urban surroundings. It was not uncommon for the second and third sons of Tokugawa village families to be sent as apprentices (*detchi*) to the cities, to make some provision for their lives. Ishida, following this custom, was sent to a

trading house in Kyoto when he was eleven. Although he was forced back to his family when he was fifteen because of the bankruptcy of the trading house he served, he was sent to another one in Kyoto, the Kuroyanagi family, when he was twenty-three, where he served for more than twenty years. In total, he spent twenty-eight years as a merchant in Kyoto, and he continued to live in the city until his death in 1744.

Neither of the two trading houses Ishida served was related to, or had close ties with, his family. But, even for an apprentice from an unknown family outside the kinship network, one could expect a gradual promotion in Tokugawa trading houses. Recruited at the age of ten or so, one usually served an apprenticeship of ten years or thereabouts. If one's performance was deemed sufficiently sound, then one was promoted to 'clerk' or 'retainer' (*tedai*) in one's late teens. A clerk could occupy an important position in the house, and could eventually establish himself as an independent manager of a branch house if he was sufficiently gifted and his services were well recognised in the household.[1] Ishida was expected to follow this path, but the unfortunate experience of his early days prevented him from establishing himself as a merchant. The bankruptcy of the trading house he served in his youth left an 'indelible stain' on his career, although the incident could hardly be seen as attributable to the services performed by Ishida himself. He became a chief clerk (*banto*) of the Kuroyanagi family in his late thirties, but the head of the household neglected to confer the headship of a branch house (*noren wake*) on him, a crucial step if a shop clerk were to set up in business on his own.

Thus, one could hardly argue that Ishida was hugely successful in trading. On the other hand, his career as a merchant was contributory in establishing him as a popular thinker: He was never removed from the economic and social realities of the Tokugawa trading houses, and with his knowledge and experience of trading, he had a far better understanding of the life of the townsmen than thinkers who had spent most of their lives in predominantly 'academic' environments. With the daily practices of merchants in mind, Ishida articulated the idea of work prevalent among the Kyoto merchants, and diffused it through lectures and the writing of family precepts of trading houses. At the same time, he fused the idea of 'learning of the mind', which originally derived from the Neo-Confucian ideology of the pursuit of 'true' mind, with the practicalities of trading; he laid down a system of cultivation that commoners could practise in everyday life. In short, he played a crucial role as a medium through which the tacit idea of work as embraced by merchants was conceived and fertilised with ideology, and was thus imbued with intellectual expression.

Tokugawa trading houses trained their men in reading, writing and calculating, and Ishida, like other apprentices, received such an education during the course of his service. He, however, did not confine his learning to the acquisition of such basic skills; although he did not receive any formal education in classical learning, he gradually but steadily accumulated knowledge of the Chinese classics, including such Confucian writings as the Analects, Mencius, and the Mean. Ishida did not have an affiliation with any particular school of the Tokugawa intelligentsia; nor did he pursue a prolonged scholarship under the direct instruction of any distinguished scholar of the time. He was a common man who was self-educated throughout. Although his teaching was later called by his pupil 'Sekimon Shingaku', or 'Ishida's school for the learning of the heart', he did not have sustained contact with scholarly representatives of any *shingaku* school in Japan.[2]

Ishida gave his first lecture in Kyoto in 1729, when he was forty-five. His lectures involved the so-called 'Four Chinese Classics' (*Shisho*); the Analects of Confucius, Mencius, the Great Learning, and the Mean. Lao tzu and Chuang tzu were also used in his lectures. These difficult texts were rarely accessible to the common people of that time, but through referring to everyday occurrences in his discussion of sublime texts, and giving question and answer sessions in lectures, Ishida made the content of the texts relatively understandable, and in fact drew a large popular attendance. No tuition was required to attend lectures by Shingaku scholars. No references of any kind were necessary either. Those factors all contributed to the popularity of Shingaku.

Ishida's leadership ended at his death in 1744, fifteen years after he first began lecturing. His disciples however continued to spread the teaching of their founder. Its popularity grew steadily in the first fifty years, and grew with more rapidity in the Tenmei period (1781-88). At its zenith, Ishida's teaching prevailed among more than thirty-six thousand pupils in over sixty domains. In later years, however, the Shingaku movement tended to be downgraded into a common morality movement, particularly after the proclamation of the Kansei Prohibition of Heterodox Learning in 1790.

Ideological background

Ishida was not a thinker who produced numerous ideological works. Tohi-Mondo and *Seikaron* ('Discourse on the Wise Government of the Household') are virtually the only accounts written by Ishida himself with the assistance of his pupils. Another source of Ishida's thought is the twenty-four-volume *Ishida Sensei Goroku* or 'Memoirs of our teacher, Ishida', a retrospective collection of Ishida's lectures and question-and-answer sessions made by his pupils. Tohi-Mondo is Ishida's chief ideological discourse, which includes not only moral and behavioural teachings for everyday life, but a metaphysical assessment of the origins of the universe, man, and all other beings.

Research by Shibata Minoru has shown that Tohi-Mondo draws on a total of seventy-eight different sources, with

Ishida's thought on work and the economy

references being mostly to the Analects of Confucius (referred to 133 times and quoted 75 times) and to Mencius (referred to 116 times and quoted 54 times). The Great Learning and the Mean are referred to twenty times each; other sources of Confucian, Buddhist, and Shinto thought appear much less frequently (twenty-one accounts are used only once each).[3] Thirty-one volumes of Buddhist accounts are either used or referred to (as against thirty-eight Confucian accounts), however only once in most cases.

What, then, is the ideological content of Tohi-Mondo? Ishida argues in Tohi-Mondo that the ultimate aim of both Buddhism and Confucianism is the same - to attain unity with one's nature (*ten* or *sei*). But diversity looms, he argues, when it comes to the means of attainment. Buddhism, in Ishida's view, requires the adherent to follow a specific path to attainment in an environment dissociated from secularity[4], while Confucianism recognises one's pursuit of moral practices in the secular context as the path to fulfilment:

> Confucianism equates the practice of the ways of *Gojo* and *Gorin* [5] in a secular context with the 'Way of Heaven' [as the ways to attain unity with one's nature], while Buddhism does not have such ways[6] . . . Buddhism and Confucianism share their ideas concerning the concept of man's nature [*ri* or *sei*], while they differ greatly from each other in terms of the means of attaining it.[7]

As shall be shown later in this chapter, Ishida argues that the means of cultivation lies in secular activities, particularly in one's everyday work. He dissociates himself from Buddhist thought in this respect. Ishida's view of Buddhism may need some qualification, however. Japanese *Zen* popularisers, Suzuki Shosan (1579-1655), for instance, regarded secular pursuits in everyday life as the means to attainment.[8] On the other hand, Confucian scholars of Sung China (960-1279) and thereafter developed articulated methods of cultivation marked by scholasticism and sublimity. From then on, the Neo-Confucian concept of cultivation emphasised the practice of formalised methods of self-refinement alien to the everyday life of the people. The only exception was a sect of the Wang Yang-ming school of Neo-Confucianism, which did identify moral action in a secular context with the means of cultivation.[9] It seems that Ishida was not profoundly concerned with these differences in ideas that existed between the sects and schools within Buddhism or Confucianism. He expressed his concept of cultivation in Confucian language, but he did not propound the elements of the scholastic method of cultivation advocated in Neo-Confucianism.

Ishida Sensei Jiseki or 'The Vestige of Our Teacher, Ishida' suggests his association with Shintoism at an early stage in his life; it shows that he intended to become a private Shinto preacher when he went to serve at a second merchant house in Kyoto at the age of twenty-three, and was consistently pursuing an orthodox 'morning Shinto practice'.[10] His references to Shinto texts, however, appear much less frequently in both Tohi-Mondo and Seikaron, compared with the intensity of reference to Confucian sources. The influence of Shinto upon Ishida's later thought may ultimately have been marginal, despite his early acquaintance with the religion.

Studies conducted up to the present time show that Ishida's thought reflected the ideas of all the major East Asian teachings - Confucian, Buddhist, and Shinto. No scholar has so far been successful in determining which of these formed the chief ingredient of Ishida's thought.[11] However, it could be argued that his thought has a stronger association with the Confucian mode of thought, particularly with that of Mencius, than with the other two; Mencius was extensively referred to by Ishida, particularly when composing his core argument. On the other hand, his idea of the cosmos reflects the metaphysics of Chou Tun-yi (1017-73) and Chu Hsi (1130-1200), two of the preeminent Neo-Confucians in Sung China who composed a concrete and structural mode of metaphysics encompassing both the universe and man. Uekawa Kisui (1748-1817), a Shingaku disciple, stated that Ishida's thought followed on directly from the ideas of Chu Hsi, while Kamada Ryuo (1754-1821) argued that it had a direct affiliation with the thought of Chu and Chou.[12] In fact, Chou's Diagram of the Supreme Ultimate (*Taikyoku Zusetsu*) was frequently referred to by Ishida in his discussions of the cosmos in Tohi-Mondo, as were the works of Chu Hsi.[13]

The ultimate aim of a Neo-Confucian was to become a sage, the state in which one attained moral purity and was unified with the cosmos. Neo-Confucians stressed moral cultivation and signified intellectual investigation as essential activities in preserving self from evil impulses and human desires and maintaining unity with one's own nature (*sei*).[14] Cultivation was also sought in order to unify oneself with the pattern of change in the cosmos, thereby affecting the transformation of things in society and the cosmos.[15] Specific methods advocated by Neo-Confucians to achieve these ends were the investigation of things and the extension of knowledge (*kakubutsu-chichi*), adherence to seriousness (*kyokei*), and exploring or 'fathoming' principle (*kyuri*).[16] For Ishida, being at one with one's own nature was also of prime importance, as was the necessity of refining and spiritually disciplining self. However, although for the Neo-Confucians the orthodox means to this end were study and meditation, for Ishida the answer lay in the everyday world, namely, in one's intensive devotion to work.

Ishida's thought: Work as the process of self-cultivation

> One shall be aware that one's standing is the actualised state of Heaven's will [*tenmei*]. This is duly what Confucius teaches us also. If one were aware of this, how could one be negligent of one's *shokubun*?[17] [In other words,] one's

> being is the nature [*ten-sei*] itself . . . samurai are samurai, peasants are peasants, and merchants are merchants . . . if one is loyal to Heaven's assignment, and is devoted to it, one shall certainly reach the state of fulfilment.[18]

Ishida argues here that each man born in this world is the actualisation of Heaven's will; those belonging to each occupational group have assigned tasks to pursue. His ideas thus look almost identical to the Neo-Confucian conception of man and his duty. However, what distinguishes Ishida from the Neo-Confucians is that he recognised immersion in assigned tasks as the means to fulfilment. And, through it, he advocated that people could become active entities in the process of self-cultivation, as this excerpt from Tohi-Mondo shows:

> While the assignment might differ from one person to another, one's nature is the same [*ri wa ichi nari*] . . . all people, from the Sage to commoners, are entitled to cultivate themselves; how can the people of each status group - samurai, peasants, artisans, and merchants - be different from one another in cultivating self?[19]

Ishida draws on the classic Confucian tradition to argue for self-cultivation as the universal right, which is not the case in the later Neo-Confucianism. This thesis of Ishida is noteworthy, for it has at least two important implications. First, it suggests that cultivation could be sought not only by a particular sector of the population (the ruling class) through sublime means but equally by people in all status groups. As has been pointed out by Watanabe Hiroshi, Neo-Confucianism aimed to cultivate the ruling class or 'upper strata' of the population. The elite was entitled to self-cultivation, and thereby to influence and transform society and the cosmos. On the other hand, Neo-Confucianism does not designate any means of cultivation for the masses.[20] Indeed, such accepted methods of cultivation in Neo-Confucianism as *kakubutsu*, *chichi*, and *kyuri* required a lengthy and intensive commitment to particular formalities, which could in practice be pursued only by a certain elite population. The masses were the indirect recipients of this influence, passive entities to be transformed by the force of the cultivated elites. H.D. Harootunian states that 'in Neo-Confucianism, the fundamental division was between the sage who possessed a certain kind of knowledge and the people who did not, between ruler and ruled. Knowledge entitled some to rule; it also required the acquiescence of those who had not attained knowledge.'[21] An important division is assumed here between ruler and ruled; between those who were entitled to cultivate themselves and those who remained mere passive recipients of influence from the cultivated population. Although the issue may still be debated, conventional Neo-Confucian methods of cultivation were designed exclusively for the upper strata of the population.

Ishida identified the work of each status group with cultivating action, thereby breaking away from the conventional assumption regarding cultivation in the Neo-Confucian mode of thought. Neo-Confucianism, with its emphasis on the scholarly and the contemplative, was pushed to the background and everyday work was promoted as a means to fulfilment. Refinement of self was at last no longer solely within the reach of the learned.

The second implication is that it was not only the practice of 'moral constants' in the secular context that Ishida emphasised as the means of cultivation. That he strongly argued that self-cultivation could be attained through devotion to one's 'work' is clear from the following:

A man asked Ishida: Is it the practice of 'Thirty-three hundred acts of *rei* [courtesy] and *gi* [righteousness]' which you are referring to as 'practical action'? If it is so,

peasants like us are not entitled to pursue that action; unlike the academicians, we cannot [afford to] practise such an action.
Ishida replied: The 'action' I am talking about is not thus. The learning of *rei* and *gi* which you mentioned might enhance the learning of dignity, but it might foster, as Confucius says, 'partial learning'. I shall explain the 'practical action' which I meant to advocate: If you are a peasant, you shall work from dawn to dusk. You shall devote yourself [to agricultural work] extensively; cultivate in spring, weed in summer, harvest and stock in the autumn. You shall always think of the way to produce more, even down to a single grain of rice . . . What I shall stress here is that if one is aware of one's own nature [*kokoro*], and work extensively, one shall be blessed with a great feeling of pleasure despite physical exhaustion.[22]

Here Ishida identifies the pursuit of agricultural tasks with cultivative action. The means of cultivation is not confined only to such 'moral practices' as the pursuit of the five moral constants and five social relationships; an intensive devotion to one's occupation preserves heart and cultivates self.

Researchers on East Asian religions have pointed out that Shingaku teaching emphasises the profound reflective contemplation and other contemplative means, which were the commonly advocated methods of self-cultivation in the orthodox Ch'eng-Chu teaching in China. R.N. Bellah argues that Shingaku teaching stressed the pursuit of 'quiet-sitting' so as to "exhaust the heart" (*kufu* or *seiza*)[23], while William T. de Bary, following Bellah, propounds that Shingaku's concept of self-cultivation followed on from Ch'eng-Chu teaching and practice, which emphasised more on the exercise of spiritual and moral discipline in order to 'fathom' self than on 'investigation'.[24]

It is true that the pursuit of such sublime practices - alien to the life of ordinary people - were increasingly emphasised in the later Shingaku movement in the post-Ishida era, particularly in the early nineteenth century. However, the vital element of Shingaku teaching in Ishida's time lay, as we have seen, in its emphasis on devotion to work. He stressed no sublime practice, such as quietistic detachment ('quiet sitting') or scholarship, as the primary means of practice, although he did recommend *kufu* as a secondary practice to be carried out in one's 'spare time'.[25] The following observation by Ishikawa Ken supports this view:

> Few thinkers were more enthusiastic than Baigan in discoursing the way of household work [*kashoku/kagyo*] . . . He revealed the origin of *kashoku*, the importance of it, and explained it in detail with numerous examples. He was not an example of the ordinary [Japanese] Neo-Confucians who tend to advocate only ethical discourse of a general kind; he explained moral actions along with the idea of *kashoku*.[26]

Indeed, Ishida himself experienced his first enlightenment (*satori*) when he was totally absorbed in caring for his sick mother, while the conscious efforts he had made for reflection before that did not get him anywhere.[27] In other words, he was enlightened through an intensive involvement in secular action, not through "quiet" reflective effort or study of any kind. Neo-Confucian advocacies of the investigation of things and the extention of knowledge may both be considered as 'active' elements of the means of cultivation, while adhering to seriousness and the 'fathoming' of principle may be categorised as 'quietistic' elements of the means. 'Active' as well as 'quietistic' means may both be needed in an ultimate sense to cultivate self. In Ishida's thought, it was the 'active' means - one's devotion to assigned work - that was emphasised, while quiet-sitting was recognised as a secondary means to attain self-cultivation.

Ishida's theories on cultivation invariably had major

The perception of work in Tokugawa Japan

implications for his views of the Tokugawa social structure. As the following passage from Tohi-Mondo suggests, people - the 'cultivated entities' - are all active entities in forming a part of the social process and its betterment:

> Samurai are retainers as they stand; not only samurai, peasants are also the retainers of the nation on the rice field; merchants and artisans are the retainers in the town; ... merchants serve society with trade ... society cannot stand without the contribution of all people in the form of the pursuit of their own assignments.[28]

The people in each status group were the retainers of the nation, and the assignment of each was a task which invariably involved the enhancement of social well-being. In Ishida's thought, commoners were to fulfil the assigned tasks for social good as the great figures of the past did:

> Yao devoted himself to fulfilling the way rulers are supposed to; Shun devoted himself to fulfilling the way pious men are supposed to; Duke of Chou devoted himself to fulfilling the way bureaucrats are supposed to; and Confucius devoted himself to fulfilling the way scholars are supposed to. They are, in Mencius's words, following the intention of their nature [sei] ...[29]

It thus became possible, at least in theory, for the masses to cultivate themselves so as to attain unity with nature, and actively participate in social betterment, which had until then been possible for the small number who could afford to go through particular processes of investigation and meditation. Furthermore, economic activities such as production, distribution and exchange had ideologically come to be recognised as a cultivating activity.

A school of thought that emphasised learning, self-development or self-cultivation through secular means had already developed in seventeenth century Japan. According to Kojima Yasunori, an intellectual historian of Tokugawa Japan, thinkers in the 'Classical School' (*Kogakuha*), Yamaga Soko and Ito Jinsai in particular, advocated a practical and 'action-oriented' method of training in attaining cultivation, while casting doubt over what they perceived as the 'static' method of training such as contemplation, adherence to seriousness, and fathoming principle, the accepted methods of cultivation in Neo-Confucianism.[30] Yamaga refrained from any reflective or contemplative means of cultivation, which he believed to be as elusive a means as trying to make a mark on water (*mizu ni shirushi wo nasu ni hitoshi*), and advocated instead the deployment of a more tangible, specific method of training as a way of refining one's being from the exterior, that being the practice of decorum and civility in everyday occasions.[31] Ito Jinsai argued, in the words of Najita, that 'metaphysical absolutes could not be known by the limited human mind, so the "observation" of nature should not be thought of as a reliable epistemology that would lead the human mind to such grandiose discoveries ... "Observation" cannot serve as an approach to reach conclusions as to transcendent and timeless norms of goodness that Neo-Confucian cosmologists have claimed.'[32] Both Ito and Yamaga expressed a strong inclination toward practical, tangible means of learning to be practised in a secular context, although the 'secular action' they refer to has more to do with 'moral' action than to one's assigned work.

The practical learning (*jitsugaku*) school, as it is generally termed, emerged not only among the Tokugawa intelligentsia but in the intellectual schools of other East Asian states. In fact, it developed in China much earlier than it did in Japan. According to Yu Ying-shi, a sect of Wang Yang-Ming's school of Neo-Confucianism which emerged in the sixteenth century, identified the secular deeds of peasants, artisans and merchants as the 'way' of cultivation, and emphasised learning through daily pursuits.[33] The emergence of the schools of *keisei chiyo* and *riyo kosei*, two of the preeminent practical learning schools in Korea, was a major intellectual sprout in the nation, particularly after the seventeenth century.[34] But Yu's study does not sufficiently describe the overall impact of the thought of Wang's school upon the common people of China. Some studies even claim the contrary point of view; Minamoto Ryoen, for instance, argues that the growth of practical learning schools stagnated in the late Ming (1368-1644) and early Ch'ing (1616-1912) China, and did not prevail over the orthodox Neo-Confucianism which was in favour of meditation and scholarship.[35] According to Pak, practical learning schools emerged in the second half of the seventeenth century in Korea and flourished in the early nineteenth century.[36] But one can hardly claim that this thought system infiltrated beyond the realm of the intelligentsia and into the masses as a popular, practical means of cultivation in everyday life.[37] Japanese *jitsugaku*, in contrast, not only exhibited a major intellectual *elan* from the early stage of the Edo period but also spread through to samurai, merchants, and peasant leaders both as thought and as a practical means of self-development.[38]

De Bary argues that the peculiarity of *jitsugaku* lies in the 'shift in the center of gravity from an early emphasis on moral substantiality and metaphysical truth to the pursuit of objective, empirical investigations serving utilitarian ends'.[39] It served to construct the 'preconditions' for the development of proto-scientific empirical rationalism as well as a radical moral activism.[40] The thought of Ishida differs itself from the *jitsugaku* of de Bary's description in that it does emphasise the quest for 'metaphysical truth' and the refinement of self, and it is not designed so much to serve utilitarian ends. One might argue, however, that the predominance of *jitsugaku* as a substantial intellectual trend in Tokugawa Japan certainly encouraged Ishida to improvise a powerful and widely acceptable method of cultivation. As a thought system which advocated 'work' as the means of cultivation, Ishida's method gained considerable support among the common people in the mid-Edo period.

Ishida's thought: The justification of trading

The second half of the seventeenth century saw a rapid expansion of transport systems on both the land and sea throughout the whole of Japan, thanks to the massive extension of road systems and other communication infrastructures. Great trading houses such as Mitsui, Konoike, and Sumitomo extended their businesses not only in the Kinai region but in Edo and its environs, diversified their businesses, and founded large shops in the cities. The era was marked by trade expansionism, however, increase in trading house bankruptcy followed shortly; trade growth had begun to slow down by the beginning of the Genroku era (1688-1703), due largely to the saturation of the domestic market and the unavailability of foreign trade occasioned by the seclusion policy. Some succeeded in stabilising and laying down solid business foundations after the era of rapid expansion, while a substantial number of trading houses, particularly those run by second or third generation shop owners and managers, faced difficulties; in fact, memoirs and diaries of the Genroku and Kyoho (1716-1736) eras show that numerous shops closed down; traders in these eras were demoralised through the loss of the unlimited business opportunities for expansion which their predecessors had fully enjoyed. Many became indulgent (*hoto*) and lazy, and lost business incentive.[41]

Samurai also began to face economic difficulties in the Kyoho era, and from then on were often in a state of constant poverty. The prosperous state of some rich merchants provoked, notwithstanding the fact that numerous trading houses were closing down, no little antagonism, as this account by Ogyu Sorai shows:

Merchants' accumulation of wealth was never so enormous as it has been for the last one hundred years . . . All stipends are absorbed by the hands of merchants, and samurai have become poorer every day.[42]

Ogyu attributed the impecunious state of the samurai to excessive exploitation by the merchants. Their "sleight of hand" in circulating goods whilst absorbing profit for their own ends and at the expense of others was condemned.[43] In fact, the Kyoho period of the mid-Edo could be seen as the time when antagonism towards the activities of merchants first became apparent. And it was exactly at this time that Ishida began his career as a Shingaku master. With the prevailing atmosphere as it was, what Ishida needed to do as a popular thinker was twofold: he needed to formulate a new meaning for trading not based on mercantile expansionism, in order to provide demoralised merchants with renewed incentives in an era of limited economic growth. On the other hand, he had to establish the legitimacy of trading and a *raison d'etre* for the merchants so as to eschew fierce criticism of them from others, particularly, the samurai. With these aims in mind, he argued the following:

If all the merchants were involved in peasantry or artisanship, there would exist no function for the exchange or circulation of money or goods. That would, without any question, bring about a paralysis in society. Samurai, peasants, artisans, and merchants are all mutually interdependent entities in the machinery of society. If society did not have any one of them, there would be serious difficulties in the functioning of society.[44]

Here Ishida spoke of the functional indispensability of all occupational groups in Tokugawa society, including merchants, without whose undertakings such as trade and distribution society would not be run. He also remarked:

> . . . samurai, peasants, artisans, and merchants all have their own ways. Not only the people in those classes, even a beggar has his own way.[45] How can the way of the merchants differ from that of the people in other status groups? As Mencius said, there is only one way for the people of each status group; how could there be two ways?[46]

Ogyu condemned merchants for unfair profit-making designed to benefit only their own group. In contrast, Ishida was supportive of mercantile activity, for it functioned as a medium through which shortcomings and oversupply in society were met. A merchant's devotion to his task was the righteous 'way' in the secular context which not only served to increase the merchants' profit but also benefited the people in other status groups. Ishida even went so far as to legitimise mercantile profit-making in the following way:

> Artisans' earning from their crafts is equivalent to the stipend. Peasants' making their living through agrarian work is also equivalent to the stipend.[47] Accumulation of the profit from sales is the 'way' of merchants . . . the profit from trading is also equivalent to the stipend.[48] Without profit, it is impossible to sustain a merchant's household business.[49]

He thus compared merchants' profits through trading to the samurai's stipend. He argued that both were the product of devoted action to one's occupation, and thus it was neither legitimate nor fair to castigate merchants for their profit-making.

On the other hand, Ishida was aware of the existence of merchants who practised unfair trading for the sake of one-sided benefit. To clarify the 'righteous' way of trading, he pronounced the following cautious words:

> The way of the merchant is based upon a mutually

beneficial way of trading. A ruffian trader tries to cheat his customers, in order to make a profit on that one occasion only. A merchant of this sort should not be considered as equal [to righteous merchants].[50]

Here Ishida denounces traders who are out for short-term profitability at the expense of their customers, and do not care about a long-term partnership with their clients leading to a prolonged beneficial mutuality. Such traders received no respect from the rest of the population; nor did they develop a solid basis of trading with which to continue their assigned task. Ishida did not support such traders.

On one occasion, he pointed out that the 'paddy which merchants have to cultivate exists in people's mind'.[51] Every act of trading or other assigned task should be conducted - as a peasant would cultivate his soil - with the greatest care. Here then is the bedrock of Ishida's perception of commerce and the social role to be played by merchants: trading was, in his view, not a matter of merely circulating goods, but also of cultivation. It was the prerogative of merchants to provide their customers with invaluable information and those goods and services best suited to them. Merchants, as specialists familiar with both the customer's needs and the products available, were entitled to act as mediators between the two sides, in order to enrich their customers with goods and services and to provide the producers with information regarding the customer's requirements. The activation and betterment of this interactive process was the merchants' mission: through it the customer's mind was enriched, as was that of the merchants with the practical knowledge of trading they acquired, and, ultimately, with insight into human society. Thus, 'careful cultivation' and 'mutual benefit' appear at the heart of righteous trading in Ishida's thought. He also said the following:

Customers are the 'providers' of your income. If you take

the best care of your customers with sincerity, most of the commodities you intend to sell will suit the customer's mind, and will be sold. If you make your best effort to provide customers with the best suited goods, you will have nothing to worry about in your career as a merchant.[52]

Customers were to be treated with integrity by traders whose good intentions became objectivised in the form of suitable goods and services. In turn, traders received their income, profit or 'stipend', as a reward for the caring effort they made. Mutual beneficiality continues thus.

One might wonder how Ishida assessed profit in the case of an economic *force majeure*. He remarked:

> A commodity which is worth 100 *me* may be sold at 90 *me* at times due to market fluctuations. You will suffer a loss when the market fluctuates thus. Then there are times you could sell it at 120 to 130 *me* . . . Such a rise and fall in price constitutes a *force majeure* caused by the 'manoeuvre' of Heaven; it has nothing to do with the merchants' will.[53]

It is arguable that there was a degree of market manoeuvring at the hands of mercantile giants in the mid-Edo period. It would not be appropriate to conclude from the above statement that Ishida, after serving trading houses for three decades, was not aware of the existence of this. However, neither in Tohi-Mondo nor in Seikaron is the market itself discussed to a great extent; Ishida seems to have concentrated more on the justification of the merchants' place in society, their assigned tasks, and their necessary attitude in daily life.

By focusing on these subjects, however, Ishida successfully set out a thesis through which merchants could view themselves as not essentially inferior to other people in different status groups, and their deeds as legitimate compared to other tasks: trading was of mutual benefit to both producers and consumers. Profit making was justifiable as long as it was the result of one's fervent action aimed at the fulfilment of that objective. Ishida's thesis thus legitimised the then disregarded merchants and their economic activity.

On the other hand, Ishida argues that trading was an assigned role given to merchants, through which they should cultivate self. He formulated this system of cultivation with reference to both the Neo-Confucian concept of attainment and the work of merchants. The everyday work of the common people, even those in the lowest ranks of the Tokugawa social strata, was identified with the idea of self-cultivation in the thought of Ishida. As such, members of all status groups were empowered to become active participants in their own self-refinement.

Notes
1. For customs and trading practices in Tokugawa merchant households, see Miyamoto Mataji's studies. Miyamoto Mataji, *Kinsei Shonin Ishiki no Kenkyu: Kakun Oyobi Tensoku to Nihon Shonindo*, Yuhikaku, Tokyo, 1942. Miyamoto Mataji, *Kamigata no Kenkyu*, Seibundo, Osaka, 1977.
2. A concise summary of the development of *shingaku* (learning of the mind and heart) in East Asia can be found in J. Anderson Sawada, *Confucian Values and Popular Zen: Sekimon Shingaku in the Eighteenth Century*, University of Hawaii Press, Honolulu, 1993. She argues that the "learning of the mind" originated in the Neo-Confucian revival of Sung China (960-1280). It reached Japan in the sixteenth and seventeenth centuries, after successive modification efforts by Chinese and Korean Neo-Confucians.

Such Japanese Neo-Confucians as Kaibara Ekken (1630-1714) and Nakae Toju (1608-1648) were the early recipients of the idea of 'learning' in Tokugawa Japan. By the middle of the Tokugawa period, *shingaku* came to be identified with the teachings of Nakae Toju and his disciple, Kumazawa Banzan (1619-1691). Anderson Sawada, *op. cit.*, pp. 1-3.

While the *shingaku* started by Ishida Baigan - named '*Sekimon Shingaku*' - emphasised such issues as "purifying the self", "learning of the heart", and "cultivation of the self", these were commonly advocated also in the preceeding *shingaku* thought and movement of Toju and Ekken. However, Ishida's *Sekimon Shingaku* differed from other schools in terms of its emphasis on the 'method' of cultivation; to cultivate the heart, it emphasised the pursuit of everyday work, not a particular, sublime method such as investigation and meditation. Hereafter, '*Sekimon Shingaku*' will be abbreviated to 'Shingaku' to differentiate it from other *shingaku* schools.

3. Shibata, *Baigan to sono Monryu*, pp. 13-15.
4. *IBZ*, vol. 1, p. 117.
5. *Gojo Gorin no Michi* (五常五輪之道) = five moral constants and five social relationships; *Gojo no Michi* are, benevolence, righteousness, courtesy, wisdom, and faithfulness: *Gorin no Michi* are the duties between sovereign and minister, father and son, husband and wife, elder brother and younger, and those pertaining to social intercourse between friends: from *Doctrine of the Mean* chapter 20-8, Clarendon Press, Oxford, 1893. Translated by James Legge.
6. *IBZ*, vol.1, p.116.
7. *Ibid.*, p.117.
8. See Nakamura Hajime, 'Suzuki Shosan, 1579-1655, and the Spirit of Capitalism in Japanese Buddhism', *Monumenta Nipponica*, 22, 1-2 (1967). Also, Bellah, *Tokugawa Religion*, pp. 78-79.
9. The T'ai-chou branch of the Wang Yang-ming school of Neo-Confucianism in late Ming China (1368-1644) advocated that the masses were also entitled to attain 'sagehood'. In their view, self-cultivation could be achieved through morally responsible activity, including work. Judith A.

Berling, 'Religion and Popular Culture: The Management of Moral Capital in *The Romance of the Three Teachings*', D. Johnson et. al. (eds.), *Popular Culture in Late Imperial China*, University of California Press, Berkeley, 1985, p. 217.
10. *IBZ*, vol. 2, p.621.
11. Ishikawa Ken has compiled a variety of theses concerning the ideological origins of Shingaku from existing scholarship. See Ishikawa, *Sekimon Shingakushi*, pp. 38-57. Although he briefly discusses conflicting views about 'origins', he seems to have refrained from stating any conclusive thesis himself. Recently, Anderson Sawada attempted to discuss the issue, only to conclude, perhaps following Ishikawa, that the 'Shingaku openness to different religious elements was shaped by a fundamental premise: human beings can reach moral perfection by experiencing the true nature of the mind. Religious doctrines and practices function in the Shingaku system according to their compatibility with this credo'. Anderson Sawada, *Confucian Values*, p. 4; Ishikawa, *Sekimon Shingakushi*, p. 54. Although one can assert that Shingaku had never been 'syncretic', in which religious situation conflicting and incoherent ideas are brought together (Anderson Sawada, *op. cit.*, p.4), it seems that the only possible conclusion is that Shingaku duly embraced a 'synthetic' element in its thought, despite its stronger inclination toward Confucianism.
12. Uekawa Kisui, 'Kyōchō Gorakusha Shingaku Shōden no Zu', Shibata Minoru (ed.), *Iwanami Nihon Shisō Taikei, vol. 42: Sekimon Shingaku*, Iwanami Shoten, Tokyo, 1971, pp. 202-203. Ishikawa, *Sekimon Shingakushi*, p. 39. Shibata, *Baigan to sono Monryu*, pp. 145-46.
13. Chu Hsi was a preeminent Chinese Neo-Confucian, who synthesised and completed the early Sung philosophers' re-assessment works on Confucianism in China. He strengthened the theoretical aspect of Confucianism mainly through the formulation of a metaphysics encompassing both the universe and man. Maruyama Masao, *Nihon Seiji Shisoshi Kenkyū*, Tokyo Daigaku Shuppankai, Tokyo, 1952.

A classic work by Fung in 1942 presents a concise discussion of Chu Hsi metaphysics. Fung, Yu-lan, 'The Philosophy of Chu Hsi', *Harvard Journal of Asiatic Studies*, 7 (1942-1943), pp. 1-51. Translated by Derke Bodde. For details of Neo-Confucian terminologies, see Ch'en Ch'un's *The Pei-hsi tzu-i*, translated into English in Wing-tsit Chan, *Neo-Confucian Terms Explained*, Columbia University Press, New York, 1986. Other sources which discuss this issue in some detail include Maruyama Masao, *Nihon Seiji Shisōshi Kenkyu*. Later scholarly works tend to be more focused on individual thinkers who belonged to particular branches and schools of the Neo-Confucian thought system, and not many 'general' accounts can be found. However, a good overview can be found in M.E. Tucker, *Moral and Spiritual Cultivation in Japanese Neo-Confucianism: The Life and Thought of Kaibara Ekken (1630-1714)*, SUNY (State University of New York) Press, Buffalo, New York, 1990.

14. Maruyama, *Nihon Seiji Shisōshi Kenkyū*, pp. 23-5.
15. Tucker, *Moral and Spiritual Cultivation*, pp. 60-1.
16. See de Bary, Wm. T., *Neo-Confucian Orthodoxy and the Learning of the Mind-and-Heart*, Columbia University Press, New York, 1981, esp., Part II (pp. 67-185).
17. *IBZ*, vol.1, p. 38.
18. *Ibid.*, p. 473.
19. *Ibid.*, pp. 215-16.
20. Watanabe Hiroshi, 'Tokugawa Zenki Jugakushi no Ichi Joken', *Kokka Gakkai Zasshi*, 94-1,2 (1981), pp. 67-69.
21. H.D. Harootunian, 'Metzger's Predicament' in the 'Review Symposium: Thomas A. Metzger's Escape from Predicament', *Journal of Asian Studies*, 34-2 (February, 1980), p. 254.
22. *IBZ*, vol. 1, p. 10.
23. Bellah, *Tokugawa Religion*, p. 151.
24. de Bary, *Neo-Confucian Orthodoxy*, pp. 206-209.
25. Shibata Minoru, *Shingaku* (Nihon Rekishi Shinsho), Shibundo, Tōkyō, 1967, p. 190. Ishikawa Ken also argued that it was not *seiza* or *kufu* which Ishida stressed as primary means of cultivation. It was one's active conduct of thrift and labour. Ishikawa Ken, *Ishida Baigan* (Nihon

Kyoiku Sentetsu Sosho), Bunkyō Shoin, Tokyō, 1943, pp. 24, 30-31.
26. Ishikawa, *Sekimon Shingakushi*, p. 178.
27. *IBZ*, vol. 1, pp. 8-9.
28. *Ibid.*, p. 82.
29. *Ibid.*, p. 4.
30. Kojima Yasunori, 'Kinsei Nihon Shisoshi ni okeru 'Kokoro' to 'Katachi'', Minamoto Ryoen (ed.), *Kata to Nihon Bunka*, Sobunsha, Tokyo, 1992, pp. 98-116.
31. *Ibid.*, pp. 101-105.
32. Najita, *Visions of Virtue in Tokugawa Japan*, p. 44.
33. Yu, Ying-shi, *Chugoku Kinsei no Shukyo Rinri to Shonin Seishin*, Heibonsha, Tokyo, 1991, pp. 158-66. This account was translated from Yu, *Ying-shi, Zhong-guo jin-shi zong-jiao lun-li yu shang-ren jing-shen*, Taipei, 1987, by Mori Noriko.
34. Minamoto Ryoen, *Kinsei Shoki Jitsugaku Shiso no Kenkyu*, Sobunsha, Tokyo, 1980, pp. 81-91.
35. *Ibid.*, pp. 79-81. Also, Hiraishi, 'Kinsei Nihon no "Shokugyo" kan', pp. 40-1.
36. Pak, T., 'Richo Koki ni okeru Seiji Shisō no Tenkai', *Kokka Gakkai Zasshi*, 88-11, 12 (1975), pp. 629-91.
37. Minamoto, *Kinsei Shoki Jitsugaku*, p. 101.
38. *Ibid.*, pp. 101-102.
39. de Bary, Wm. T. and I. Bloom (eds.), *Principle and Practicality: Essays in Neo-Confucianism and Practical Learning*, Columbia University Press, New York, 1979, p. 25.
40. *Ibid.*, p. 33.
41. A record of numerous examples of trading house bankruptcies can be found, for instance, in the diary of Kawachiya Yoshimasa, a landholder who also ran liquor shops in the Province of Kawachi. Nomura Yutaka and Yui Kitaro (eds.), *Kawachiya Yoshimasa Kyūki*, Seibundo Shuppan, Osaka, 1970 (first published in 1955). Ishida Baigan also lamented the notorious situation of trading house bankruptcies where he found 'seven or eight houses out of ten collapsed'. *IBZ*, vol. 1, p. 197. It would be risky to assume any statistical reliability in this statement.

Ishida's thought on work and the economy

However, the record of Kawachi, and the 'impression' given by Ishida on the state of things, give an authentic picture of the economic situation the trading houses were facing in the eras of Genroku and Kyoho.
42. Ogyu Sorai, 'Seidan, vol. 2', Nishida Taichiro, Maruyama Masao, *et. al.* (eds.), *Iwanami Nihon Shiso Taikei, vol. 36: Ogyu Sorai*, Iwanami Shoten, Tōkyō, 1973, p. 307.
43. *Ibid.*, pp. 306-45.
44. *IBZ*, vol. 1, p. 82.
45. *Ibid.*, p. 76.
46. *Ibid.*, p. 90.
47. *Ibid.*, p. 82.
48. *Ibid.*, p. 78.
49. *Ibid.*, p. 82.
50. *Ibid.*, p. 87.
51. *IBZ*, vol. 2, p. 283.
52. *IBZ*, vol. 1, p. 88.
53. *Ibid.*, p. 81.

Chapter 4

Skill, management, and workers' initiatives in Ishida's thought

In Ishida's view, the fulfilment of role assignment in the secular arena leads to the refinement of 'inner self'. It was not he alone, however, who related work to the inner cultivation of self. As we have already seen, Suzuki Shosan in the late seventeenth century argued that agricultural work and trading were the process of *shugyo* itself, which enriched one's spirituality. However, Ishida's thought was considerably more specific and interrelated with actual business process in trading than Shosan's; as a thinker with active experience of life in trading houses, he spoke of commerce, the skills necessary for the conduct of household business, and the importance of such 'economic' matters as management. This chapter examines selected elements of Ishida's discourse on work with reference to such economic concepts as 'skill', 'management', and 'work initiative'.

The concept of 'skill' in Ishida's work thought

The valuation of skill in the West
One of the essential elements consistently referred to by economic historians and sociologists in the discussion of work is 'skill'. In Paul Thompson's words, skill has been 'fundamental' to European cultures for centuries, and 'already had the double sense of mental reasoning and discrimination with practical ability in its medieval usage'.[1] Charles More defines skill as a combination of the ability to perform complex manual operations and the knowledge of materials and tools.[2] Braverman quotes in his *Labor and Monopoly Capital* the following description of 'skilled work':

> skill covers his ability to imagine how things would appear in final form if such and such tools and materials were used . . . he can estimate accurately both aesthetic appeal and functional utility, organise his tools, his power and his materials in a way which accomplishes his task and gains him livelihood and recognition . . .[3]

Although the word 'skill' was not yet the preeminent linguistic representation of artisanal presence in the first half of the eighteenth century in Europe, and its solid conceptualisation did not occur until the early period of industrialisation, it had already been recognised by artisans of the age as an 'individual technical property', as a means of distinguishing themselves from 'ordinary' workers; it was 'deeply embedded in the culture and consciousness of the artisans, as was the assumption of the respect of others for it'.[4] Skilled workers retained, as Marx argued, considerable power to safeguard their interests in the 'period of manufacture', because, in those days, handicraft skills remained the technical basis of manufacture.[5] As industrialisation progressed, the combination of capital-intensive factory operations and cheap labour began to erode their 'property'[6]; the trend brought with it the gradual replacement of handicraft skill by another kind, and eventually culminated in the social phenomenon called 'degradation' and the 'deskilling' of work.

Deskilling is defined as the 'incorporation of the crafts, knowledgeable practices and elements of job control held by workers into the functions of management, or operation of machinery'.[7] In other words, it is the subordination of those skills and knowledge, which had long been possessed (supposedly) by the workers in pre-industrial times, to the capitalists. This has been regarded as a major ingredient in the alienation of work, and thus also in the deterioration of the sense of satisfaction in the practice of work.

H.A. Turner stated in his account of nineteenth-century English cotton spinning workers that those who belonged to a social group which was recognised as a 'skill group' did not need to be skilled in reality, as long as they belonged to the group; the sharp demarcation between skilled and unskilled, due largely to traditional apprenticeship, gave individual workers in the 'skilled' group recognition.[8] Turner's argument, however, needs to be viewed with some qualification; for a skill group is an 'economic' institution and the maintenance of a 'genuine' skill level among individual members is essential for its very existence (and for the construction of that skill). Nevertheless, it is important to recognise that skill is not an automatic consequence of any given technological advance. As has been emphasised by recent sociological studies of work, it is a social construct which is a product of various value-adding elements. These studies distinguish between 'genuine' (or technical) skill which arises from a technology, and the 'socially constructed' skill which results from the artificial distinction of a particular skill through the control of entry to the social group which possesses that particular skill, for example, by apprenticeship.[9] They stressed that it was this 'artificial' construction, rather than a worker's actual technical competence, that added (or generated) scarce value to a skill.

E.P. Thompson argued that 'when the people search for legitimations for protest (in industrial disputes), they often turn back to the paternalist regulations of a more authoritarian society, . . . artisans appeal back to certain parts (e.g. apprenticeship regulation) of the Tudor labour code'.[10] That 'paternalist' regulation included apprenticeship regulation, through which a particular skill group could set up a demarcation line between skilled and unskilled, and thus make themselves 'exclusive' from the rest. They could preserve their skill and its social importance by that means, and this was presumably one of the primary reasons why protestors harked back to their past customs and regulations.

While this is not the place to examine the continuing debate on the term 'skill' in European history, it could be argued that skill represents the 'technological superiority' of individuals, and has been decisive in the economic and social career of the workers. For this reason, skill itself has continuously embraced recognition and social value.

In contrast, 'technology' of the 'individual' has not been manifestly posed as an important element of work in Japan, even in the modern period. The period after 1890 saw a rapid mechanisation of industries related to textile production. However, studies on industrial disputes show that neither workers nor industrial agitators vocally demanded the reinstatement of skill among individual workers during the disputes that occurred at that time.[11] The number of disputes increased sharply in the 1920s following the end of the economic boom thanks to the Great War of 1914-1918. But the restoration of a 'household-like' system (*kazokuteki keiei*), which embraced the 'benevolent' employment relationship, was the dominant linguistic feature of the industrial disputes.[12]

In the Edo period, skill was linguistically represented in such terms as *waza, giryō,* and *takumi*[13], and was the mark of artisanal presence. Skill and technological superiority was regarded as an important asset in agrarian as well as artisanal society. The advancement of agricultural technology was marked by the emergence of such agrarian technologists as Okura Nagatsune. Okura, along with other technologists, produced numerous agricultural handbooks (*nosho*).[14] These contained detailed explanations of advanced technologies. Peasants were keen to obtain these handbooks, and apply them in practice. However, most aimed to improve the economic welfare of the household, not to enhance an individual's potential to improve his economic status nor to raise the technological superiority of that individual over others.

Acumen in trading (*shosai*) and precision in calculation (*san'yo*) were seen as important assets in the Tokugawa mercantile environment.[15] But the recognition of those skills was not affiliated with individual recognition so much as with the succession of the business entity, the merchant's household (*shoka*). Ishida Baigan's thought on work recognised the importance of skill acquisition, but it was important as an 'instrumental' element to attain an end, which was the maintenance of the well-being of the household.

True, the occupational group which is most concerned with individual skill levels is the artisans. In the Edo period, artisans comprised only about five per cent of the population throughout the era. The percentage would be even smaller if one were solely concerned with those most skilled artisans who possessed a saleable skill.[16] One might argue that the absence of social valuation of skill in Tokugawa Japan was a logical outcome of this. But this is a common demographic feature of pre-industrial societies. A large proportion of the British population, for instance, remained agrarian even in the industrial period; a study shows that the bulk of the British population lived in an agrarian environment until the 1830s, and that the largest single occupational group of the male population still worked on the land.[17] As far as the 'form' of employment is concerned, only five to six per cent of the working class were self-employed even in London, by far the largest centre of artisanal production, by the end of the eighteenth century.[18] The employment relations of most artisans retained a patriarchal tinge in the eighteenth century, although the relationship increasingly became freer throughout the period.[19] Skill was, however, taking on an intrinsic social value in British society. The praxis of the skilled artisan was one of the axes of industrial bargaining, despite the scarcity of a truly skilled population and its diversity. What then was the factor which made the individual technological property of 'skill' an important but less socially valued element of work in Edo Japan? What was the alternative notion of skill in Japanese social history?

The work environment of the Japanese trading houses and skill

As we saw in Chapter 2, work in Tokugawa society was viewed as role-play, in which the tasks involved were plural. The succession of the household, the perpetual entity of lineal continuation, was the medium within which members identified themselves and maintained work motivation in agrarian households. Work in agrarian settings depended on skill of a less specialised but nonetheless plural kind, and was labour intensive both in agrarian and proto-industrial settings. The ability to work in consonance, to coordinate and allocate the existing labour force, were even more important than individual skill speciality.

The stable succession of the household business, and of the household itself in an ultimate sense, were of the highest priority in the trading houses of Kyoto in the second half of the eighteenth century, especially in large houses. Workers were recruited at an early age, and internalised job rotation was practised in order to enrich the workers with various types of job experience. A long-term employment system was already becoming an integral element of large trading firms. The labour market was internalised in these firms, and competition was enhanced within a certain demarcation (the household).[20] In short, workers were trained in-house from an early stage in their lives, and were expected to give a household a lifetime's service. They were trained to be 'skilful' in trading in the course of their service, but were expected to be adaptable to any tasks allocated to them. The skill of each worker needed to be of a plural nature in this job rotation system.

In such a work environment, single skill speciality was not a value in itself; value was attached to the secure continuation of the household, and the various skills which contributed directly to that continuation were considered of some importance. As the chart on the following page suggests, skill can be differentiated into three distinct kinds: first, there is 'genuine' skill which involves one's knowledge of materials and tools, and basic methods of carrying out complex material operations. Second, in addition to 'knowledge' and 'method', there is practical ability which embraces one's 'know-how' in utilising one's genuine skill in actual business, usually learned through on-the-job training.[21] Third, there is a skill of an even more general kind, namely, one's adaptability to varied tasks, one's capacity to facilitate consolidated task implementation such as communication between workers, and one's ability to organise an efficient workgroup and maintain good relations between workers and superiors. While these three aspects are inter-related in the actual implementation of tasks, they nonetheless constitute distinct kinds of skill. It was the 'genuine', individual skill, and the ability to practise it, which was generally recognised as 'skill'. The above discussion on skill in the West suggests that it was this type that was recognised as 'technological property' and imbued with social value. In contrast, it seems that skill of a general kind was considered of prime importance in

Japanese trading houses in the mid-Edo period. Except in employment relations where highly specialised skills were prerequisite, i.e., in artisanal society, no skill of a technical kind embraced a predominant social value in itself in the Tokugawa work scene.

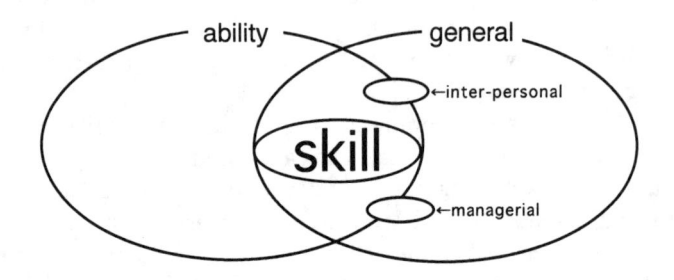

Diagram: Two overlapping ellipses labelled "ability" and "general", with "skill" at the intersection. Arrows point to "inter-personal" and "managerial".

Ishida's thought: The justification of skill acquisition
Ishida served two trading houses in Kyoto. Based on his own work experiences in trading houses, Ishida stressed the importance of skill of the third type - 'general' skill - involving one's coordinative capacity to organise the workgroup, communication skill in sharing business information and work experience, and the ability to maintain good relationships with one's co-workers. These skills may be termed 'managerial' and 'inter-personal' skills, calculated to enhance the efficiency of household business, and to avoid the disruption of the stable continuation of the household:

> The master of a household shall be keen to form a consensus in every business decision that the household makes. Business matters shall be consulted first among the chief clerks [*banto*]. If no agreement is reached, then all the retainers [*tedai*] in the household must be summoned to discuss the matter. If retainers are hesitant to express their say, then employ a ballot [*nyusatsu*] to settle the

matter.[22]

The above is an extract from Ishida's "Memorandum for the Well-Being of the Household", which was collected in his 'Memoirs', and was copied by his pupils when they formed their own family precepts (*kakun*). Here, Ishida refers to the importance of communication between workers and superiors. Communication, as he understood it, was not solely the expression of a superior's 'benevolent care' towards his retainers but a two-way information-exchange through which all - regardless of their position - were fully involved in the process of commercial decision-making. The memorandum even suggested a way in which the views of 'silent retainers' could be expressed - through a ballot system. Ishida also stated the following regarding the clerks (*tedai*) of the trading houses:

> *Tedai* retainers of a household shall always be concerned with each other; they shall be keen to consult with each other, and even a tiny matter shall be discussed among them so that a consensus is reached.'[23]

An influential factor here is Neo-Confucian ideology which valued concern for others, the practice of mercy, loyalty, and so on.[24] However, these were taught not as 'moral' or 'ethical' practices but as necessary abilities in the running of a household business. Retainers were not merely to be ethically concerned with each other but were entitled to consult each other regarding business affairs, and to get involved in the mercantile decision-making process. In short, Ishida emphasised the practice of managerial and inter-personal skills, geared to activate information transmission among co-workers and improved the workers' sense of participation.

The following words collected in Ishida's Tohi-Mondo also illustrate the importance of the skills discussed above. Responding to a question concerning personnel affairs and promotion within a household business, he argued that

> ... if there be no difference in *kiryo* [between the two retainers], the retainer who started his service to the house earlier shall be promoted sooner; ... if there be a difference in *kiryo* between them, the superior shall be promoted to the higher position sooner; ... the difference is caused by "Heaven's intention"; not attributable to individuals.[25]

Here Ishida spoke of the meritocratic settlement of personnel affairs. Worthy of note here is his use of the term '*kiryo*' (器量); it suggests his strong concern with abilities regarding inter-personal matters. Indeed, if he were concerned only with an individual's competence in trading, perhaps Ishida would have employed such terms as *waza* or *giryo*, the terms in existence in the Edo period that best correspond to the English word 'skill', and/or *shosai* (acumen in trading) or *san'yo* (precision in calculation). Instead, he used the term '*kiryo*'. The word consists of two distinct elements of human ability. *Ki* (器) or *utsuwa* means simply a 'receptacle', but it also means one's 'capacity'. *Ki* in the context of '*kiryo*' means the knowledge and power to carry out a task. The word *ryo* (量) also has two distinct meanings; it literally means 'quantity', but its secondary meaning is one's ability to 'read' another person's mind. The term *ryo* in the context of *kiryo* also means a place or a man fulfilled with virtue (*toku no mitsuru tokoro*).[26] The word *kiryo* therefore means not only individual technical competence in a speciality, but the ability and willingness to be concerned with others, through which good inter-personal relationships can be maintained. Ishida's use of the term *kiryo*, not *giryo* or *waza*, thus expresses the importance he places on managerial and inter-personal skills.

Retainers' initiatives and subjectivity in work

The secure succession of the household was prioritised in trading houses, but the stability of the household was not sought through the enforced submissiveness of the household members; as we have seen, retainers were encouraged to have their say. Ishida spoke of retainers as subjective entities who were self-contained in thought, initiative, and judgment. He commented in this way in his 'Memoirs':

> ... A man should rise to his feet [*ware wo tateyo!*] when he conducts his household work [*kagyo*]; think of *kagyo* as if it were an inseparable part of the body [*teashi no gotoku hanarezaru*] ... Be firm of will, hold onto your principles; one should be concerned to act upon the will; one's willingness and effort to be self-reliant constitute an expression of loyalty.[27]

Modern Japanese scholars have long focused on Ishida's emphasis on retainers' devotion to a lord, and failed to account for his discourse on the subjectivity, initiative, and spontaneity of retainers.[28] Ishida's thought tended to be regarded as yet another inducement for internal constraint, loyalty and submission, through which the status quo of the household unit, and, in an ultimate sense, of Tokugawa society itself was maintained. The degeneration of Shingaku into a common morality movement in later days has been attributed to this element of Ishida's thought. While Ishida spoke of the importance of a retainer's devotion to his lord on occasion, this must not be confused with a mere admonition of 'blind submission'; Ishida spoke openly of the right of retainers to express their own opinions, and emphasised on workers' subjectivity in work.

One might still wonder that, despite Ishida's advocacy of relative autonomy for retainers, they were never given sufficient decision-making power to topple their superiors; ultimate power rested in the hands of the superior (*kacho*) in the trading houses of Tokugawa society, and thus there was, in reality, no room for retainers to manipulate business, or to be 'subjective' in their conducting of business matters. On this point, Ishida argued:

> Retainers [*tedai*] shall attempt to expostulate even their superior, if his deeds are judged unrighteous[29] . . . If the master be selfish, or indulge in dissipation, retainers should call for a discussion session so as to work out the means to stop the master's indulgence; if the master do not stop, retainers should jointly call for his retirement from the headship, because it will seriously damage the ancestors of the household.[30]

Thus, for Ishida, the retainers of trading houses were not mere 'vassals' submitting blindly to the will of their superior, but had the power to influence managerial decisions, including those concerning personnel management at the highest level.

As discussed in Chapter 2, work was seen in Tokugawa society as a role to be played by the members of each status group. Ishida also viewed the work of each status group as the 'given' one. Contrary to, say, the Calvinist concept of work, which assumed the commoners' right to choose their own work[31], individuals were not offered the opportunity to choose an occupation. This being so, how could the opportunity exist for an individual to act 'subjectively' in carrying out his work? Here it is necessary to distinguish between freedom to choose the task to be pursued, and subjectivity in conducting the task itself. The freedom to choose work was almost unthinkable in Tokugawa society, where all tasks were recognised as 'sanctioned' role-play. A subjective attitude in the carrying out of one's task was however a matter of great concern, and, according to Ishida, a man could pursue his task with his own judgment, initiative, and spontaneity albeit within the limits of a given work circumstance. Moreover, job selection itself was, it appears, not a matter of great importance in the Tokugawa work context: for job valuation stemmed, as we saw earlier in this chapter, not from the type of job an individual dealt with but from his ability to sustain the household; the level of an individual's technical skill was important, but value was not attached to the level of skill itself. Furthermore, the mastery of managerial and inter-personal skills was valued regardless of job-type. In a work environment of this sort, one could argue that freedom in the choice of task loses its relative importance; the ability to practise general skills in any field of business was of greater importance.

The quality of work performance within a business enterprise depends on the ability and the degree of skill-specialisation possessed by the individual workers. Equally important factors which sustain that quality include organisational and human relational elements present in the work process. The organisation of the workgroup, its relations with superiors and management, the degree to which workers have control over decision-making, and the extent of communication between workers are all crucial in the efficient running of a business. Ishida was aware of this, and emphasised the importance of management and human resource coordination skills. He spoke of the potential of these skills to fully activate the abilities the household retainers possessed.

Ishida held that household work was in itself the process of self-cultivation. Individual competence in trading was an important asset, and immersion in trading was regarded as an act of enrichment. Hard work alone would not lead to self-refinement, however. For Ishida, 'process' meant not merely an intensive labour input but embraced the practice of managerial and inter-personal skills, and involvement in business decision-making in a household. It calls for the workers' 'subjective' participation, not merely a 'passive' adaptation or submission to one's superior in a collective entity.

The recognition of the importance of these skills, and the identification of them with work, are worthy of note, for they could be seen to represent a widening of the perception of work to include social relational and inter-personal elements. Furthermore, the recognition of these abilities had begun to shape the actual meaning of work; a meaning that had arisen not merely from an individual's gain for the sake of personal profit, but from his role as an activator of human resources and as a contributory agent in the stable continuation and betterment of the household.

As was mentioned in the last chapter, there were thinkers and schools of thought which identified secular pursuits and the acquisition of practical knowledge with cultivation even before Ishida, not to mention the *Zen* popularisers of seventeenth century Japan. The T'ai-chou branch of the Wang Yang-ming school in late Ming China regarded the pursuit of morally responsible activity in the secular context, including work, as the process of cultivation. But, surely, the integration of such skills as coordination and management into the scope of work was found for the first time in the thought of Ishida. As such, it can be seen to mark a crucial development in the enlargement of merchants' perception of work in eighteenth century Tokugawa Japan.

Notes
1. Thompson, P., 'Playing at Being Skilled Men: Factory Culture and Pride in Work Skills among Coventry Car Workers', *Social History*, 13 (1988), p. 45.
2. More, C., 'Skill and the Survival of Apprenticeship', S.

Wood (ed.), *The degradation of work?: Skill, De-skilling and the Labour Process*, Hutchinson, London, 1982, p. 109.
3. The quoted lines are from M.C. Kennedy's unpublished PhD thesis. Quoted in H. Braverman, *Labor and Monopoly Capital: The Degradation of Work in the Twentieth Century*, Monthly Review Press, New York, 1974, p. 444.
4. Rule, J.,'The Property of Skill in the Period of Manufacture', Joyce (ed.), *The Historical Meanings of Work*, p. 104.
5. Marx, K., *Capital, vol. 1*, Lawrence and Wishart, London, 1983 (L&W version first published in 1954), chapter 14: Division of Labour and Manufacture. German edition, *Das Kapital*, was first published in 1867. English edition first published in 1887.
6. Rule, 'The Property of Skill', pp. 104-6.
7. This definition is quoted from 'Glossary of Labour Process Terms' in P. Thompson, *The Nature of Work*, Macmillan, London, 1989 (first published in 1983), p. xiv.
8. Turner, H.A., *Trade Union Growth: Structure and Policy*, George Allen and Unwin, London, 1962, pp. 110-14.
9. H.A. Turner was probably the first who noticed the constructed element of skill in 1962, although he did not clearly state it as a 'social construct'. He has subsequently been followed by authors including Phillips and Taylor, 'Sex, Class in the Capitalist Labour Process' - paper presented to Windsor conference, 1978, Wood (ed.), *Degradation of Work?*, Pahl (ed.), *On Work*, and so on.
10. Thompson, E.P., *Customs in Common*, Merlin Press, London, 1991, p. 10.
11. For a detailed description of the nature of labour relations and of industrial disputes in modern Japan, see Hazama, 'Japanese Labor-Management Relations and Uno Riemon' (*Roshi Kyocho no Teiryu*), *Journal of Japanese Studies*, 5-1 (Winter, 1979), and S. Garon, *The State and Labor in Modern Japan*, chapters 1 and 2.
12. One might argue that the Japanese workers' call for the restoration of the 'household-like system' in industrial disputes is almost synonymous with the English workers' call for the 'reinstatement of paternalist regulations'.

However, it has to be noted that the chief aims of the disputes by the Japanese workers were the improvement in the treatment of employees (*taigu no kairyo*) which embraces the 'benevolent relationship' between the employer and employees, and the improvement of one's 'respectability' (*chii no kojyo*). Smith, *Native Sources of Japanese Industrialization*, esp. pp. 236-47. It did not aim to preserve a certain 'skill' and the stake of a skill group based on a particular skill. See also Hazama, *Nihon Romu Kanrishi Kenkyu*, pp. 14-121, and A. Gordon, *The Evolution of Labor Relations in Japan*.

13. 'Skill' is generally translated into *jukuren* in contemporary Japanese. But the Edo words mentioned in the text stood for technical skill and instrument [*waza* = Kindaichi, *et. al.* (eds.), *Nihon Kokugo Daijiten*, vol. 20, p. 638], one's level of ability in accomplishing tasks [*giryo* = *Ibid.*, vol. 6, p. 293], and skilfulness [*takumi* = *Ibid.*, vol. 12, p. 712].

14. For Okura's agricultural treatises, see Iinuma, *et. al.* (eds.), *Nihon Nosho Zenshu.*, vols. 14 and 15.

15. Miyamoto Mataji, *Kinsei Shonin Ishiki no Kenkyu*. Najita, *Visions of Virtue in Tokugawa Japan*.

16. Sekiyama Naotaro, *Kinsei Nihon no Jinko Kozo*, Yoshikawa Kobunkan, Tokyo, 1958, pp. 275-307.

17. 'Occupational Structure of Great Britain, Males, 1841-1921' in B.R. Mitchell and P. Deane, *Abstract of British Historical Statistics*, Cambridge University Press, Cambridge, 1971, p. 60.

18. Schwarz, L.D., 'Income Distribution and Social Structure in London in the Late Eighteenth Century', *Economic History Review*, 32 (1979), pp. 256-57.

19. Marx, K. and F. Engels, 'The German Ideology' (1845), J. Cohen, E.J. Hobsbawm, *et. al.* (eds.), *Collected Works*, 5, Lawrence and Wishart, London, 1976, pp. 65-67. However, E.P. Thompson argues that paternalist control over the whole life of the labourer was being eroded in the first six decades of the eighteenth century. E.P. Thompson, *Customs in Common*, pp. 35-38.

20. Saito Osamu, *Shoka no Sekai, Uradana no Sekai*, Riburo Pooto, Tokyo, 1987, esp. pp. 38, 101-102, 123,

165-66.
21. Saito Osamu, 'Jukuren, Kunren, Rodo Shijo', Kawakita Minoru (ed.), *Shiriizu Sekaishi eno Toi, vol. 2: Seikatsu no Gijutsu, Seisan no Gijutsu*, Iwanami Shoten, Tokyo, 1990, pp.170-71.
22. *IBZ*, vol.1, p. 270.
23. *Ibid.*, p. 271.
24. In fact, mutual care and 'concern' in inter-personal contexts tended to be regarded as 'ethical practice'. See, for instance, Takenaka, *Sekimon Shingaku no Keizai Shiso*, Mineruva Shobō, Kyōto, 1962, pp. 445-49. Miyamoto Mataji even argues that the admonitions of the family precepts concerning inter-personal care were the 'remains' of feudal elements, and dismissed them as 'negative' (*shokyoku teki*) elements of the precepts. Miyamoto Mataji, *Kinsei Shonin Ishiki no Kenkyu*, pp. 73-87. On the other hand, advocacies on such 'individual' skills in commerce as acumen in trading (*shosai*) and precision in calculation (*san'yo*) were regarded as 'positive' elements of the trading house precepts.
25. *IBZ*, vol. 1, p.74.
26. Kokushi Daijiten Henshu Iinkai (ed.), *Kokushi Daijiten vol. 4*, Yoshikawa Kobunkan, Tokyo, 1983, p. 458. As for the term *ryo* (量), see also Niimura (ed.), *Kojien*, p. 2,518. See also Matsumura Akira (ed.), *Daijirin*, Sanseido, Tokyo, 1988, p. 658.
27. *IBZ*, vol.1, pp. 336-37.
28. Minamoto Ryōen and Sakasai Takahito, however, focus on Ishida's advocacy for retainers' subjectivity in their respective studies. See Minamoto Ryoen, 'Ishida Baiganron', Imai Atsushi and Furuta Shokin (eds.), *Ishida Baigan no Shiso*, Perikansha, Tokyo, 1979, pp. 73-120. Sakasai, 'Sekimon Shingaku ni okeru Jissen Tetsugaku no Tenkai'.
29. *IBZ*, vol. 1, pp. 270.
30. *Ibid.*, p. 271. A similar clause can be found in the family precepts of other trading houses of eighteenth-century Kyoto. Such a large trading house as Mitsui had a clause in its precepts which legitimised the expelling of a prospective heir if he were indulgent. Clause 15, 'Mitsui

Constitution of 1722'. Quoted in J.G. Roberts, *Mitsui: Three Centuries of Japanese Business*, Weatherhill, New York, 1973, pp. 501-502 (Appendix A).
31. Weber, M., *Purotesutantizumu no Rinri to Shihon Shugi no Seishin*, Iwanami Shoten, Tokyo, 1991, pp. 305-17. This is the third revision of *Purotesutantizumu no Rinri to Shihon Shugi no Seishin*, originally translated by Kajiyama Tsutomu from *Die protestantische Ethik und Der Geist des Kapitalismus, Gesammelte Aufsatze zur Religionssoziologie*, Bd. 1, 1920, SS. 17-206, and published by Yuhikaku in 1938. This account has been revised and translated by Otsuka Hisao.

Chapter 5

The spread of Ishida's thought on work

In the foregoing two chapters, Ishida's thought on work has been examined from several different perspectives. The impact of his thought was partially explored in Chapter 4, but one cannot ascertain the overall effect of his thought on the mercantile environment of the Tokugawa era and, more generally, on the emergence of the perception of work in Tokugawa Japan, without a careful assessment of its actual diffusion. This chapter aims to deal with this issue.

The chronology and the process of the spread of Shingaku have already been covered in two major studies by Ishikawa Ken; *Sekimon Shingakushi no Kenkyū* and *Shingaku Kyōka no Honshitsu Narabini Hattatsu*.[1] In addition, Shibata's research closely examines the discourses of successive Shingaku leaders such as Teshima Toan, Uekawa Kisui, and Kamada Ryuo.[2] Miyamoto Mataji's classic work on the family precepts of the trading houses shows Shingaku's influence on the everyday life of merchants.[3] However, apart from Robertson's account on Teshima Toan and Anderson Sawada's recent work on the later Shingaku movement[4], no research on the Shingaku movement after Ishida's death has yet appeared in the English language. Moreover, Robertson's work deals with the methods employed by Ishida's successor, Teshima Toan, to organise and transmit the ethical element of Ishida's teaching, but how Ishida's thought on work and commerce influenced merchants of the era did not concern her. Anderson Sawada has dealt substantially with both the method of transmission and the concept of cultivation inherited by Ishida's pupil, but the impact of Ishida's work thought is left untouched. With all this in mind, this chapter will consider the impact of Ishida's thought on merchants of Tokugawa society in the running of trading houses in eighteenth century Japan.

We will start with a brief sketch of the nationwide spread of the Shingaku movement, based upon the research of Ishikawa and Shibata, to be followed by a discussion of the 'ingredients' of the teaching in the later Shingaku movement. The final section, we will trace the influence of Shingaku upon the family precepts (*kakun*) of trading houses.

The nationwide spread of Shingaku

Fifteen years of pre-eminence as leader and as chief lecturer of Shingaku came to an end when Ishida died in 1744 at the age of fifty-nine. The Shingaku movement, however, showed no consequent sign of decline but continued to grow under the leadership of his successors. Sugiura Shisai (1711-1760) succeeded to the lecturership at Ishida's old house in Kyōto, and also lectured in Ōsaka. The lecturership was succeeded to by his son, Muneyuki (1733-1809).[5] Teshima Toan (1718-86), perhaps the most recognised of Ishida's followers, not only lectured throughout Kyōto, Osaka, and the surrounding areas but initiated the establishment of Shingaku academic centres, generally called *bosha*. The *bosha* system not only provided pupils with meeting places, but organised Shingaku into an entire 'movement'; it enhanced the regular and systematised delivery of lectures and the further extension of its membership. With the rise in popularity of Shingaku, such centres as *Shuseisha* (1773), *Jishusha* (1779), and *Meirinsha* (1782) were founded in Kyoto. Five centres were also founded in Ōsaka in the first few years of the Tenmei period (1781-1788), along with those three Kyoto centres (both Ishida and Teshima delivered lectures in Ōsaka but academic centres were not built until this time).[6] While the usual number attending lectures in Ishida's time was forty to fifty, Teshima's lectures attracted from three to four hundred people up to a maximum of a thousand.[7] Teshima himself lectured in fourteen cities in seven different provinces where the centres were newly founded. Including the centres which were in the care of his pupils, Shingaku extended its influence to fourteen provinces.[8] Shingaku reached Edo when Nakazawa Doni (1725-1803) built academic centres in Kanda and Nihonbashi in 1783. Thus, Shingaku centres were in place in the three major cities of Japan by the time of Teshima's death in 1786.[9]

Teshima Wa'an (1747-1791), Toan's son, and Uekawa Kisui (1748-1817), an adopted son who succeeded to the Uekawa family (*chokkei* of Toan's mother) inherited the leadership of the three centres in Kyoto, and administered the movement in the Kinai and its environs.[10] They also contributed to the spread of Shingaku to western Japan, and to Shikoku; three academic centres being founded in the domains of Awa and Tosa.[11] Meanwhile, Nakazawa continued to spread Shingaku not only within urban Edo but throughout the entire Kanto region. Ishikawa's research shows that the development of Shingaku centres was concentrated on the districts of Kinai in the years of Tenmei, while the Kanto region saw extensive development in the years of Kansei (1789-1800) and Kyōwa (1801-1803).[12] Shingaku spread also to the Hokuriku and Tōhoku regions in those years, owing largely to the efforts made by Nakazawa, and the number of Shingaku academic centres increased in the San'yō, San'in, and Shikoku regions in the years of Bunka (1804-1817) and Bunsei (1818-1829). Eventually, Shingaku reached all four corners of Japan, except Ezo (Hokkaidō), the northern part of Tohoku and Kyushu, by the end of the Bunsei era. Shingaku reached Kyushu in the following Tenpo years (1830-1843), but the movement began to decline in Kanto at that time, due largely to the great famine.[13] Evidence shows that it was superseded by Ninomiya's more practical *Hotoku* movement, and his *shiho* programme (cf. the villages of Kamado Shinden and Oda; see note 24 of this chapter).

In sum, twenty-two Shingaku academic centres were founded in the years between 1745 and 1786 (Toan's era), and fifty-nine were founded by his successors from 1787 to 1803. Another fifty were founded in the subsequent Bunka and Bunsei eras. As a result, the number of *bosha* reached one hundred and thirty-one by the end of the Bunsei era (1818-1829).[14]

Shingaku is largely believed to have been a townsman's movement, spread only among the mercantile, urban population. However, its influence was not limited to this. Ishikawa's research shows that a total of 179 Shingaku centres were established, and of these, 58 were located in towns which were not castle towns (*jokamachi*), and 62 of them were in rural areas.[15] This shows that although the spread of Shingaku was mainly within the urban population in Ishida's time, it gradually extended to the provinces and to rural areas.

The teaching strategy in the later Shingaku movement

Teshima and his followers made an effort to popularise Shingaku, notably by using accessible and simple vocabulary in lectures. Ishida taught sublime classics such as the Analects and Mencius in his lectures. Teshima also used these classic texts, but he declined to use difficult words and always couched his teaching in an easier vocabulary, often using words in five-seven-five syllibus (*shichigochō*) in both written and verbal teachings. A typical example of this is *Jijo Nemuri Samashi* ('For Boys and Girls: Waking Up from Sleep'), a collection of ethical discourses in easy *shichigochō* words.[16] His teaching strategy of 'casual transmission', coupled with the establishment of Shingaku academic centres (*bōsha*), could be seen to contribute significantly to the accumulation of a large following and to the spread of the movement. Ichimura's study of the teaching strategy of Nakazawa Dōni also reveals an emphasis on accessibility in the later Shingaku movement.[17]

Apart from the strategy employed to improve teaching methods, Teshima also adopted a strategy designed to target people by age group. For instance, *Zenkun*, which literally means 'provisional training', was the lecture programme designed to educate the young. Boys between the ages of seven and fifteen and girls between seven and twelve were encouraged to attend the programme, but it was also open to adult newcomers. Like the ordinary Shingaku lecture programmes, it did not require tuition of any sort. Lectures were held every ten days, usually in the afternoon. The contents of the teaching were not substantially different from that of the regular sessions, but the words and phrases used were made appropriate to the age of the students.[18]

A movement without a figurehead needs a clear ideological premise with which to determine direction. The Shingaku movement, which lost Ishida in 1744, needed to establish a creed for this reason, and in answer to that need Teshima Toan wrote *Kaiyu Taishi* or 'Creed of the friends of the Shingaku association' in 1773. It opened as follows:

> *Kaiyu Taishi   Kogi Shishu* [Main theme of the lectures]:
> What our teacher Ishida taught us is to get to know the 'original mind' [*honshin*] of the Sages, and to be keen to preserve enlightenment brought about by these Sages. In order to know the original mind, one needs to be frugal,

keen in self-refinement in everyday life, and diligent in cultivation.[19]

To do this, Teshima advocated, through short articles in *Kaiyu Taishi*, the practice of the five social relationships.[20] Following those ethical teachings, he spoke of immersion in one's household work (*kagyo*):

> *Kagyo* of any kind - agricultural, artisanal, or mercantile - is not an occupation reflecting the intention of the individual; it is the task which is "wonderously" assigned by Heaven [*fushigi ni shite uke'etaru kagyo nareba kore tenmei nari*]. One shall thus not be negligent in the pursuit of *kagyo*; . . . If one is not properly conducting *kagyo*, one will face great difficulties in life, disturb one's parents, and will end up betraying the virtuousness inherent in the original mind.[21]

As shown in *Kaiyu Taishi*, the practice of refinement through secular activities was the chief ingredient of Shingaku advocacy. The pursuit of the five social relationships and household work were recognised as the means whereby one becomes familiar with the 'essence of the Sages' and attains enlightenment. Teshima, following Mencius's words, argued that the 'way' lay not in the pursuit of the sublime practices of study and meditation but in everyday activities, particularly in the practice of diligence, frugality, and social relationships. Thus, the tenor of teaching in Teshima's era was not alienated from Ishida's teaching.

Alienation from secularity in the later Shingaku movement
Shingaku, however, gradually alienated itself from practical learning. It began to emphasise more 'extraordinary' activities such as study and meditation.[22] Under Nakazawa Doni who took the initiative to spread Shingaku to the Kanto region, it was reduced to an ethical doctrine.

Nakazawa emphasised the importance of following ethical teachings rather than the practice of cultivation through everyday work. Moreover, he ultimately emphasised the 'obedience' of the people. He frequently used the term '*shitagau bakkari*' which means 'just obey', and was in part responsible for the eventual dwindling of Shingaku to a mere morality movement which encouraged passive adaptation to the social order.[23] True, Ishida did argue that the people should be fully suited to their given social environments and inherent assignments, but he also strongly advocated the subjective addressing of action toward an object of work. In contrast, submissiveness was the sole exhortation of Shingaku teaching under Nakazawa.

This propensity in the later Shingaku movement coincided with the great famines in the Kanto region in the first half of the nineteenth century. Shingaku was unable to cultivate people's attitude to counter the economic difficulties. For this reason, the movement's popularity declined sharply in the region in the late Edo period. Thus the way was paved for the more practical Hotoku movement of Ninomiya Sontoku, and his shiho programme.[24]

Shingaku thought in the family precepts of trading houses

The era of great trade expansionism gradually faded away as the seventeenth century came closer to its end. In the eighteenth century, trading houses began to pay more attention to the foundation of a solid business system for the sake of stability, and this was sought through a formalised system of education for household members geared to create the necessary tact, know-how, and appropriate 'attitudes' among employees, and to standardise their performance. The common method employed for that purpose was the formation of the family precepts (*kakun*). Some houses used different names such as *tensoku* (rule of the shop), *tenho* (law of the shop), and *misesadame* (provisions of the shop) instead of the term *kakun*.[25] Moral and ethical admonitions usually constituted a large part of the precepts, but they also involved descriptions of trade regulations, and 'concepts' and methods of trading. The family precepts of a radical sort, that of the Yano family, for instance, involved specific methods for efficient management, the 'way' to read the market, and secret know-how in dealing.[26] Miyamoto Mataji shows that the employment of the family precepts became almost fashionable in the second half of the eighteenth century not only among the big merchant houses but also among middle and small merchant households.[27]

Of note here is the fact that Shingaku pupils were active in the writing of the family precepts. The following extracts are taken from the precepts of the *Omiya* trading house in Kyoto, composed by the head of the house, Saitō Masakado in 1769. They exhibit Ishida's influence; some passages are quoted virtually *verbatim* from Ishida's 'Memorandum for the Well-Being of the Household' in *Ishida Sensei Goroku*, mentioned in the last chapter:

> 1. Needless to say, each member of the shop shall pursue his role to the best of his ability; [in addition,] there should always be mutual assistance in the pursuit of household business; from clerks to apprentices, all shall respect harmony and consort with one another in the household . . . If a member be selfish and pursue 'unrighteous' quarrels, that will always be to the detriment of the household . . . Members shall always be righteous and be in agreement for that is the way to preserve the well-being of the household. [article 4]
>
> 1. If the master of the household were not performing his duty, or if there were a need for amendment to the household rules, the problem shall be discussed immediately by all members. The master shall be expostulated constantly for his wrong doing. If no sign of improvement appears, all members shall [consult with one another and] even decide to confine the master; for the

continuation of the household shall be prioritised above all. [article 3]

1. If a retainer thought that the earning of extra profit even through the deployment of unfair means is a mark of loyalty to one's master, such retainer's thought shall be corrected. [article 15]

1. Not to mention a business with a frequent customer, even the sale of a small cut of cloth [with an unfamiliar customer] shall be conducted with a heartfelt care . . . A man's business continues through the mercy of the customers; they are like the parents of the business. [article 17]

[28]

The essence of articles 15 and 17 appeared in Ishida's discourse in Tohi-Mondō, and the importance of 'mutual care' was manifest in his 'Memorandum' in the *Goroku*. The retainer's right to terminate the service of an ill-serving household head is also listed in the precepts. Saitō was a merchant who studied under Ishida, and became one of his closest pupils in the final years of his leadership. The following is taken from 'A Provision of Household Business' (*Kagyo no Sadame*) written by Sugiura Munenaka, and is another example of the influence of Ishida's thought on the family precepts of trading houses:

. . . Regarding the 'origins' of the existence of the merchants; merchants exist in order to meet the surplus and shortfall of goods and services; they are entitled to make their living through transactions . . . To make their fortune through these activities is the way of the merchants. The parents of this fortune are the people . . . Be conscious even of a penny, and give a heartful care to the commodity you intend to sell; if you do this, the goods will suit the customer's wishes and will be sold . . . Furthermore, the merchants' activities will circulate fortune amongst the people, and profit all corners of society.[29]

As we saw in Chapter 3, Ishida spoke of the functional indispensability of merchants, and also of the legitimacy of the profit made by them. The above passage duly reflects Ishida's those ideas concerning commerce and merchants. Also, eleven short articles followed this passage, their subjects ranging from specific methods of trading and the treatment of house customers to the precepts of the 'righteous way of trading'.[30]

Both Saito and Sugiura studied in the Shingaku school under the direct headship of Ishida, and one might thus argue that the reflection of Ishida's thought in their family precepts was a natural outcome. Its influence, however, extended beyond the Shingaku school: Yura Shichihei of *Tanbaya*, a cotton wholesaler in Osaka, wrote two family precepts, 'Code on the Way of the Family' (*Kafu Shikimoku*) in 1796 and 'Provisions' (*Okite*) in 1797, when he handed over the headship of the family to his son, Hisahide. Takenaka reveals that Shichihei's precepts followed those of Saito Masakado. Twenty-three out of the thirty-five articles of Saito's precepts were either copied directly or were of the same tenor; twenty-five of the thirty-four articles of *Okite*, six out of the twenty-seven of *Kafu Shikimoku*, and two of the four supplementary articles were adopted from passages in Saito's precepts, according to Takenaka.[31] In later years, Hisahide began to involve himself increasingly in Shingaku and became one of the lecturers at the *Meiseisha* in Osaka.

According to Miyamoto Mataji's study, the precepts of the Yano family reveal the considerable influence of Shingaku thought, despite the fact that no direct link between the house and the Shingaku school is identifiable. An ethical precept of the house, *Enju Hoshinki*, stresses such virtues as selflessness, thrift, and recognition of one's role (in both the household and society) and devotion to it.[32] The twenty-

The spread of Ishida's thought on work

fourth and twenty-fifth articles of *Monmo Hajigaki*, written in 1845, warn against selfish decision-making in business, and stress the importance of consultation with other household members and of consensus in both written and verbal means of communication.[33] According to Miyamoto, 'it seems that Shingaku masters wrote the family precepts for various households in townships at the request of those households'.[34] He also argues that 'a fundamental similarity between the ideologies of households and the ethics of Shingaku thinkers is identifiable in numerous examples (of the precepts in various households), and thus the contribution of the Shingaku school in the formation of the 'norm' of the merchants is highly likely'.[35]

Shingaku as a movement declined in the late Edo period. Many of its academic centres were closed down in the years from late Edo to Bakumatsu, especially the ones in the economically difficult Kantō region. However, Shingaku thought, particularly the thought on work developed in its founder, Ishida, formed an intrinsic part of the precepts of trading houses.

Shingaku masters maintained their contact with trading houses even in the modern Meiji era. A prime example is their association with the Sumitomo family, a mercantile giant of the Edo period, which grew to become *zaibatsu* conglomerate in the Meiji period. One of the executive members of the Sumitomo family, Kokura Masatsune, began to employ Shingaku teaching for the education of the Sumitomo employees in the early Meiji period. Kokura continued his association with Shingaku, and later became the president of the Sekimon Shingaku Association in the post-war year of 1952.[36]

Notes
1. Ishikawa, *Sekimon Shingakushi*. Ishikawa, *Shingaku Kyoka no Honshitsu narabi ni Hattatsu*.
2. Shibata, *Baigan to Sono Monryu*.
3. Miyamoto Mataji, *Kinsei Shonin Ishiki no Kenkyu*. Miyamoto Mataji, *Kamigata no Kenkyu*.
4. Robertson, J., 'Rooting the Pine: Shingaku Methods of Organization', *Monumenta Nipponica*, 34-3 (Autumn, 1979). Anderson Sawada, *Confucian Values and Popular Zen*.
5. Shibata, *Baigan to sono Monryu*, p. 167.
6. *Ibid.*, pp. 170-71.
7. Ishikawa, *Sekimon Shingakushi*, p. 272.
8. *Ibid.*, p. 272.
9. Shibata, *Baigan to Sono Monryu*, p. 178.
10. Ishikawa, *Sekimon Shingakushi*, pp. 312- 433.
11. *Ibid.*, pp. 399-400.
12. Ishikawa, *Shingaku Kyoka no Honshitsu*, p. 192.
13. Ishikawa, *Sekimon Shingakushi*, pp. 739-82, 978-87.
14. *Ibid.*, p. 555.
15. Ishikawa, *Shingaku Kyoka no Honshitsu*, pp. 211-24.
16. Teshima Toan, 'Jijo Nemuri Samashi', Meirinsha (ed.), *Teshima Toan Zenshu*, Meirinsha, Kyoto, 1931, pp. 47-67.
17. Ichimura Yuichi, 'Shingaku Dowa to Komyunikeishon', Bito Masahide Sensei Kanreki Kinenkai (ed.), *Nihon Kinseishi Ronso*, vol. 2, Yoshikawa Kobunkan, Tokyō, 1984.
18. Teshima Toan, 'Zenkun', *Teshima Toan Zenshu*, pp. 69-93.
19. Teshima Toan, 'Kaiyu Taishi', *Ibid.*, p. 97.
20. *Ibid.*, p. 98.
21. *Ibid.*, p. 98.
22. Anderson Sawada, *Confucian Values and Popular Zen*. Anderson Sawada argues that Shingaku provided the commoners with methods of cultivating the 'original mind' by themselves. Neo-Confucian texts failed, in Sawada's words, to prescribe a feasible method of cultivation for busy merchants, artisans and farmers. In contrast, a peculiar element of Shingaku teaching lies in its sensitivity to the 'context of everyday life'; it amalgamated the Neo-Confucian concept of cultivation and "casualised" Zen

practices for attainment, and provided the commoners with practically employable means to "quest the mind". *Ibid.*, pp. 4, 8, 165, 166.

Anderson Sawada was right in pointing out the importance of the concept of cultivation in Shingaku teaching. However, Ishida argued in Tohi-Mondō that cultivation could be achieved through the daily activities of the populace, that is, through work, not through 'group study' or 'contemplation'. Anderson Sawada, in contrast, argues that Shingaku methods of cultivation lie in such 'extraordinary' activities as study and meditation. *Ibid.*, pp. 91-109. Indeed, Sawada describes the means of cultivation and educational programmes developed in Shingaku teaching in the post-Baigan era, but most of these were alien to the pursuit of daily activities. This may well have been the propensity in Shingaku teaching in the post-Toan era, while it was certainly not the case in Baigan's time, nor, probably, in the first half of the Toan era. After all, Shingaku's alienation from secular means was a major factor behind the loss of pupils to more practical, production-oriented movements, such as the Hōtoku movement in the nineteenth century. (see note 24 below).

23. Nakazawa Doni, 'Dōni-O Dōwa', *Iwanami Nihon Shisō Taikei, vol. 42: Sekimon Shingaku*, pp. 207-32 (esp. pp. 210-1). This view of the later Shingaku movement is also shared by Ishikawa in his *Sekimon Shingakushi*, pp. 492-584 (esp., p. 532), and by Tsuda Hideo in his 'Kyoiku no Fukyu to Shingaku', Asao Naohiro, Ishii Susumu, *et. al.* (eds.), *Iwanami Koza Nihon Rekishi, vol. 12 (Kinsei 4)*, Iwanami Shoten, Tokyo, 1976, p. 164.

24. Kobayashi Heibei, a village headman of Kamado Shinden village in the Province of Suruga, was an active member of the Shingaku movement in the Bunsei era (1818-29). He 'transferred' himself from Shingaku to Hotoku after 1837 when Ninomiya Sontoku came to inspect the village. He became a leading figure as well as a chief financial provider of the shiho implementation in the village. Niki Yoshikazu, 'Odawarahan Kamado Shinden

Mura no Hotoku Shihō ni tsuite', *Rikkyō Keizai Kenkyū*, 45-3 (January, 1992), pp. 123-62.

Similar transitions occurred in other villages in the Kanto region. The villages of Yatabe and Oda in the Province of Hitachi, for instance, abandoned the Shingaku academic centres established in the villages and started to adapt the shiho programme in the Tenpo era (1830-44). For Yatabe's Shingaku, see Oto Osamu, 'Kanto Noson no Kohai to Sontoku Shiho', *Shiryōkan Kenkyu Kiyo*, 14 (supplement volume; September, 1982), pp. 131-66.

25. Miyamoto Mataji, *Kinsei Shonin Ishiki no Kenkyū*, p. 154.
26. *Ibid.*, p. 156.
27. *Ibid.*
28. Articles extracted from the 'Precepts of Household Matters in Omiya Jinbei of Kyoto' (*Kyoto Omiya Jinbei Kaji Kyokun)'*. 'Jinbei of Kyoto Omiya' was Saito Masakado, an Ishida disciple. The original of Saito's precepts has been kept by Professor Miyamoto Matao of Osaka University, son of Mataji. The unabridged articles of Saito's precepts are also available in Takenaka, *Sekimon Shingaku no Keizai Shiso*, pp. 446-50.
29. Sugiura Munenaka, the 'Rule of the Household Work' (*Kagyo no Okite*), quoted in Takenaka Yasukazu, *Nihonteki Keiei no Genryu*, Mineruva Shobo, Kyoto, 1977, pp. 150-51.
30. *Ibid.*, pp. 151-55.
31. *Ibid.*, pp. 155-57.
32. Miyamoto Mataji, *Kinsei Shonin Ishiki no Kenkyu*, pp. 244-46.
33. *Ibid.*, p. 243.
34. *Ibid.*, p. 148.
35. *Ibid.*, p. 164.
36. Miyamoto Mataji, *Kamigata no Kenkyu*, pp. 221-22.

PART III NINOMIYA SONTOKU

Chapter 6

The idea of work in the thought of Ninomiya Sontoku

Ninomiya Sontoku

Ninomiya Sontoku, as a representative of agrarian leaders working for the rehabilitation of villages that had been deserted in the late Edo and Bakumatsu eras, is a figure of considerable historical importance. Like other rural leaders and technologists, he was a man of common origin who lived most of his life in villages. He held governmental office at both national and provincial levels, but his chief concern lay not in politics but almost solely in the improvement of economic conditions in the villages, some of which had reached a desperate state by the beginning of the nineteenth century, particularly in the northern Kanto region. Ninomiya is also important as a popular thinker who represented the new thrust of thought on work and the economy which emerged in the late Edo period. Although he was not a vanguard representative of the commercialisation of the agrarian economy, he played a critical role in accumulating underlying ideas of agricultural work to which he added ideological meaning, and in feeding this back to the agrarian commoners of the era. He was the founder of the movement for agricultural rehabilitation - later called the *Hotoku* movement - which spread extensively in the Kantō region in the first half of the nineteenth century, and at a national level in the subsequent Bakumatsu and Meiji eras.

Ninomiya was born in 1787 into a farming household in Kayama, a village in the domain of Odawara, Suruga Province. Kayama village was approximately three miles north of Odawara (town), the principal castle town of the domain. The household to which he belonged had two *chō* and three *tan* of wet paddy, a considerable area of arable land for a farmer to hold. His family was one of the richer peasant households in the region, but the great flood in the early 1790s destroyed all its fortunes: the Ninomiya family into which Sontoku was born was a branch family, newly established by Sontoku's grandfather. As was often the case with new families, the Ninomiyas' paddy and house were located not on the ideal side of the village, but alongside the bank of the River Sakawa, and were vulnerable to natural disasters, particularly floods.[1] The great flood of 1791 swept away the entire land area belonged to the Ninomiyas. What was even worse, Sontoku lost his father, Riemon, when he was thirteen, and this was followed by the death of his mother two years later. Sontoku and his two younger brothers were left to fend for themselves, and experienced a time of extreme hardship.

By 1810, however, he had restored his farmland and his household, thanks to help from relatives and by dint of his own efforts. The restoration he undertook was recognised by the domain of Odawara, and the domain, looking for a 'good model' of diligence with which to admonish its peasant producers, awarded Ninomiya for his efforts. He was employed by the domain in 1811 as a member of a restoration project for the Hattori family, one of the retainers of the domain lord, Okubo. In 1816, he began in the service of Okubo Tadazane, the Lord of the time, and immediately joined domainal village reconstruction programmes. Two years later, he was appointed the leader of the Hattori family project, an unusual honour for a person of agrarian origin. In 1822, at the age of thirty-five, he was appointed the leader of the village rehabilitation programme in the domain of Sakuramachi in Shimotsuke Province. From then on, he devoted himself to the rehabilitation of deserted villages and domains in the entire northern Kanto area. He was also in charge of similar projects in more far-flung domains, such as Soma in the Tohoku region.

Ninomiya became a retainer of the Tokugawa Shogunate (*bakushin*) in 1842, and participated in the project for the refurbishment of the bank alongside the River Tone. Even after he left Government office, he continued to serve village and domainal projects until he died in 1856 at the age of seventy at the administration office of the Nikko project. He was involved in as many as twenty-three village rehabilitation projects in thirty-four years. Including the villages which employed Ninomiya's schemes but had no direct contact with him, the total number of the villages affiliated with Ninomiya is believed to have reached six hundred.[2]

Ninomiya's adolescence was thus devoted to the restoration of his own household, and the rest of his life was spent in the restoration of deserted villages and domains. He had no formal instruction or academic education, except for a few opportunities to get acquainted with Neo-Confucian teaching from domainal lectures when he was serving the Hattori family in Odawara. This fact is responsible, in turn, for the construction of his thought, which was marked by its practicality. As we will see in the next chapter, agricultural topics predominate in his theoretical accounts. He used words and phrases from Neo-Confucian rhetoric, and even used Neo-Confucian diagrams to express his ideas, but they were all related to the productive work of agriculture.

Although his thought may not be as intellectually refined as other Tokugawa schools of thought, the actual influence it had on the rural populace, and its contribution in restoring village morale and agricultural productivity cannot be discounted.

Ninomiya produced several written works in which his thought on work, society and nature was expressed. But he was not a thinker who composed theory only; he also formed the village rehabilitation programme called *shiho*, in which he specifically designed work in actual terms. Since he expressed his idea of work in two different modes - ideological 'discourse' and the economic measures of the shiho programme - and the level of thought in each differs, we need to deal with them separately. Ninomiya's thought on work as expressed in his philosophical writings is to be examined in this chapter. His ideas as reflected in the workings of the shiho programme will be dealt with in Chapter 7. The findings of the two chapters will be consolidated and the impact of his work thought on the economic activities of the peasants of the era will be analysed in Chapter 8.

The philosophy of work (1): Virtues of industry and planning

The title of Ninomiya's main treatise, *Sansai Hotoku Kinmoroku* (abbreviated as *Kinmoroku* hereafter), illustrates his idea of nature, man and work: *Sansai* means 'three abilities', which were the abilities of Heaven (*ten*), earth (*chi*), and human beings. The title literally means 'the use of the three abilities of Heaven, earth, and man as recompense for the virtues received'. 'Virtue' as it is used here has little to do with moral excellence or righteousness. As we will see in this chapter, it refers to the 'gift from nature' given to man in one form through the birth of ancestors, and in another form through the consistent supply of 'sources of life', such as the soil, water, and seeds: nature provides man with these natural gifts. The physical birth of man is brought about by his parents, ancestors, and, in an ultimate sense, by nature. A living man's existence has been made possible by the diligence and industry of his ancestors in bringing to fruition the natural gifts. Living human beings, the product of both nature and the predecessors, are obliged to work hard in order to continue and further cultivate the received virtue (natural gifts). This act, in Ninomiya's view, corresponded to remuneration for the blessings received from nature.

Kinmōroku appeared in 1834. Its content comprises revised versions of manuscripts and jottings written in his diary in an informal manner mostly in the 1820s and early 1830s, when Ninomiya was vigorously involved in village projects. *Kinmōroku* was, in other words, a culmination of his thought as it developed concurrently with his idea of work and the economy during the course of the actual village rehabilitation processes. Ninomiya's written works, *Kinmōroku* and others, are all preoccupied with words that enhanced man's industry and planning within an agricultural context due largely to this fact. The words and diagrams in the following pages were taken from the *Tenmei Shichigenzu* of 1836, which encourages man's industry.

In the diagram of riches and poverty, *yaku* (約 = frugality) is placed along with 卯二月, February in the old calendar, which is the beginning of spring, and with 東, the 'East', the direction of the rising sun. *Tomi*, wealth and/or abundance, is placed with 午五月, May, the beginning of summer, and with 南, the 'South'. *Ogori* (奢 = extravagance) is placed with autumn and the 'West', and *hin* (貧 = poverty) with winter and the 'North'. Ninomiya compared the cycle of riches and poverty to the seasonal ups (summer) and downs (winter), and with the compass; frugality leads to the season of abundance (summer) and extravagance will result in poverty (winter). Similarly, he composed a diagram of fulfilment and loss. *Tsutome* (勤 = industry) is the beginning of fulfilment (得 = *toku* or *eru*), while indulgence (惰 = *da* or *namake*) will result in loss (失 = *shitsu* or *ushinau*). For Ninomiya, eco-

The perception of work in Tokugawa Japan

Diagram A: Riches and Poverty

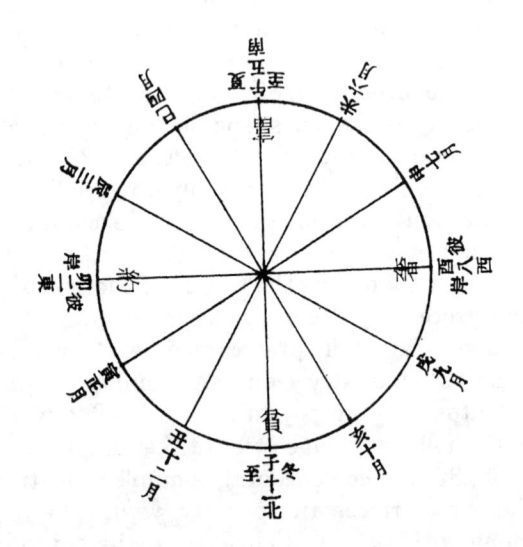

[3]

... If you practise frugality and economy, you will be rich; if you indulge in a luxurious life you will be poor. For years, this law will never be changed or reversed.³

Diagram B: Fulfilment and Loss

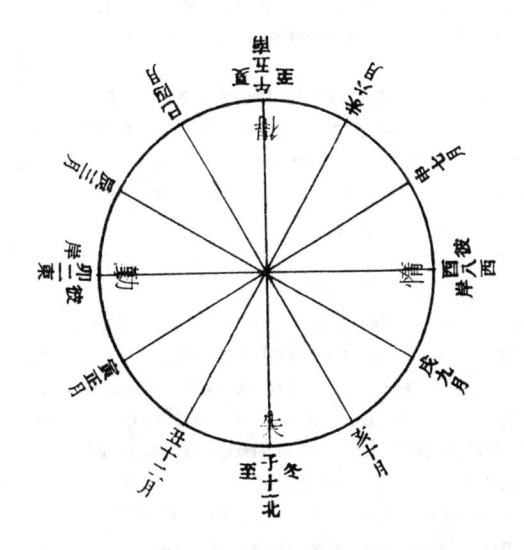

[4]

... If you are industrious, you will acquire prosperity and be fulfilled; if you lose your industriousness you will lose prosperity. As such, this law will never be changed or reversed.[4]

nomic ups and downs depend on the degree of industry, and on the amount of frugality practised. He also stated the following:

> Wealth and poverty both exist in human society. One might think this is accidental, but it is not. There is always a cause for this difference. Wealth resides with a frugal man; it disintegrates if it resides in an extravagant man . . . Neither wealth nor poverty is caused by accident.[5]

In Ninomiya's view, people were not destined to be poor or rich by *force majeure*; industry and frugality could overcome even difficult circumstances and bring about fortune. Moreover, he did not just limit himself to preaching admonitions for industry and frugality. Specific formulas for efficient production were devised as the diagrams C and D on the following pages show.

Diagram C is a daily production schedule. *Yontoki* is about eight hours on the present day-scale. According to this daily production schedule formulated by Ninomiya, peasants are advised to work at least two different times a day, making a total work time of approximately eight hours per day.[6] Work hours are also calculated on an annual basis. The length of work time and the number of tasks to be dealt with vary according to seasonal demand. Collective and lengthy work is carried out in peak seasons. Work time also varies due to the expansion and contraction of one *toki*, the length of which differs according to the length of daylight hours; night-time *toki* expands and daytime *toki* contracts in winter and *vice versa* in summer. However, it is important to note that, in this standardised daily work schedule, time is objectified and represented in a diagram, and used to constitute an ordered formula for everyone to rely on when dealing with productive activities. Ninomiya also devised a diagram for annual yield (Diagram D), which set out seasonal yield in a form that could provide the basis for a

Diagram C: A Labour Plan
(daily production schedule)

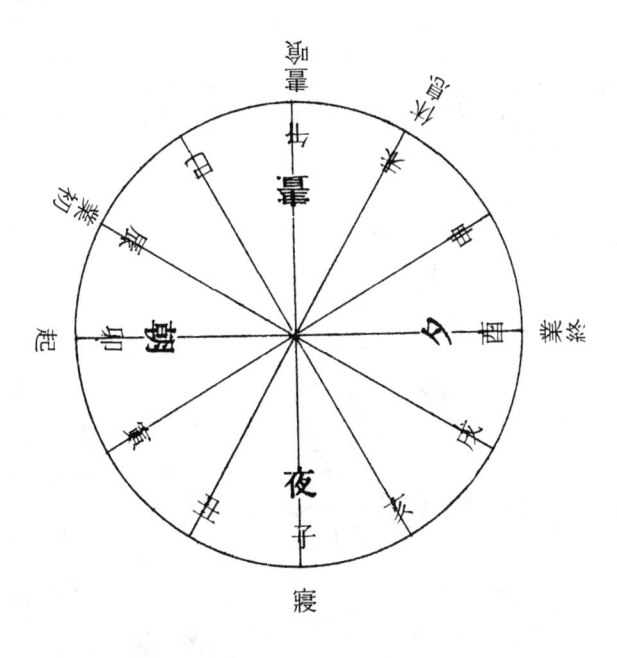

[7]

Deduct *muttsutoki* of night time [approximately half a day] from *jyuunitoki* [twenty-four hours = one day]. Within the other *muttsutoki*, you have your breakfast between sixth time [*muttsudoki*] and fifth time [*itsutsudoki*] in the morning. You should work for two *toki*; one in between fifth and fourth times [*itsutsudoki* and *yottsudoki*], and the other between fourth and ninth times [*yottsudoki* and *kokonotsudoki*]. You have your lunch break at ninth *toki*, and have a rest until eighth *toki*. You should work for two *toki* again; between eighth and seventh, and seventh and

The perception of work in Tokugawa Japan

sixth *toki*. From the sixth *toki* in the evening to the sixth *toki* in the following morning, you have a rest. In total, you have *hattoki* [approximately sixteen hours] of rest hours and *yontoki* [approximately eight hours] of work hours in a day. Within one year [four-thousand three-hundred and twenty *toki*], you will rest for two-thousand eight-hundred and eighty *toki* and work for one-thousand four-hundred and forty *toki* [two-thousand eight-hundred and eighty-hours]. That means, 33 per cent of your time will be spent working, and 66 per cent resting.[7]

Diagram D:"*Ten*'s Order of Annual Yield"
(annual production schedule)

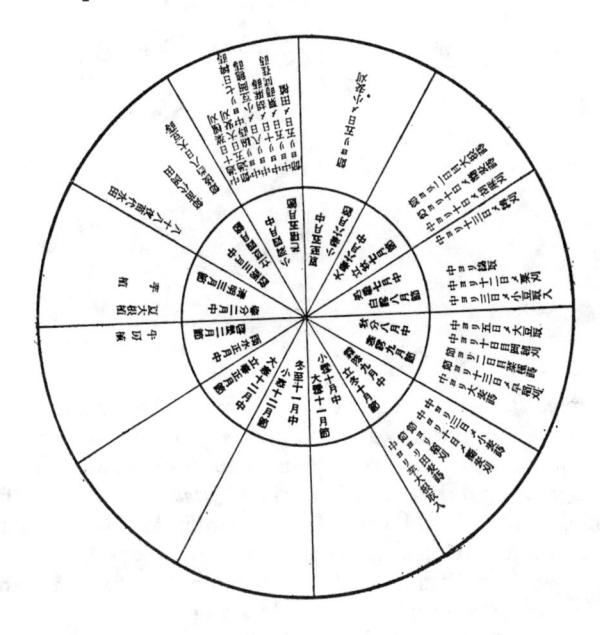

[8]

yearly work schedule. In other words, the productive cycle of nature was not just viewed as a 'natural occurrence' but was assimilated in diagrammatic form and used as an invaluable source of information for judicious task organisation and production scheduling, enabling man to manipulate time in the elaborate process of multi-crop production; man was no longer merely submissive to time and the 'rhythms' of nature.

T.C. Smith's study shows that time-orientation was already becoming an integral element in agricultural work by the early stages of the Tokugawa period. Knowledge of farm management and planning were apparent in the *Hyakusho Denki* of 1680. The assertion of agricultural knowledge and well-timed planning were a dominant feature of the agricultural treatises (*nosho*), which appeared in abundance in the late eighteenth century. Commercialisation and the spread of proto-industry in rural areas further fostered the integration of time-orientation into agrarian work. Time was regarded, Smith argues, 'as fleeting and precious, and great moral value attached to its productive use.'[9] The prevalence of this view of time certainly helped Ninomiya to instil into the peasants the concept of planning as a decisive factor in production increase.

Agriculture requires man to follow nature's rhythms in many respects, and one might argue that time-orientation would not have fit into the mode of production common in agriculture for this reason. However, spread of proto-industry and other agricultural bywork - often for the production of commercial goods - transformed the mode of production decisively. Since land resources were utterly limited for most Tokugawa peasants, double-cropping was widespread, and peasants had to implement intricate timetables for multi-purpose planting, growing and harvesting procedures developed alongside rice production. In such a case as this, the mode of production could no longer be purely task-oriented. The introduction of time-oriented planning as a 'pace-maker' in rationalisation of agrarian work was essential. Such 'scheduling devices' as Ninomiya's diagrams seen earlier aid in the distribution of labour timing to facilitate complex crop rotation systems, thus man can maximise the potential productive capacity of nature.

Thus, the industry in agricultural production which Ninomiya advocated represented not merely an increase in the amount of 'labour input', but the execution of appropriate management involving accurate estimation and planning; it was a 'plan rational' industry geared towards efficiency. His *shihō* programme, which will be examined in the following chapter, was the culmination of this feature of his thought; it was a programme for production improvement, formulated with well coordinated absorption and utilisation of labour, finance, and other resources with a view to efficiency maximisation.

Ninomiya also emphasised the continuation of industry and planning for successive generations for the sake not only of individual prosperity but of the well-being of the household. As was seen in Chapter 2, the Japanese household developed as a unit of agricultural production as well as an entity of perpetual continuum with which its members identified themselves. According to Ninomiya, initiatives in industry and planning were to sustain this perpetuality. The following words and diagram, called *Hotokukun*, is taken from Ninomiya's *Kinmoroku*:

> The origin of parents is to be found in the will of Heaven and earth [霊命]. The origin of a human being is found in the birth and care [生育] given by the parents. Succession to children and grandchildren depends on the parents' nourishment [配偶]. The prosperity of parents is brought about by their ancestors' industry and accomplishments [勤功]. Our prosperity is indebted to the concealed virtuous act [陰徳] of our parents. The prosperity of descendants is dependent on our (present member's) efforts [勤労]. Our

own growth and prosperity depend upon the following three things: clothing [衣], food [食], and shelter [住]. These three necessities are realised by paddy and field, woods and forests [樹藝]. It is our vigor [竭力] in cultivation which brings these to fruition and nurtures ourselves. The yields of today are brought about by the productive act [産業] of yesterday. The yields of next year will be brought about by the exertions and hardships [勤難] of this year. Do not forget your duty of giving recompense for virtues you receive year in and year out [年歳].[10]

Diagram E: *Hotokukun*

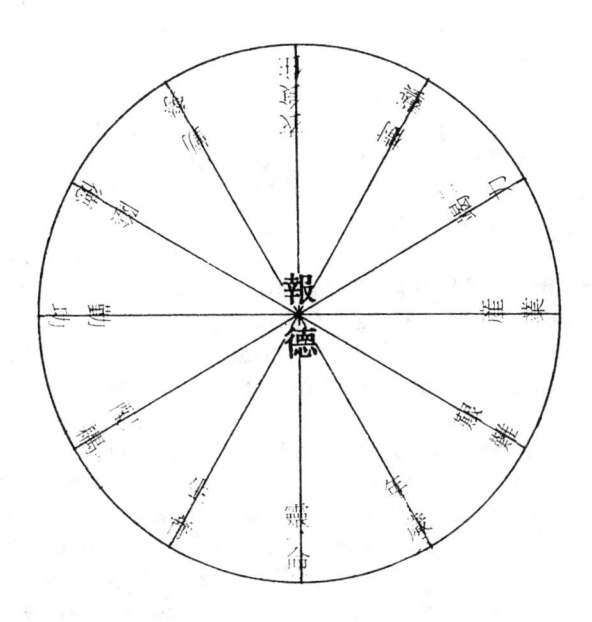

[10]

The perception of work in Tokugawa Japan

Human beings receive virtue from Heaven and earth in one form in the birth of parents (ancestors), and in another in the supply of soil, water, and seeds - the sources of existence. Human beings in turn are to formulate plans, and invest manpower to make the best possible use of these received virtues in order to nourish themselves and to maintain the prosperity of the household. Moreover, the life of the present members is dependent on the accomplishments of the ancestors, and of the successive generations. Industry, predecessors' devotion, and 'good deeds' were not merely to promote the prosperity of a person or a generation but acted as 'cumulative agencies' for the successive betterment of the prosperity of the household. Present members were obliged to fulfil their part through industry in order to participate in this cumulative effort for the benefit of future generations. The creative force of nature, the industry of the ancestors, and the diligence of the present members were all unified in this continuous act. The concept of industry was not only central to this interactive process, but was dependent on it. Industry was encouraged because it promotes the well-being of the household, and constitutes the virtuous act. In this way, *ie* ideology became inseparable from economic activity; in turn, the ideology incorporated economic rationale into its organisational principle.

Ninomiya's thought appears contrastive to mere intellectualism. On one occasion, Ninomiya attacked Confucianism for teaching empty courtesies which did not provide the populace with any means of enriching themselves. According to 'Sage Ninomiya's Evening Talks', edited by Fukuzumi Masae, a Ninomiya disciple, Ninomiya wrote:

In Confucian teaching, you are taught not to see, listen to, speak of, or act upon anything not associated with courtesy [*rei*]; in real life, however, the practice of courtesy alone is not enough; I thus advocate that you do not see, listen to, speak of, or act upon anything which does not benefit yourself and people; I decline to believe anything, even the teachings in the classic texts, unless it provides people with actual benefit.[11]

Neo-Confucianism aimed, as we saw in Chapter 3, to cultivate self, and so influence and transform society and the cosmos. It certainly aimed to 'benefit' self and society in this respect. However, the thought system prescribed the means of cultivation only for the elite population, while it prevented the masses from any prospect of becoming active participants in cultivation. Moreover, neither contemplative means nor scholarship could serve to improve the economic conditions of the Kanto villages where Ninomiya spent a considerable part of his life. The villages had suffered serious economic decline. The orthodox measures advocated by Confucians, and the more scholastic methods of Neo-Confucianism, were alien to productive action of any sort, and could do nothing to ease the peasants' predicament. The sole means to alleviate those chronic conditions was the provision of practical devices to bring about the rehabilitation of the economy. Ethical teaching had to be geared toward activating the economy, not observing courtesies. In the following passage, Ninomiya castigates the son of a wealthy farmer. The son was to be sent to Yushima Seido at Edo to study Neo-Confucianism, but Ninomiya accuses the son of becoming involved in the meaningless study of intellectualism and admonishes him on the importance of 'practical learning':

> However rich a farmer may be, he must have a good knowledge of agricultural affairs, and whatever amount of gold a rich man may possess, he must lead a life of thrift and industry and concede whatever possessions he can spare, so as to enrich and beautify his native place . . . You engage in your studies with the overwhelming idea that

agriculture is a low occupation and a farmer is a lowly person, the learning you acquire will make you still more vainglorious, and there is no doubt that you will finally bring ruin to your house . . . Even were you to continue to study [at Yushima Seido] for the rest of your life, you would never be able to see this truth.[12]

In Ninomiya's view, practical knowledge, which was mainly concerned with the promotion of agricultural production, was of the utmost importance. The scientific observation of things and its practical use in agriculture, these were what enriched individuals, the household, and society as a whole, not the practice of courtesy and righteousness.

The philosophy of work (2): Concepts of Tendo *and* Jindo
Ninomiya viewed the cycle of nature as a continuous process of creation. In his philosophy, this process was termed *Tendo*, which literally means the 'Heavenly Way'. *Kinmoroku* includes the following words and diagrams which illustrate Ninomiya's idea of creation inherent in the Way of Heaven.

> No creature can be born without the force of the 'source of all lives' - the Great Ultimate. It has been said that the Great Ultimate was at the beginning a nebulous entity without a division between Heaven and earth, nor was there a division between yin and yang; it was like an egg.[13]

The diagrams of the Great Ultimate and the 'Development of the world' on the following page illustrate the separation of Heaven and earth, the creation of such life-forces as wind, fire, water, and soil, and the emergence of man (我). A more specific assessment of the development of life is given in *Banbutsu Hatsugenshu*, 'Collection of Ninomiya's Words on Things', which sets out his discourse on the

The idea of work in the thought of Ninomiya Sontoku

Diagram F: Great Ultimate

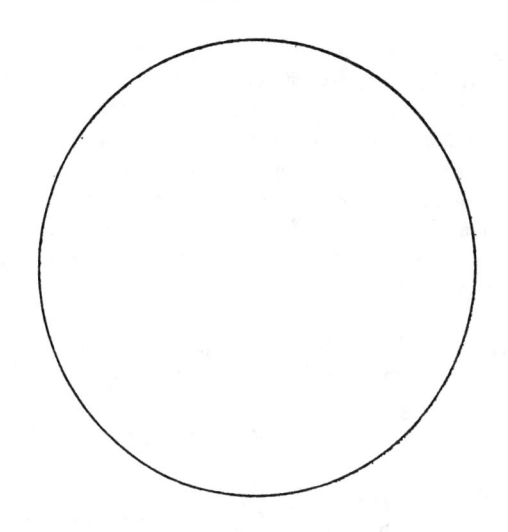

[13]

Diagram G: Development of the World

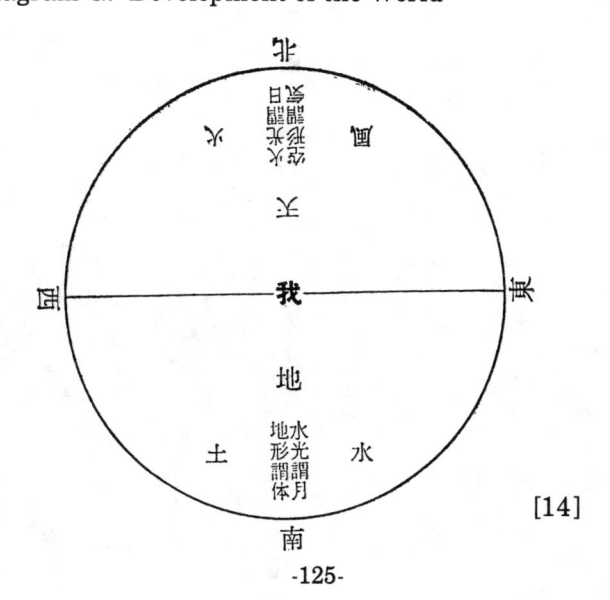

[14]

The perception of work in Tokugawa Japan

'chain process of creation' brought about by *Tendō*:

> ... The sun shone and rain fell, and moss grew on the earth; it was the first living thing on the earth; it withered in the autumn; but the withered moss nurtured the soil, on which grass could grow; grass withered in the autumn; then trees grew because of the soil enriched by the grass; small animals emerged, thanks to the nourishment of the fallen leaves of the flora; ... next, these small animals nurtured birds and beasts; ... all the flora come out in the spring; they all wither in the autumn...[15]
>
> The seed [実] is the will of Heaven [*Tenmei*] itself; the continuation of Heaven's will [seed] is the tree and grass; its flourishing is the flower [華]; its culmination is the seed [実].[16] If one sows rice, it grows, flourishes, and culminates in rice. If one sows wheat, it grows, flourishes, and culminates in wheat.[17]

Diagram H: The creation of Living Things (1)

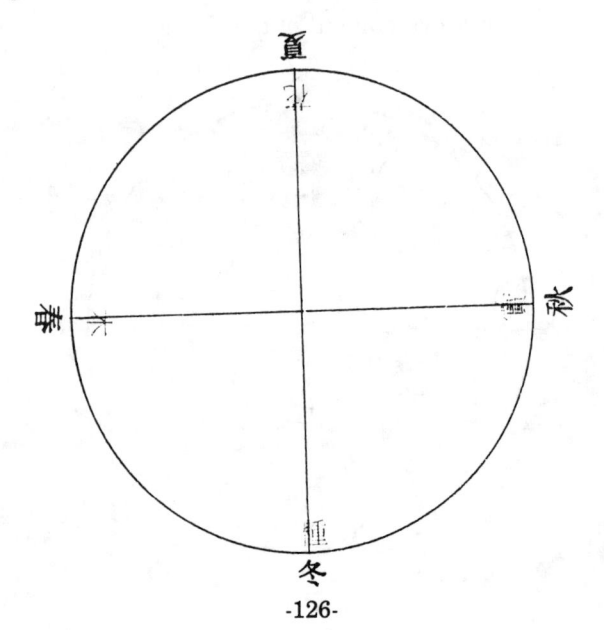

[16]

Diagram I: The creation of Living Things (2)

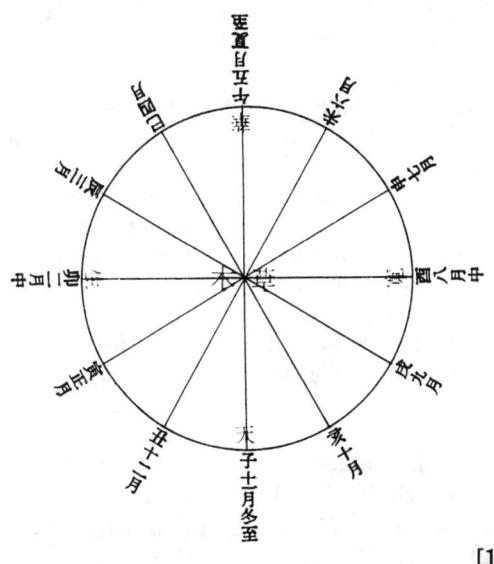

[17]

A creature flourishes and dies in accordance with the seasonal changes set by nature (the will of Heaven). On the one hand, a creature reproduces itself; on the other hand, the life-force of a creature nurtures another creature of a superior rank into fruition. Ninomiya spoke of the successive and cumulative ascendancy of the household in his *Hotokukun*. Similarly, he argues here for the cumulative betterment in the creative cycle of nature; a creature's death contributes to the growth of a creature of a superior rank, and this cumulative cycle spirals upwards. Calamities in the cycle of nature not only brought about the extinction of creatures but also brought about the creation in one way or another.

Nature, however, turns out to be destructive to human

beings if left uncontrolled. Man must thus accurately assess the conditions of nature, implement tasks in an ordered form, and make tireless efforts to maintain prosperity. For Ninomiya, the pursuit of such planned industry represents *Jindo*, the 'Humanly Way', as against *Tendo*, the 'Heavenly Way':

> The Sage says that *Tendo* is the way nature arbitrates and works; *Jindo* is the way which is to be pursued [intentionally] by human beings. The two ways shall not be confused and seen as the same 'way': *Jindo* is to be sustained by a human's intentional efforts so as to meet *Tendo*'s [natural] undoing force. If human beings failed to do so, the force of *Tendo* would destroy river banks, dry up rivers, destroy bridges, and ruin houses. *Jindo* should be pursued [by human beings] in order to erect river banks, regularise the flow of rivers, mend bridges, and build houses . . .[18]

Ninomiya distinguished *Jindō* - human beings' constructive action - from the natural way of Heaven, as has been clarified by Maruyama Masao in his classic study.[19] Ninomiya's thoughts on the separation of the two Ways marks an ideological departure from orthodox Confucian teaching, which recognised human beings' existence and actions as 'given' or 'natural', and advocated efforts to conform to nature as the 'supreme order'. Ninomiya's strong emphasis on man's initiative, interpreted here as man's efforts in agricultural and other development projects, expresses his sensitivity to man's subjectivity in production.

Ninomiya, however, viewed nature - the Heavenly Way - as a supplier of 'virtues' on the one hand, and as an 'undoing force' on the other. It might seem hard to reconcile his bipartite view of nature, but this contradiction serves to legitimise his emphasis on industry and planning: natural calamities occur with no regard for human desires. Man has

The idea of work in the thought of Ninomiya Sontoku

to plan ahead in order to avoid possible disasters. Nature on the other hand prepares the 'seeds of prosperity' for life, but the seeds would never be brought to fruition without consistent industry and appropriate planning by human beings. Ninomiya upheld man as an entity capable of activating the creative capacity of nature to the maximum degree. But man by no means possesses the ability to dominate nature. He attempted to clarify this point, and illustrated the action to be taken by man with reference to the motion of a hydraulic turbine:

> Sage says that *Jindo* is . . . like [the motion of] a hydraulic turbine; half of the turbine is in the water, and moves along with the flow; but half of it remains outside, and going in the opposite direction. If the entire turbine were in the water, it would be washed away; if no part was in touch with the water, it wouldn't turn . . . The same applies to agriculture: land may be covered by weed. This is what *Tendo* brings about. A man has to cut the weed and develop the land. *Tendo* also provides us with the opportunity to grow grains in the spring. We follow these blessings of *Tendo* and sow seeds. We follow *Tendo* on the one hand, and go against it on the other. This is what *Jindo* is all about.[20]

Thus, Ninomiya in no way suggested the domination of man over nature, although production initiatives *within* the creative fabric of *Tendo* were vigorously encouraged. People suffer famines because of their ignorance of nature, their lack of awareness of its movements, and of the efforts they should make to respond to it. With the investment of an abundance of human resources, the potential of nature can be taken advantage of and even increased. Ninomiya stated that,

> A land is, no matter how potentially rich it may be, useless without the developing force [of human beings]; paddies and ploughlands are useless fields without peasants . . . It is

the effort of human beings that brings about crops; a man shall note this point and devote himself extensively to the development and cultivation of the land.[21]

The philosophy of work (3): Production as shinden kaihatsu

The other notable element of Ninomiya's thought is its amalgamation of physical deeds and spiritual affairs. He relates agricultural work to the cultivation of humanity, and the mental and physical worlds, without losing sight of the importance of efficiency.

Diagram J: The 'Virtue From the Paddy' as the Source of Humane Life

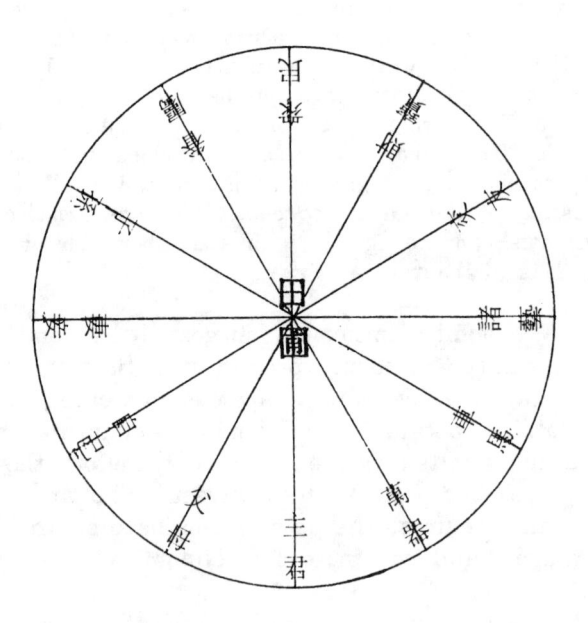

[22]

The idea of work in the thought of Ninomiya Sontoku

> ... If there is no paddy, no living things [human beings] could grow. There is [human] life because there is a paddy and field ... People can all live because of the virtue from the paddy. Because of that virtue, fortune grows, humane intercourse between friends develops, and people maintain their belongings. Without a paddy and field, no one can pursue a humane life. Cultivation of land has thus continuously been pursued from the era of *Amaterasu* in Japan, and from the era of Yao and Shun in China. The heralds of the gods took the initiative in agriculture, and let people learn agriculture. None of us should forget this.[22]

Ninomiya speaks here of agricultural work and yield, and its importance as the source of fortune, prosperity, and every human relationship. Yield - the basic constituent of humane life - was regarded by Ninomiya as 'virtuous'. Virtue refers to physical gifts from nature in his main treatise, *Kinmoroku*. Here in the above passage it effectively means yield. The concept of virtue is intermixed with agriculture and its product, and one's extensive involvement in agricultural production is the source of every human fortune, and the 'way' which leads to humanity. On the other hand, he argues in 'Evening Talks' that a cultivated human heart would bring about the cultivation of the land, and ultimately the prosperity of the nation:

> Desolation of various kinds is caused fundamentally by the desolation of the human heart. My task thus starts with the cultivation of this battered human heart [*shinden no kaihatsu*]. If the heart is returned to good, paddy and field will be reclaimed. Through a succession of reclamation efforts, a nation will easily be strengthened.[23]

> ... My aim is to cultivate the desolated *kokoro no ta* [the 'paddy of the human heart]; sow the paddy [heart] with

good seeds such as *jin, gi, rei,* and *chi* which we received from Heaven, harvest good seeds from the paddy [heart], and sow them again . . . When a desolate man's mind is cultivated, thousands of acres of paddies and dry fields can be developed without any difficulty.[24]

An abundant yield brings about humanity; the refinement of the human heart brings about the development of paddies and dry fields. While no orthodox method such as meditation or investigation was emphasised for the cultivation of heart in Ninomiya's thought, agricultural production in an ordered and calculated form was directly linked to the cultivation of inner self. He also attempted to diffuse this thought to the masses through *waka* (the 31-syllable Japanese ode). The following are thought to have been composed by Ninomiya in 1832:

Honen no aki no monaka no maki-doki wa, hotoke ni masaru satori narikeri[25]
(Sowing of wheat in the autumn of a fruitful year; it will lead you to spiritual enlightenment [*satori*] more than to the level attained by Buddha.)

Maki uete tokini tagayashi kusa kirite, minori matsu mi wa tanoshi karikeri[26]
(Sow the land with seeds, cultivate the land, and mow the grasses; you labour, and wait for a fruitful harvest. You are blessed with joy on that very occasion.)

Ninomiya composed *waka* on various occasions, as a vehicle for his thoughts and often included them in correspondence with his people. The rhythmic *waka* made it easier for the populace to remember the content, and as a means of transmission it was far more effective than an admonitory discourse involving difficult words.

Ninomiya identified agricultural production as an act

The idea of work in the thought of Ninomiya Sontoku

through which 'virtuous interactions' between Heaven, earth, and human beings were to be executed. And that was seen as the source of humane living and the continuous prosperity for generations. It was however not a mere input of 'labour' which Ninomiya emphasised in the execution of that virtuous act; he referred to the management of time, labour allocation, and judicious planning to fully activate the productive potential of nature, not 'hard work' alone. It was the consolidated action of the creative forces of nature, the industry of ancestors, and the diligence of the present members of the household that actualised the building of cumulative prosperity.

Notes
1. Morita Shiro, *Ninomiya Sontoku* (Asahi Sensho), Asahi Shinbunsha, Tokyo, 1989 (first published in 1975), pp. 4-9. Newly established branch families needed their own paddies to support their own households. But the land areas allocated to - or newly developed for - these households tended not to be the most desirable ones. Due largely to the shortage of land areas, new development was often confined to sites near the river, or which were less convenient for water allocation. Branch families tended to be vulnerable to natural calamities for this reason. See Otsuka Eiji, 'Kinsei Koki Kita-Kanto ni okeru Shono Saiken to Hotoku Kinyu no Tokushitsu', *Nihonshi Kenkyu*, 263 (July, 1984), pp. 32-33.
2. Sasai Shintaro, 'Kaidai', *NSZ*, vol. 1, p. 1.
3. *NSZ*, vol. 1, p. 274. The same diagram can be found in *Ibid.*, pp. 302, 319.
4. *Ibid.*, p. 277. The same diagrams in *Ibid.*, pp. 304, 322.
5. Saito Takayuki, 'Ninomiya Sensei Goroku vol. 2, No.127', *NSZ*, vol. 36, p. 378. Ninomiya's words of a similar tenor can be found in numerous places; not only in

his *Kinmōroku* and other philosophical accounts but in letters and correspondence with villagers and proprietors during village rehabilitation.

6. Eight hours is the standard length of work time per day in present-day industrial society, but it does not seem to have been common in many pre-industrial, agrarian work settings. Even so, Ninomiya argues that eight hours was still 'inadequate' for a preson to be called a 'diligent workman'. *Ibid.*, p. 21.

7. *NSZ*, vol.1, p.146. Similar diagram was employed in Ninomiya's *Kinmoroku*. *Ibid.*, p. 21.

8. *Ibid.*, p.20. A prototype of this diagram can be found in *Ibid.*, pp. 147-48.

9. Smith, *Native Sources of Japanese Industrialization*, chapter 9. Smith presents a number of examples which illustrate the 'time-awareness' of Tokugawa peasants and their productive use of time. From the viewpoint of socio-economic history, Ninomiya's diagram may be seen as a mark of the prevalence of the notion of time even in the economically backward areas of northern Kanto.

10. *NSZ*, vol.1, p. 35. Also, *Ibid.*, p. 544.

11. Fukuzumi Masae, 'Ninomiya-O Yawa vol. 5, No. 227', *NSZ* vol. 36, pp. 820-1.

12. 'Ninomiya-O Yawa vol. 4, No. 166', *Ibid.*, p. 783.

13. *NSZ*, vol.1, p. 7.

14. *Ibid.*, p. 13. The same diagram in *Ibid.*, p. 68.

15. *Ibid.*, p. 338.

16. *Ibid.*, p. 16.

17. *Ibid.*, p. 38.

18. Fukuzumi, 'Ninomiya-O Yawa: A Sequel, No.1', *NSZ*, vol. 36, p. 831.

19. Maruyama, *Nihon Seiji Shisoshi Kenkyu*, pp. 308-9. Ninomiya consistently spoke of *Jindo* as 'intentional effort' or the 'initiative' of human beings. [cf. Fukuzumi, 'Ninomiya-O Yawa', *NSZ*, vol. 36, pp. 680, 831] Maruyama was perhaps the first to clarify this element of Ninomiya's thought. It should however be noted that Ninomiya spoke of man's initiative in industry and planning as a triggering mechanism for the maximum activation of the potential of

nature, not as an act to arbitrate nature. In this respect, Naramoto Tatsuya's assessment of Ninomiya's conception of the two Ways in later years could be seen as more accurate than Maruyama's view. Naramoto Tatsuya, 'Ninomiya Sontoku: *Sansai Hotoku Kinmoroku* wo chushin toshite', *Shiso*, 548 (February, 1970), p. 83.

20. Saito Takayuki, 'Ninomiya Sensei Goroku vol. 2, No. 134', *NSZ*, vol. 36, p. 380. Similar discourse is to be found in Fukuzumi, 'Ninomiya-O Yawa vol. 1, No. 3', *Ibid.*, p. 679.
21. *NSZ*, vol. 1, p. 553.
22. *Ibid.*, p. 31.
23. Fukuzumi, 'Ninomiya-O Yawa: A Sequel, No. 24', *NSZ*, vol. 36, p. 841.
24. Fukuzumi, 'Ninomiya-O Yawa vol. 2, No. 59', *Ibid.*, p. 718.
25. *NSZ*, vol. 1, p. 891.
26. *Ibid.*, p. 891.

Chapter 7

The *shihō* programme

1) *The economic setting and the programme*
Ninomiya not only expressed his thought on work in written form but designed and organised work in the actual village rehabilitation process. He composed and implemented the *shiho* programme[1] which demonstrated the close relationship that existed between his thought and economic reality. It is this relationship that distinguishes him from other thinkers and explains the high level of practical influence his thought gained.

This chapter analyses four main features of a comprehensive shiho programme implemented in the domain of Sakuramachi (a domain in northern Kanto): (1) the investment of capital, the mobilisation of financial, land, and other idle resources; (2) the incentivising and training of labour; (3) the improvement of technology; and (4) the provision of social welfare. Amongst the economic measures which comprised these four elements, the most influential ones in the development of the perception of work were:

a) The fiscal reform package, namely, the setting of

bundo and *suijo* (to be discussed in section 2-1). The package was designed to impose strict financial control upon both the proprietor and the peasants. It clarified the demarcation between 'subsistence' and 'surplus', and helped cultivate a sense of financial planning in the minds of peasants.

b) The way the injection of start-up capital was made; loans were offered not to the domain proprietor alone but also to the household producers. The households were attempted to have been made financially semi-autonomous entities responsible for their own production (section 2-2).

c) Communal schemes; organised labour projects for land reclamation and infrastructure development were carried out, often involving intra- and inter-village task-forces (section 2-4). Projects were financially assisted by the capital which was communally pooled and controlled. This capital was also used to finance the collective purchasing of tools and fertilisers, and the poor-saving schemes (sections 2-2, 4-1). These measures helped develop communal sensitivity in the pursuit of work.

d) Introduction of an award system. This promoted competition among villagers and raised the overall standards of work intensity (section 3-1). At the same time, measures were taken to aid the poor peasants by integrating them into the economic fabric of the village (section 5-1). The sense of 'competitive cooperatism' was promoted in the minds of peasants.

e) Ninomiya's educational efforts during the process of village rehabilitation cultivated productive and managerial initiatives among peasants in the pursuit of their work (section 3-2).

As we shall see later in this study, shiho achieved a significant degree of success in rehabilitating villages in the domain of Sakuramachi. Such economic measures as the mobilisation of capital not only increased work opportunities but gave greater opportunities for technological improvements; and, through it, work took on greater variety and

The shiho programme

complexity. The deployment of such economic measures, in turn, enlarged the *scope* of work. On the other hand, such opportunities were taken up only where peasant producers were able to respond to them. What we are concerned with here is this process of correspondence between the economic measures applied and the peasants (the subject of work by whom the measures were effected).

It is not possible here to analyse the form work took *before* the implementation of the shiho programme (we may call this the 'base structure' of work). But given the fact that shiho was successful, it would be reasonable to assume that there was a meaningful set of interactions between the economic measures employed and the base structure of work of peasants, during which process the economic measures successfully drew out the villagers' economic capacities, and, a new, more institutionalised structure of work emerged. This new structure (or new 'form') set out clearer reference points for peasants in their perception of work. In other words, the shihō programme provided them with a framework within which work was carried out, and thereby institutionalised the structure of work. The purpose of this chapter is to define this institutionalised structure of work which Ninomiya attempted to create through the implementation of the economic measures included in his shiho programme.

[1-1] The village economy in early nineteenth century Japan

Before entering into the details of Ninomiya's shiho programme, it may be appropriate to sketch the village economy of the late Tokugawa era, and in particular that of the northern Kanto region, in order to identify the economic factors which were responsible for the emergence of the programme. The first half of the nineteenth century, particularly the period after 1820, was marked by an overall growth of economy in national terms.[2] The population started to increase after experiencing steady decline throughout the eighteenth century.[3] Agricultural production also grew, owing in part to the increase of arable land area, but mainly to the growth of land productivity as a result of the increased use of manures and fertilisers, the introduction of fertiliser responsive and high-yielding seed varieties[4], the spread of double cropping[5], and the further intensification of labour in response to these technological advancements.[6] The penetration of the agrarian economy by commercial institutions in urban areas was as intensive as ever. It stimulated the rural proto-industrial development started as *nokan yogyo* in western Japan in the second-half of the eighteenth century. It began to spread to the east, and the provinces of Shinano, Kozuke, Iwashiro, Musashi, and Kai in eastern Japan, for instance, became leading regions of raw silk production by the middle of the nineteenth century.[7] Income per capita grew steadily due both to the increase in agricultural production and to the flourishing of proto-industry.[8]

On the other hand, the domains generally suffered from chronic budgetary deficits throughout the second half of the Edo period. Their revenues were no longer secure in an era of ever-increasing economic dynamism; inflation alone caused serious financial difficulty for samurai. To counter the difficulty, the domains attempted to carry out fiscal reform, or, so-called *hansei kaikaku*. Some attempted to increase their revenue through financial reform, the implementation of domain-scale cultivation and land-reclamation, and, notably, the encouragement of special local production (*tokusan*). *Tokusan* varied from the making of wax, paper, and ceramics to cotton manufacturing in western domains. Several domains in the Tōhoku region specialised in silkworm growing and silk reeling, and other textile industries.[9] But there were many domains which could not afford such forward-looking plans. Most of the domains in the northern Kanto region possessed neither advanced technology in

The shiho programme

agriculture nor substantial proto-industrial output, even in the early nineteenth century. Domain officials, alienated from the land and without any experience of agricultural production, often turned to the more educated agricultural technologists such as Okura Nagatsune. Alternatively, they turned to the Shingaku school to raise the peasants' morale[10], even though 'moralistic' measures alone were not effective in promoting productivity.[11]

[1-2] The northern Kanto villages in distress

The northern Kanto villages without substantial growth in either agricultural or proto-industrial output were drawn into the nationwide extension of commercial economy.[12] At the same time, the region was hit by the great famines of Tenmei in the late eighteenth century and of Tenpo between 1833 and 1839 (the severest damage was inflicted in 1833 and 1836), which were mainly caused by cold weather. The severity was reflected in population decline, revealed in a study by Sekiyama Naotaro. The overall population in Japan decreased slightly from 26,065,425 in 1721 (Kyoho 6) to 25,086,466 in 1786 (Tenmei 6), and then increased to 26,602,110 in 1822 (Bunsei 5). Sekiyama's index on the Kanto region shows a decline from 100 (1721) to 85.40 (1786), and to 82.81 (1822 = Bunsei 5).[13] The decline was far sharper in the northern Kanto region. The index shows that the population in Shimotsuke Province declined from 100 (1721) to 77.4 (1786), and to 61.1 (1834). Hitachi Province's population declined from 100 (1721) to 72.2 (1786), and to 64.2 (1834).[14]

Famines decimated the population in the northern Kanto region, which further deteriorated its production capability. To counteract this vicious cycle, measures were finally taken by domain administrators of the region in the form of a 'village rehabilitation programme by the head of the domain' (*ryoshu shiho*), which consisted of land reclamation and infrastructure development projects, and a scheme to increase the population. Typical examples included *Moka Daikan Shiho*, which started in the Kansei era (1789-1800), and the *ryoshu shiho* in the village of Nishi Takahashi. Ninomiya's *Sontoku shiho* retained some elements of the *ryoshu shiho*.[15] But Ninomiya's (Sontoku) shiho was decisively different from that of the domain: its primary aim was not the increase of the domain's income, but the nourishment of villages and households; for instance, Sontoku shiho was designed to limit the revenue of the domain and to return the surplus to peasant producers for their reproduction purposes. This not only helped struggling peasants but motivated them to work.

Tokugawa agriculture, even that in the most advanced areas, was marked by labour intensity. Given the abundance of labour and the scarcity of land, successive technological advancement centred around labour intensity, and required individual peasant producers to work even longer hours, be equipped with better technological knowledge, and invest tireless effort in producing with limited land resources. Labour saving technology did not develop substantially even in the advanced regions of western Japan in the first half of the nineteenth century.[16] Given that technological peculiarity, success in agriculture depended on the intensity of the peasants' labour and 'care'; each worker's care, knowledge, and initiative were seen as vital factors for successful production.

This peculiarity in the form of Tokugawa agriculture was closely linked to a fundamental cause of the economic decline that occurred in the Kanto villages from the late eighteenth century onwards. The devastating famines were certainly a major cause of economic stagnation in the villages, but one needs to distinguish between the 'triggering' cause and the 'substantial' or 'real' cause, which was a deterioration in the nature of the peasants' 'attitude' towards work. A positive approach was indispensable for this form of labour intensive agriculture. Kaiho Seiryo (1755-1817) illustrates the atmos-

The shiho *programme*

phere in the Kanto villages thus:

> People in Bushu [the Province of Musashi] tend to be lazy [*zurukegachi*]. They are not like the people in the five provinces of Kinai. Lazy men are always negligent. They prefer eating dull food without work to producing good quality food through work.[17]

Musashi was one of the provinces in the Kanto region. The difference between the people in the Kanto and the Kinai in terms of 'attitude' to work is clear in Kaiho's statement. This fact, in turn, suggests that the restoration of the Kanto villages did not have to be accompanied by measures involving massive investment, i.e., investment in such labour-saving technologies as heavy machinery, a large number of domestic animals or tools, usually too costly for poor domains to afford. Village restoration could be sought through providing the idle labour force with incentives, and nurturing their ability to manage the production processes of their own. Ninomiya's shiho programme consisted of such measures.

[1-3] The case of Sakuramachi

The domain of Sakuramachi in Shimotsuke Province, approximately 100 kilometres north of Edo, was the place where Ninomiya's shiho was implemented for the first time in 1822. Like other domains in the northern Kanto region, it had been suffering a severe decline in production. It produced more than 3,000 *hyo* of rice per annum in the late seventeenth century, but a succession of great famines reduced the productivity severely, so that in the early nineteenth century it was producing less than 1,000 hyo per annum. There were 433 households when the Utsu family, a branch of the Okubo family of Odawara, was posted to govern the domain in 1698. But the number of households had declined sharply to only 156 by the time of Ninomiya's survey in 1821.[18]

The perception of work in Tokugawa Japan

Sakuramachi consisted of three villages: Yokota, Tonuma, and Monoi. The domain was governed by Utsu Hannosuke when Ninomiya started his preliminary research in 1821, and had been in a chronic economic difficulty for years. It was constantly being given financial and other assistance from Odawara. Ninomiya, having already been recognised by Lord Okubo Tadazane through the former's success in the Hattori family's financial project in the late 1810s, was considered suitable to lead the Sakuramachi restoration project. He was officially posted to the domain in 1821.[19] He was sent to Sakuramachi only as a village headman (*nanushi*) from Odawara, but given a mandate to run the rehabilitation project himself. He did not receive any instructions from Odawara; nor was he under obligation to report on progress to the domain. He had sole power to control and utilise the surplus from the yield. Okubo appointed Ninomiya the sole delegate for the next ten years, and promised that he would not be brought back to Odawara whatever might occur during that period.[20]

2) *Capital investment, the mobilisation of capital, land, and labour resources*
[2-1] Fiscal reform

The chief aim of the comprehensive shiho programme was the recovery of production in rice and other crops. Equally important was the establishment of a financial system that would ensure a consistent supply of self-generated capital for investment. Only by attaining both, Ninomiya believed, could the domain secure its succession. The first and the most immediate task of the shihō programme was financial rehabilitation.

First, Ninomiya submitted a statistical report to the Utsu family in order to make his case. The project started with a preliminary investigation carried out in 1821 (Bunsei 4), one year prior to the official start of the programme. Production studies, including assessments of labour, land, and

The shiho *programme*

equipment resources, were conducted in that year. Annual output was calculated for the previous ten years, between 1812 (Bunka 9) and 1821. A document called *Goshuho Gododaikin Heikincho*[21] was produced late in 1821, which showed the yield of each village in the region, including local grains (*zakkoku*). In the early Edo period, Sakuramachi was considered to have produced nearly 4,000 *koku* of rice per annum. The production record book, *Kokin Seisui Heikin Dodaicho*,[22] of the region suggests that as much as 3,116 hyo of rice was produced annually between 1698 and 1716. But Ninomiya and his shiho group's study shows a quite different picture; an average of 962 hyo of rice and 130 *ryo* worth of other crops were produced annually between 1812 and 1821.[23] The cultivability of the entire land area in Sakuramachi was studied and reported on in 1821, and the outcome officially recorded in the *Kaihatsu Denbata Tanbetsu Hikaecho* of 1824. It shows that there was 226 *cho* and 1 *tan* of wet paddy, but land under use consisted of less than half of this; only 104 cho and 1 tan was under cultivation.[24] On the basis of these studies, Ninomiya concluded that the domain's feasible production level was 2,039 hyo - an average of 3,116 and 962. The official report including these figures was submitted to the Utsu family in the form of the *Shuho (Shiho) Dodaicho* in 1823.

Secondly, Ninomya distinguished between 'subsistence' and 'surplus' to make a case for capital accumulation, and conceptualised it with such terms as *bundo* and *suijo*. As we have seen, the 'sustainable level of production' was determined on the basis of average productivity and investigation of land feasibility. It was, in Ninomiya's view, the 'given capacity of production' (*tenmei shizen no bun*) for the region. Based on the production estimate, a set of financial plans was formulated. Financial control based on the foregoing calculations was called *bundo*. The proprietor of a village or a domain was to observe *bundo*. Individual households were also instructed to calculate their 'given' capacity, define

The perception of work in Tokugawa Japan

bundo, and observe it:

> A nation, a province, a district, a village, and a household . . . each of them has its own stipend [based upon its productive capacity]. This is the 'given' [capacity] of nature. Determining one's expenditure based upon given capacity is [the setting and observation of] *bundo* . . . If one strictly observes *bundo*, a surplus [*yozai*] will begin to appear, and will enrich the nation and the people.[25]

This passage is from the 'Memoirs of Teacher Ninomiya', a collection of his thoughts expounded during the shiho programme. Ninomiya argues the need for financial control in each household, so that each could make a consistent self-generation of capital.

Once this *bundo* was met, and surplus had begun to appear, the next stage was to accumulate the surplus. A scheme to meet this end was called *suijo*, and the accumulated capital was pooled and controlled under the direct supervision of Ninomiya and his shiho leaders. The accumulated capital was called *Hotokukin* (the Hotoku Capital) and used as principal to buffer any shortage of food supply caused by poor crops, to loan capital to peasants struggling without any start-up funds, and to invest in new facilities such as tools and fertilisers, and in the development of infrastructures.

These devices, however, did not end up with the provision of a systematic model for capital accumulation and investment; since *bundo* and *suijo* were to be practised by all members of the village, they helped develop financial awareness and a sense of long-term planning among peasant producers. Whether or not the schemes were successful in cultivating peasants' financial awareness and their willingness to practise their own financial control could be judged from the result of the shiho programme; for the continuation of the programme - and the sustaining of the

The shiho programme

village economy - depended totally on the consistent practices of *bundo* and *suijo* by individual peasant households, through which the self-generation of capital for reproduction was realised. Indeed, as tables 1 and 3 suggest, shiho showed an overall success in rehabilitating the villages. This fact in turn suggests that the necessary capital had been reproduced, and the programme could continue on that basis. It would therefore be safe to assume that the schemes successfully cultivated the financial awareness of peasants. The attitude of peasants in maintaining *bundo* is also clear from the letters written to Ninomiya from peasants in 1829:

> From the peasants of Yokota village, Zenzo, Yasugoro, Genzo, Kouhachi, and Uhei: We were able to restore our village through the implementation of the shiho programme, which was carried out under your [Ninomiya's] instruction . . . All five of us will eagerly maintain our frugality, maintain our *bungen* [*bundo*] assigned to us, and be diligent in agriculture . . .[26] (10 letters of similar content were sent in April, 1829 alone. Four of them were from the ordinary peasants.)[27]

This is the letter produced after a small rebellion organised against Ninomiya by a group of peasants in 1828.[28] The ordinary peasants, not only village headmen, wrote directly to Ninomiya expressing their willingness to observe the fiscal reform package.

[2-2] Local credit facilities

The Hotoku Capital amounted only to 71 ryo at the beginning of the Sakuramachi project, but it had reached 10,000 ryo by the time the Nikko project was started in 1853. The Capital enabled indebted peasant households to release themselves from difficult financial situations.[29]

Those households which borrowed from the Hotoku

Capital were expected to repay the money in annual instalments, which were usually spread over five years. They were also required to pay back 'blessing money' (*myogakin*) as an expression of 'gratitude' for the loans after the completion of the yearly instalment payments, the amount corresponding to one year's instalment. However, the Hotoku Capital loan system enabled indebted peasant households to enjoy virtually interest-free loans for the instalment years. In addition, the Capital was offered without any security or mortgage, which made funds available even to struggling peasant households.[30] Loans at the initial stage were all recorded in *Toza Kingin Deiricho*, *Toza Kingin Kome Zeni Deiricho*, and other record books in 1823.[31] Sasai calculated that the amount spent in assistance for each household reached 168 ryo; loans totalled 27 ryo. Expenses for fertiliser, tools, and rice were also covered by the amount.[32]

The loans saved peasants from economic difficulties, but more importantly, allowed them to maintain their own households and thus retain their economic as well as ideological integrity, the very existence of which was the source of household members' identity and motivation. Indeed, as mentioned in Chapter 2, the household became a semi-independent unit of agricultural production during the course of Tokugawa economic evolution. In the shihō programme, most of the loans were allotted to the head of the household (*kacho*) to allow this unit to enjoy a relative financial autonomy; one record book, *Yuzu Muri Toki Kashicho* of 1824, for instance, shows that fifteen out of eighteen loans were offered to the household head in the village of Tonuma, and one to the leader of a 'quasi-family' unit in the village.[33] In short, Ninomiya did not attempt to abolish the autonomy of the households by concentrating power and financial capability in the hands of the proprietor. Rather, each household was offered loans in order to sustain its financial capability, and thereby the fundamental

The shiho programme

necessity for autonomous management of production was met.

[2-3] The rehabilitation programme

Despite all the financial schemes, Sakuramachi did not have the financial capability to support these schemes when the programme was launched in 1821. The income of the domain of Sakuramachi was determined at 2,039 hyo; however, for a domain which had produced an average of only 962 hyo per annum for the last decade, 2,039 hyo per annum looked unachievable. To counter the initial difficulty, Ninomiya employed two emergency measures: first, he lowered the income of the domain for the next ten years in order to make investment capital available. *Shuho (Shiho) Dodaicho* of 1823 states,

> For the next one decade [until 1831], the amount of tax [*gochigyo*] shall be limited to 1,005 hyo of rice, 127 ryo worth of dry-paddy products such as soya bean, and other sundry products. Nothing beyond this should be requested.[34]

1,005 hyo and 127 ryo in fact represented the total yield in 1821, and were representative of the preceding ten years' production levels. Significantly, this policy limited the 'income' of the proprietor to a level which was possible for peasants to produce at the initial stage, thereby returning a prospective surplus resulting from that limitation to peasant producers to be used for reproduction purposes. This 'emergency *bundo*' imposed upon the proprietor functioned to defend peasant producers from excessive exploitation; returned capital was to be used as Hotoku Capital for reproduction purposes.

Indeed, as the chart below shows, production rose to 1,326 hyo and 137 ryo in 1822, the first year of the shiho programme, and surplus for *suijo* began to appear. It rose

The perception of work in Tokugawa Japan

further to 1,825 hyo and 137 ryo in 1827, and to 1,987 hyo and 138 ryo in 1834; which accumulated the surplus of 8,543 hyo and 210 ryo in fifteen years. In short, Ninomiya's approach was characteristically rational, and was reasonably close to the modern understanding of macroeconomics: by cutting down expenditure for a while, one could restore production activities; once they were restored, such a sacrifice would become unnecessary, and production activities as a tax base would become self-financing; hence one could make the case for initial 'pump-priming'.

Table 1: Annual yield (rice) in Sakuramachi (1822 → 1836)

year	1812-21(av)	1821	1822	1824	1825	1826
hyo	962	1005	1326	1467	1006	1732
year	1827	#1828	1829	1830	1832	*1833	1834
hyo	1825	981	1856	1874	1894	1326	1987
year	1835	*1836	1837	1842	1846		
hyo	1987	803	1994	2026	2026		

[35]

\# year of the 'Toyoda rebellion'[36]
*years of the great famines in the Tenpo era

The shiho *programme*

Second, he pursuaded Odawara to lend initial capital to implement the shiho programme. Cash and rice for the project arrived in October, 1821:

October, Bunsei 4 (1821).

1. Cash: 50 ryo.
2. Rice: 200 hyo.

Total amount of capital: 112 ryo 2 bu 2 shu 78 mon [31.9 hyo of rice was convertible to 10 ryo in 1821].

The above amount of allowance was received [from Odawara]; the received rice and cash will be used to finance loan systems, awards, nourishment, and so on, for the next calendar year.[37]

Records show that rice and cash to the same amount continued to arrive from Odawara until 1836. Its currency value averaged 144.5 ryo, including the occasional 'additional allowance' in some years (Table 2).

However, the gradual increase in production and the 'lowered rate' of tax enabled Sakuramachi to depend more on the capital generated by its own increased surplus. As is apparent from Table 1, the amount of self-produced capital surpassed the amount of the allowance from Odawara from the early stages of the shiho programme.

Table 2: Rice and cash from Odawara
(bun, shu, kan omitted)

year	1821	1822	1823	1824	1825
rice (hyo)	200	200	200	200	200
cvn. rate per 10 ryo	31.9	21.0	24.0	23.8	17.8
cash (ryo)	50	50	50	50	50
total cash amt.	112.2	145.2	133.1	134.0	162.1

year	1826	1827	1828	1829	1830
rice (hyo)	200	200	200	200	200
cvn. rate per 10 ryo	17.2	26.3	20.0	19.0	16.8
cash (ryo)	50	50	50	50	50
total cash amt.	123.1	126.0	150.0	155.2	169.0

year	1831	1832	1833	1834	1835	1836
rice (hyo)	200	200	200	200	200	200
cvn. rate per 10 ryo	19.8	12.7	12.5	12.4	15.4	8
cash (ryo)	50	50	50	50	50	50
total cash amount	151.0	138.3	211.1	211.0	179.3	300

[38]

[2-4] The mobilisation of land resources
a) The restoration and new development of arable land

Reports on the land were carried out by shiho leaders in 1821 before the official start of the programme in the following year. A report based on the research of 1821-22 shows that more than half of the cultivable area was in fact not in

The shiho *programme*

use:

Area of paddies and fields in total: 501 cho 8 se 20 ho

Paddies: 226 cho 1 tan 6 se 20 ho
Fields: (approx.) 274 cho
   Cultivable paddies: 104 cho 2 tan 9 se 17 ho
   Wasted paddies: 121 cho 8 tan 7 se 8 ho

[39]

These figures suggest the seriousness of economic conditions in Sakuramachi. The following letter from village leaders to Ninomiya suggests that the leaders immediately started to organise a labour force for land reclamation:

As we attempted to lay out the paddies, we found a considerably large area of field being neglected. A large area of paddies was deserted, and not well cared for. Some areas did not have a water supply . . . Some areas can be cultivated, but we also reported that there were deserted paddies . . . The village officials understood this, and agreed to start reclamation projects; officials are vigorously involved in development projects; paddies have begun to be reclaimed gradually, so have the dry fields . . .[40]

The reclamation of paddies and fields was carried out by an organised labour force. The following *Kaihatsu Denbata Tanbetsu Hikaecho* shows an example of labour force organisation in the Monoi village:

11th day of February, Bunsei 7   [Chushichi's group]

1) Number of workers employed: 29
   [amongst the 29] 5 workers are from Den'emon's
   24 are collected from the village
   Amount of payment spent: 3 bu in cash and 3 to in rice
   The above workers reclaimed about 7 se of

Den'emon's paddy in Nishi Monoi. The above amount paid for labour.

2) Number of workers employed: 6
Amount of payment spent: 2 shu 412 mon in cash and 7 sho and 5 go of rice
The above workers reclaimed about 9 se of dry field. The above amount paid for labour.

Total amount spent for the labourers: 3 bu 2 shu 412 mon of cash and 3 to 7 sho 5 go of rice

3) Number of workers employed: 15 and a child
Amount of payment spent: 1 bu 2 shu 721 mon in cash and 1 to 9 sho 3 go and 7 shaku of rice
All 15 workers were involved in the development of the wooded area of Heizaemon's land. The above amount paid for labour.

4) Number of workers: 1
This man worked hard to reclaim the dry field. Allowance for *sake* is to be paid. Amount of payment spent: 515 mon

5) Number of workers: 1
This man worked hard for development projects. Allowance paid. Amount of payment spent: 2 shu

[41]

Within 1824, about 10 cho of paddy was estimated to have been brought back into use.[42] An additional 8 cho 2 tan and 13 ho was reclaimed in the following year.[43] Reclamation seems to have continued at the pace of approximately ten cho per annum.

b) implementation of extra tasks
Task forces were also organised for infrastructure

The shiho programme

development. Roads and bridges were constructed, and new irrigation and sewage channels, and cold water storage facilities were built. Development projects were carried out from the early stages of the shiho programme. Sasai argues on the basis of his study of Ninomiya's diaries and revenue/expenditure record books that the projects started as early as 1821.[44] Records of 1841 (Tenpo 12) are however the only available official records showing details of the actual labour organisation of those projects. The following record discusses a road construction project in that year and the labour force organised to meet the task:

> There is a hollow near the entrance to Yokohori village. Water is stagnant there, particularly on rainy days . . . It seriously disrupts men at work. The entire area needs to be refurbished, and the following roads need to be constructed: a 75 ke long, 2 ke and 2 shaku wide road to be built near Sugihama woods; a 120 ke long, 3 ke wide, and 2 to 3 shaku high road to be built; . . . overall, a 529 ke long road and four small bridges are to be built . . . Labourers are to be collected not only from Yokohori but from Tonuma and Yokota villages. Labourers are to be summoned also from the following domains: Kuwanokawa village in Kawasaki's domain, and Aoki village in Kawazoe's domain.[45]

The last two villages - Kuwanokawa and Aoki - were not within Sakuramachi. They belonged to different domains where the shiho programme was employed in later years. Shiho in Aoki village started in 1833 after persistent requests from its domain head, Kawazoe Shozaburo. This suggests that task forces consisted not only of intra-village manpower but of resources from other villages where the shiho programme was employed.

Irrigation and sewage channels were also dealt with by task forces. The following is taken from a record in November, 1842:

Regarding irrigation and sewage channels of this village: due to the drought in recent years, many irrigation channels, usually abundant in water supply, have dried up . . . Both irrigation and sewage channels have redeveloped; roads crossing the moors were also repaired. A task force is to be arranged to cope with these problems.

> Directors of the task force:
> Nakaemon of Yokota, Kishiemon of Shimo-Monoi, and two *kumigashira* from Monoi village. Total number of labourers to be employed: 158
>
> [46]

The development projects, coupled with the communal financing of these projects, helped to bring about a sense of common purpose. In addition the projects provided peasants with opportunities to earn extra cash for the speedy repayment of their debts.[47] The projects certainly enhanced the accumulation of the Hotoku Capital, which in turn encouraged reproduction initiatives.

3) *The organisation and training of labour*
[3-1] The introduction of an award system

As we have seen, the shiho programme involved a range of financial and organisational schemes for village rehabilitation. None of these schemes would have been effective, however, if the subjects of work - the peasant producers - had been left untrained. To provide them with incentive, Ninomiya employed a system of rewards. Rice, tools, and money were used as rewards for those who demonstrated outstanding performance. To choose the recipients of awards, Ninomiya let villagers themselves select the hardest workers from their fellow villagers. The system was called *irefuda*, or 'balloting'. The awards conferred between Bunsei 5 (1822) and Tenpo 14 (1843) are all recorded in the domain's award record book, the *Gohobi Hika Moshiwatashisho*.[48] The following is an extract from it:

The shiho *programme*

9th day of September, Bunsei 5

According to the regulation set by the shiho programme introduced last winter, outstanding workers are selected from the village. We have already discussed how to select valuable contributors; we have decided to call for a ballot. The following is the list of winners who received 'high vote' [*takafuda* = received many votes] in this ballot. Agricultural tools are to be awarded to them.

Announcement:
  Yokota village
  First prize winner: Kohachi   a hoe
  Second prize winner: Shojiro   two sickles
  Third prize winner: Chu'emon & Eikichi   a sickle each
  Sakai group of To'numa village
  First prize: Ichizaemon   a hoe
  Second prize: Takeshichi   two sickles
  Third prize: Sannosuke & Kitaro   a sickle each

[49]

Prizes were also given in the same manner to the workers of the Wada group of Tonuma village, Monoi group, Shimo Monoi group, and Nishi Monoi group.[50]

14th day of December, Bunsei 5

The following groups of workers have cultivated a huge area of land by their own efforts. It has been an outstanding effort, and 2 to of rice will be conferred for each one tan-ho they cultivated.

Announcement:
  Yahei's group of Tonuma village: cultivated 9 tan and 1 se-ho
    4 hyo 2 to 2 sho of rice to be given to the group
  Goemon's group of Tonuma village: cultivated 8 tan 7 se and 27 ho
    4 hyo 1 to 5 sho 8 go of rice to be given to the group

The perception of work in Tokugawa Japan

    Tsuneemon's group of Yokota village: cultivated 2 cho
3 tan 5 se and 15 ho
       11 hyo 3 to 1 sho of rice to be given to the group
Hin'emon's group of Shimo Monoi village: cultivated
8 tan 9 se and 15 ho
       4 hyo 1 to 9 sho of rice to be given to the group
Bunzo's group of Monoi village: cultivated 4 tan 9 se and
3 ho
       2 hyo 1 to 8 sho 2 go of rice to be given to the group
Heizaimon's group of Nishi Monoi village: cultivated
7 tan 7 se and 29 ho
       3 hyo 3 to 5 sho 9 go of rice to be given to the group

                                         [51]

The ballot duly reflected the villagers' view of who among them had made an outstanding contribution. For those chosen, it was a mark of the efforts they had made, and of the recognition of these efforts by their fellow villagers. It would certainly have cultivated initiative, and would have presumably had an effect on those villagers who did not win the ballot. Morita Shiro writes as follows on the 'side-effect' of the ballot system:

Electing 'outstanding contributors' from the ordinary mass must have drawn every villager's attention. Moreover, reward presumably brought about serious psychological side effects upon those who were not elected. For the villagers, Sakuramachi was the only place where they lived permanently; they knew each other well, and it was impossible to live without frequent intercourse with other villagers, their wives and their children. [A majority would have won at least one reward during the course of the shiho programme, and thus] those who did not receive any reward for years must have been branded as 'lazy men' by their fellow villagers; it must have been extremely difficult to live in such circumstances.[52]

The shiho *programme*

The awards would certainly have functioned as triggers in raising incentive in individual peasants, particularly those who had worked hard even before the award system was started. However, a more substantial effect brought about by the scheme was, as Morita implied, psychological. It raised not only the work incentive of the particular individual but the standard of performance in the village as a whole.

[3-2] Education and work initiative

Ninomiya held no official lecture sessions. But he was enthusiastic about educating the villagers, and many of his words have been collected in pupils' records such as the 'Memoirs' and 'Evening Talks'. He frequently visited the more out-of-the-way parts of the villages, admonished idlers, and rewarded diligence immediately every time he came across it. His discussions ranged from general admonition to specific criticism of one's decision-making ability. In 'Evening Talks' edited by Fukuzumi, Ninomiya spoke thus:

> The Sage [Ninomiya] says, the ability to make proper decisions [*kettei*], and care [*chūi*] are the most important of all. For things can be achieved through the making of swift decisions and the exercise of precise care; even small matters would not be attained if one did not possess these abilities . . .[53]

Here he mentioned the ability to make decisions, as well as 'carefulness' in agricultural work. The following is another example from 'Evening Talks':

> Today it is the winter solstice. It is Heaven's will that the night is long at this time of the year. A man may not like it, and he may want to shorten it, but he cannot because it is Heaven's will. A man cannot alter this. However, if he used a cupful of oil . . . and if he - exerting the 'given' ability of man - made a lamp wick thinner, he could surely illuminate the room until daybreak. This shows how

important it is for man to execute his 'humanly' [*jinji*] ability [to contrive] . . .[54]

Numerous passages of this kind can be found in the 'Memoirs' and 'Evening Talks'. This time, the central issue of his discussion is ingenuity. Ninomiya argues here that man has the capability to modify the energy of nature to meet his own needs. He speaks in these passages of judgment, carefulness, and expediency. Through the provision of production schedules and the fiscal reform package, Ninomiya attempted to teach the peasants to be self-motivated, to design their own work processes, to be cautious in carrying out that work, and in decision-making.

Thanks to both Ninomiya's educational efforts and the provision of institutional devices, the work norm of peasants showed a dramatic improvement in shiho villages. The following letter was sent to Ninomiya from a shiho leader in 1837, just after the great Tenpo famine of 1836. It clearly suggests the improvement in the peasants' attitude to work:

> Our village received blessings from the master [Ninomiya]; we were enlightened in the dark night; we were rescued from death; because of these [instruction and education], we became diligent in agrarian work . . . Those who used to sleep in the morning now rise up early. Those who were 'unrighteous' are now doing right . . . In winter, people are making ropes in their spare time . . . They work very hard from the early morning in spring . . .[55]

Indeed, this is not only illustrative of the peasants' response to instructions from their superiors (shiho leaders) but also of a change in attitude to work among idle peasants. They were working long hours, pursuing extra tasks, and, above all, they were beginning to be self-reliant in production both in economic and psychological terms. Ninomiya argued in his 'Evening Talks' that the cultivation

The shiho *programme*

of the human heart brought with it the cultivation of land. The above letter suggests that the peasants' potential to become self-reliant, diligent, and plan-rational entities was indeed cultivated.

[3-3] Settlement policy

The steady decline in production in the pre-shiho era in Sakuramachi caused a drastic reduction in population. As was stated earlier, Sakuramachi consisted of 433 households in 1698, but it had declined to 156 by the 1820s. Agriculture based upon labour intensity requires an ample population. In Sakuramachi, the decrease in production contributed to a decline in population, which in turn resulted in a further decline in production. An increase in the absolute number of peasants was thus essential in the stricken villages of Sakuramachi. Ninomiya took the initiative to bring in new households to restore manpower. A letter written in 1830 from a village leader in Machiya village in Echigo shows that five households (twenty-four peasants) were brought in from Echigo to Monoi village in Sakuramachi, and to Mooka, another nearby village where shiho was implemented. The households were headed by second or third sons of big households in Machiya village. They were brought in together with their own family members.[56] Settlement policies adapted were recorded in the *Ninbetsucho* and *Iribyakusho Toritate*. The poor condition of Sakuramachi initially attracted few settlers, and Ninomiya's attempt to foster immigration was not successful at first. Nonetheless, Sasai's study shows that nearly fifty people were brought into Sakuramachi in the first few years of the project; the records show some successful cases where workers were brought in, mainly from backward areas.[57] Sunpei, a settler from Renga village, Echigo, helped to reclaim some land and a collapsed homestead, and established himself as a producer of thirty-three koku of rice per annum. He came from Echigo in 1823, and had

The perception of work in Tokugawa Japan

cultivated 2 cho and 9 tan of new areas by the time he left for Mito in 1833.[58]

Ninomiya also took measures to discourage emigration. In 1827, he stated in a letter: 'Both men and women shall not be permitted to marry a person from another village while shiho is in operation . . . Villagers shall be strongly warned against moving away, and urged to reconsider.'[59]

4) *Technological assistance and transfer*
[4-1] The organisation of tools, fertilisers and plants

Villagers in Sakuramachi were supplied with capital at the initial stage of the programme. They were also provided with tools, fertilisers, and the necessary plants. Ninomiya purchased agricultural tools in bulk and distributed them to the villagers, thus reducing the total cost of tools, and benefiting poor villagers who could not afford efficient new tools. The purchased tools were also used as rewards for outstanding workers. *Nogu Kaiire Narabini Watashikatachō* of 1824 shows that 30 hoes and 40 sickles were purchased, and more than 36 ryō was spent altogether on the tools:

Purchase and distribution of hoes and sickles [an extract]

Hoes:
4th day of August, 1823
167 mon of cash was spent to purchase a hoe
25th day of August, 1823
1 bu of cash was spent to purchase 10 hoes
2nd day of October, 1823
1 bu 2 shu and 677 mon of cash was spent to purchase 19 hoes
Total number of hoes purchased: 30

25th day of August, 1823
A hoe was delivered to each of the following villagers:
Sahei, Chuzaemon, Kiyokichi, Kihei, Yu'emon,
Jinzaemon, Zenhei, Chushichi

The shiho *programme*

1st day of July, 1824
The following are outstanding contributors. A hoe will be awarded to each:
Ko'emon of Sakuramachi, Magozaemon of Nishi Monoi, Yu'emon of Tonuma, Chuzaemon of Yokota

Sickles:
4 ryo 3 bu 2 shu and 714 mon of cash was spent on 214 sickles. They were distributed in the following manner:
71 sickles to Tonuma group   5 to Hin'emon group
3 to Nishi Monoi
The remaining 135 were distributed through Katsumata and Takeda to:
Yokota village [35], Nishi Monoi village [an additional 45], and Sakuramachi group [55]

[60]

Ninomiya sent shihō leaders to buy fertilisers in bulk from the producers. The *Shimekasu Hoshika Jyōnōkin Toritatecho* of 1824 shows that more than 100 ryō was spent.[61] Ninomiya also arranged the collective purchase of young rice plants and young cedar buds. The *Tōza Kingin Deirichō* of 1823 recorded that 3 ryō 2 bu and 673 mon was spent on the purchase of young cedar buds that year.[62]

[4-2] Technology transfer

The nothern Kanto villages utterly lacked technological skills in agriculture, and the economic difficulties of the region were directly attributable to this. Evidence however shows a few instances where Kanto villages attempted to improve their agricultural technology. Nakai Nobuhiko's study of Ōhara Yūgaku (1797-1858), the initiator of agrarian reform and the founder of the *Seigaku* movement in Shimousa, shows Ohara's enthusiasm to introduce 'advanced' agricultural technologies from the Kinai region into the villages of Shimousa.[63] Existing research, however, tends to have ignored technological awareness within the shiho group. As a matter of fact, Sanpei Matazaemon of Sakuramachi was in touch with Okura Nagatsune, the famous agrarian technologist of the Bakumatsu era.[64] Sanpei met Okura at least three times, twice in 1829 and once in 1831, and wrote to Ninomiya in 1829 that,

> . . . Okura seemed to me to be a man with exceptional devotion to agriculture. I have already met him, and found him very interesting. He showed me some of his books concerning wealth creation in the household. I bought many copies of them, and also sent some to Odawara. He came back to me two days ago. He brought with him a couple of his newly published works. Detailed explanation was given concerning the use of cole, . . .[65]

One of the books 'concerning wealth creation in the household' was presumably Okura's *Nokaeki*, or 'Farm Family Profits'. The other book on the use of cole was *Jokoroku*, which was on ways to control insect pests in the rice paddy. Sanpei put advanced technological information on agriculture received from Okura into practice.[66] He not only used technologies in the domain he served (Sakuramachi) but also in other areas where shiho was in operation. Okura appeared also in Sanpei's letter to Ninomiya in August, 1831.[67]

The acquisition of advanced technology is important in itself, but what is crucial here is the way in which it was introduced and how it spread. Sanpei became a mediator: a person involved in the programme responded to the advanced technology and caused its use to spread without receiving any instruction from Ninomiya to do so.

Advanced technologies were actively spread by shiho leaders in other areas too. The shiho programme was introduced to three provinces in the Tokai region, Suruga, Totomi, and Mikawa by Agoin (or 'Agui') Gido-Shoshichi.

The shiho programme

Agoin did not have intensive contact with Ninomiya at any stage of his life, but he was in close contact with some of Ninomiya's pupils. He introduced such technologies as the checkrow planting of rice and the thin bedding of young rice plants.[68] These were commonly practised techniques in the Kinai region, and were adopted by Agoin for the first time in the Tokai region. Some shiho researchers emphasise the labour-intensive element of shiho, while neglecting the technological awareness of its leaders. Certainly, even the 'advanced' technologies introduced by Agoin required a heavy labour input, but it should be noted that labour intensity was not the sole ingredient of the improvement in production brought about under the shiho programme. The cases of Sanpei and Agoin reveal the technological awareness of the personnel involved in the scheme.

5) *Social welfare and village solidarity*
[5-1] The inclusion of 'very poor' (*gokunan*) peasants in the labour force

Sugano Noriko has argued that shiho was successful in rehabilitating the 'middle-class' peasants (*chunoso*), but it neglected the poorest. Based on her research on the village of Kaneko in Sagami, she stressed that shiho was the cause of the 'dissolution' of the poorest from agriculture and the 'semi-proletarianisation' of them.[69] Otsuka argues that the poorest peasants were not integrated into shiho's developmental projects and were given no reward. In his view, they were basically left out of the rehabilitation schemes of the shiho programme.[70] Both, therefore, share the idea that shiho failed to help those most impoverished, despite its overall success in the restoration of village economy through the revitalisation of the 'middle-class' peasants.

Both views may be considered accurate in pointing out that shiho could not rehabilitate the poorest peasants to the extent that they could establish themselves as semi-independent productive entities. However, one needs to consider the economic condition of the peasants in shihō villages. The poorest were not merely facing economic difficulties; what they experienced was not just the change in the 'mode' of production from agriculture to wage earning but the alienation from any means of production. In the face of this, measures had to be taken to rescue the poorest from a disastrous situation. As Sugano herself points out, extra activities for cash earning were promoted by Ninomiya in the village of Kaneko. Coupled with tax schemes (taxation on income from non-agricultural by-employment was surprisingly low compared with that from agriculture)[71], this plan rescued those in most need.

Otsuka's findings also need qualification. First, as Otsuka's research itself reveals, loans were made available even to peasant households of the poorest rank. They were provided with a greater quantity of rice assistance than those who were better off.[72] The poor could also take advantage of the loan system without providing any security. Second, measures were taken to prevent the dissolution of the poorest peasant households from the economic fabric of the village; the poorest were absorbed as a secondary labour force. For instance, Ninomiya conducted some non-agricultural bywork in the village. In 1824, he organised a task force for straw mat making[73], which included some of the poorest peasants. Yūemon and Sannosuke, villagers of Tonuma, were listed as the heads of 'very poor' households in their village, even in the survey of 1845.[74] Both, however, contributed to the project by making twenty mats.[75] Even the poorest peasants were absorbed into the labour force to carry out secondary tasks at least.[76]

Furthermore, in the daily life of the village, a variety of miscellaneous tasks were available, even for a secondary labour force. The drying of wheat, the peeling of dried beans, and the care of store rooms were tasks for the elderly.[77] The increase in labour intensity and the involvement in extra tasks created a number of miscellaneous tasks in the

The shiho programme

household.[78] For these reasons, even the secondary labour force from the poorest household was expected to take part in productive activity of one sort or another. Ninomiya's letter to Uzawa states:

> Hotoku shuho [shiho] insists on everybody's making an effort; rich and poor, village officials and ordinary peasants, working men and the retired, they are all required to be involved in one kind of task or another, so as to join in the act of creation. One should be loyal to the assignment; not only that, one should be devoted to secondary tasks, and demonstrate frugality, even after one's retirement . . .[79]

As has already been shown in the studies of Oto and Kumagawa, shiho was designed to help the most impecunious of peasants.[80] The significance of the programme, however, lies in its incorporation of the population into the unitary fabric of the village economy. 'Assistance' was given in exchange for contribution, not as a grant to be assumed by the poor. The policy arguably avoided the separation of the poor from the economic fabric, which might otherwise have resulted in the outmigration of the population to urban areas.

[5-2] The nourishment of the future labour force

One of the priorities of the shiho programme was the nurturing of children. Under the programme, children were provided for mainly in two ways: first, Ninomiya established a class for the teaching of reading, writing, and simple mathematics (*tenarai beya*). A house was prepared specially for that purpose. The education programme was supported financially by the pool money, the Hōtoku Capital.[81] Second, special aid was given to households with more than three children. The aid was offered mainly through rice.[82] The infants, the prospective labour force for future reproduction, were nurtured and educated by the pool money, which derived from the efforts of the village members.

6) *A short summary*

As we have seen, a number of schemes were employed and implemented under the control of the shihō programme. The following is a letter from Ninomiya to Uzawa Sakuemon, a leader of the shiho programme in Sakuramachi, who was later posted back to the domain of Odawara in 1838 to lead the shihō programme there. It lists the deeds implemented in Sakuramachi in somewhat self-congratulatory tones:

> ... the average production between Bunka 9 and Bunsei 4 has been studied ... and an economic formula devised ... Not only has reclamation been carried out, and new paddies and fields been developed, but roads were constructed and bridges were erected; men and horses are able to pass by. Ditches and sewers have been dug; banks erected and waterways made. Thorns, reeds, bush clovers have been mowed. Other unnecessary weeds and trees have also been cut down. Land has been raised or lowered wherever necessary. Temples and houses which had been deserted for years have been repaired; neglected branch family members and new immigrants have been brought in. With these new people, new households have been established. They have been provided with agricultural tools and some food supplies. After all the efforts that have been made for over ten years, cultivable land has increased and people have became prosperous. Villages have been restored.[83]

1836 saw the severest famine in the Tenpo era. A letter from Yokosawa, a shiho leader, shows the state of the economy in Sakuramachi in that year:

> ... After an intensive implementation of shiho, life in the villages was revived ... We have been astonished by this fact ... Even those that suffered the worst are not starving any longer. The villages are now successfully main-

tained, which in fact is a rare case in other areas. Years of hard work by the villagers, and your [Ninomiya's] foresight and judicious guidance are the factors which have brought about this situation. I heartily admire it.[84]

As was shown in Table 1, production in the domain of Sakuramachi showed considerable growth in the years of shiho implementation. The amount of rice production increased to as much as 1,825 hyō in 1827. After the settlement of the 'Toyoda rebellion' in 1828, production began to grow without fluctuation, except in the years of the great Tenpo famines. In 1842, it grew to 2,026 hyō, almost reaching the target of 2,039 hyō officially set by *bundo*. Surplus accumulated accordingly in the fifteen years of the shiho programme. Ninomiya initially pursuaded the Utsu family to temporarily lower *bundo*, and the surplus accumulation was realised largely by this political action, rather than by the success of the economic programme. Nonetheless, the accumulation would not have grown without a gradual increase in actual production. By Tenpō 9 (1838) when the economic management of the domain was handed back to the Utsu family, surplus rice accumulation had reached 8,545 hyō.[85] Financial assistance from Odawara was terminated in 1836, and Sakuramachi began to depend thoroughly on its own production.[86] An official report on the economic conditions in Sakuramachi, *Sankason Daishō Hinpu Kurashikata Torishirabe Agechō* or 'The living conditions in the three villages', which is based on the survey conducted in Koka 2 (1845) shows the following picture (Table 3): Among 188 households in Sakuramachi, 114 were listed as in 'very good' or 'good' condition, and 15 as in an 'average' condition. While 23 were considered still to be very bad, however, it is significant that nearly seventy per cent of the households were restored to 'good' or at least to an 'average' condition. Bearing in mind the devastated state of the economy in 1821, this is a remarkable recovery.

Table 3: The living conditions (of the households) in the three villages (1845)

very good	good	average	bad	very bad
55	59	15	36	23

[87]

In the course of ten years, the annual yield more than doubled, due largely to the restoration of the arable land area, which increased dramatically. On the other hand, the population had increased by only 51 per cent by the 1850s, from 722 in 1821 to 1,090 in 1853.[88] There was thus an increase in per capita production. And this was not just the result of the increase in land. It was also attributable to the amount of labour invested per person, technological improvement, and the application of the effective schemes of shiho. Moreover, the development of land resources and agricultural infrastructure was carried out at the hands of the villagers themselves. Production increase was, in the end, the fruit of the villagers' own labour.

The implementation of the shiho programme was initially to be of ten years' duration[89], but it was extended for another five years, until 1836[90] and was in effect even after 1838. The success of the rehabilitation suggests that shiho was indeed an effective programme. More importantly, it proves that the economic measures employed during the process were more than adequate in stimulating peasant work; for the key to success lies not in the programme itself but in its triumph in restoring the 'attitude' of peasants towards work. The educational as well as institutional schemes of shiho

The shiho programme

were designed to improve the labour and care capacity of peasants, and to nurture them towards an understanding of their own capabilities in the management of household work. Its success suggests that peasants were able to respond to it. One could thus argue that there existed a set of interactions between the programme and the peasants, during which process the peasants' economic potential was sufficiently fulfilled. Bearing these findings in mind, the next chapter will attempt to identify the perception of work that emerged among peasant producers.

Notes
1. The shiho programmes which Ninomiya devised and implemented can be classified into two categories: 1) The shiho practised in the Hattori family of Odawara, Shimodate and Karasuyama in northern Kantō may be termed a 'financial shihō programme' which chiefly consisted of the calculation of a family income/expenditure and the proposal for effective investment of capital. 2) The shiho programmes practised in Sakuramachi, Yatabe and Motegi, and the domain of Soma, on the other hand, were much more comprehensive economic rehabilitation programmes. As we shall see in this chapter, the comprehensive version of the shiho programme consisted of all spheres of economic activity, including financial plans, land reclamation and infrastructure development, and labour organisation. The financial shiho was primarily concerned with the control and effective use of a limited amount of capital, while the comprehensive version included radical economic plans to increase financial capability through increased production. Some large individual households also employed this type of the shiho programme. There were no less than twenty villages and domains which received direct instructions from Ninomiya in their implementation. In several

domains in such provinces as Suruga, Totomi, and Mikawa, the programme was conducted by his pupils.

The implementation of the shiho programme was usually carried out by a group of leaders consisting of Ninomiya himself, a few village headmen from the locality, and, in the case of Sakuramachi, personnel from the domain of Odawara. Ninomiya was given a mandate to conduct the rehabilitation programme, but it was usually carried out on an order from the head of the domain. Sasai Shintaro later called this '*gyosei-shiki*' or 'an administration-based programme'. In the post-Ninomiya era (after his death in 1856), on the other hand, the shiho programmes and the entire Hotoku movement were carried out by partnership groups; these may be termed, after Sasai, '*kessha-shiki*' or 'co-operative-based programme'. The latter formed a group closely related to a co-operative, which was initiated by a few leading figures in a region and formed by local sympathisers willing to contribute to the economic good of the locality. Such a group was usually called *Hotokusha* ('Society for the repayment of virtue') or '*Goho Renchu*' ('Group of people working for repayment').

Researchers on Ninomiya tend to assume that the term 'shiho' is a proper noun used only for the action taken for village rehabilitation. The word 'shiho' was used, however, in more general terms to mean 'device', 'method', or 'means' of dealing with one's difficulties. The use of the word is illustrated in Maeda Isamu (ed.), *Edogo no Jiten* (Kodansha Gakujutsu Bunko), Kodansha, Tokyo, 1991 (first published in 1979), p. 988. It was not until the second half of the eighteenth century when the villages in the northern Kanto area suffered from severe production decline, and domains began to take initiatives to restore the villages, that the term 'shiho' began to appear as a word indicating a village rehabilitation programme. The programme initiated by the head of the domain was called *ryoshu shiho*. Ninomiya's programme was usually called *Sontoku shiho* or 'the shiho programme of Ninomiya Sontoku'.
2. Shinbo and Saito Osamu (eds.), *Iwanami Nihon Keizaishi vol. 2*.

3. Sekiyama, *Kinsei Nihon no Jinko Kozo*, pp. 137-41.
4. Akimoto Hiroya's study on the Choshu economy illustrates the development of these elements of Tokugawa agriculture. See Akimoto, *Zen Kogyoka Jidai no Keizai*, Mineruva Shobo, Kyoto, 1987, pp. 34, 42-44.
5. Double cropping was practised in 60 to 70 per cent of the entire arable land area in the Hokuriku, Kinai, Sanyo, and northern Kyushu regions. In some areas in these regions, it reached 90 per cent. Tanaka Koji, 'Kinsei ni okeru Shuyaku Inasaku no Keisei', Watanabe Tadayo (ed.), *Ine no Ajiashi*, vol. 3, Shogakukan, Tokyo, 1987, pp. 320-22.
6. 'Labour intensity' has long been seen as a feature of Japanese agriculture, particularly from the eighteenth century onwards. The spread of double cropping and the accompanying technologies further fostered this tendency in agrarian labour. See Akimoto, *Zen Kogyoka Jidai*, pp. 27-51.
7. Shinbo and Saitō Osamu (eds.), *Iwanami Nihon Keizaishi*, vol. 2, pp. 15-16.
8. Hayami and Miyamoto Matao (eds.), *Iwanami Nihon Keizaishi*, vol. 1, pp. 42-47, 63-64.
9. Yoshinaga Akira, 'Tokusan Shōrei to Hansei Kaikaku', Asao Naohiro, Ishii Susumu, et. al. (eds.), *Iwanami Kōza Nihon Rekishi*, vol. 11 *(Kinsei 3)*, Iwanami Shoten, Tokyō, 1976, pp. 42-45.
10. Lord Ishikawa of Shimodate, for instance, became a pupil of Shingaku in 1792. Ishikawa invited Nakazawa Dōni, a Shingaku leader in the Kantō region, to Shimodate to deliver a lecture in 1793. *Yūrinsha*, a Shingaku academic centre, was founded in Shimodate later in that year. See Ishikawa (Ken), *Sekimon Shingakushi*, pp. 476-78.
11. As stated in Chapter 5, Shingaku followers in Kantō rural areas did not find the school's teaching effective for the restoration of deserted villages. They turned to Ninomiya instead.
12. Niki Yoshikazu, 'Nōson Fukkou no Seisan Rinri: Ninomiya Sontoku, Ōhara Yugaku', Sugihara Shiro, Sakasai Takahito, et. al. (eds.), *Nihon no Keizai Shiso Yonhyakunen*,

Nihon Keizai Hyoronsha, Tokyo, 1991, p. 203.
13. Sekiyama, *Kinsei Nihon no Jinko Kozo*, p. 141.
14. *Ibid.*, pp. 137-38. The index calculated by Otsuka, 'Kinsei Koki Kita-Kanto ni okeru Shono Saiken', p. 38.
15. A brief comparison between *ryoshu shiho* and Sontoku shiho has been made by Otsuka in his 'Kinsei Koki Kita-Kanto ni okeru Shono Saiken', pp. 36-39. He concluded that Ninomiya's Sontoku shiho programme appeared far more effective than *ryoshu shiho* practised in Nishi Takahashi village.
16. This thesis has become a commonplace in Japanese economic historiography. cf. Hayami and Miyamoto Matao (eds.), *Iwanami Nihon Keizaishi, vol.1*. Also, Iinuma Jiro, *Sekai Nogyo Bunkashi*, Yasaka Shobo, Kyoto, 1983.
17. Kaiho Seiryo, 'Goshudan', Kuranami Shoji (ed.), *Kaiho Seiryō Zenshu*, Yachiyo Shuppan, Tokyo, 1976, p. 132.
18. *NSZ*, vol. 10, p. 807.
19. *Ibid.*, pp. 791-93.
20. *Ibid.*, p. 810.
21. *Ibid.*, pp. 797-802.
22. *Ibid.*, pp. 831-33.
23. *Ibid.*, pp. 803-804, 831-33.
24. *NSZ*, vol. 13, p. 14.
25. Saito Takayuki, 'Ninomiya Sensei Goroku vol. 1, No. 6', *NSZ*, vol. 36, pp. 343-44.
26. *NSZ*, vol. 3, p. 196.
27. *Ibid.*, pp. 195-200.
28. A small-scale protest, called 'Toyoda rebellion', occurred in 1828, and resulted in Ninomiya's departure from Sakuramachi the following year.

Production in Sakuramachi increased in the first six years of shiho (1822-27), while the programme was accompanied by the intensification of labour. A group of peasants in the domain felt discontented with this, and participated in a small-scale rebellion led by Toyoda Shosaku in 1828. Toyoda was a samurai, who was sent from Odawara in 1828 in support of Ninomiya's leadership in Sakuramachi. In Odawara, he was ranked higher than Ninomiya, who by then had been promoted from peasant to retainer in the domain hierarchy. However, the apparent success in Sakuramachi under Ninomiya had earned him a recognition higher than that granted to Toyoda. Immediately after his arrival, Toyoda was deeply dissatisfied about this. Several peasants who felt uneasy with such radical economic measures as a reward system (which involved villagers' evaluation of themselves) supported Toyoda in carrying out a protest against Ninomiya's instructions. Thus, Toyoda supporters refused to attend any of the economic projects in shiho in 1828. This affected both agricultural production and infrastructure development, and resulted in a sharp decline in production in Sakuramachi that year (see Table 1 in Section 2-3 of the main text).

The contrast between the dramatic production increase under shiho and its subsequent sharp decline during the protest convinced the villagers that they simply could not sustain their economy if the shiho programme were suspended. The protest caused damage to the village economy, but, in turn, shiho's success as an effective economic scheme was proven because of it.

Ninomiya left Sakuramachi on the fourth day of January the following year (1829), and began fasting at *Shinshoji* Temple in Narita. He was away for four months, during which time economic conditions in Sakuramachi worsened. His absence highlighted the importance of his presence to the restoration of the village and of the maintenance of the shiho programme. In the end, both the village officials and the ordinary peasants in Sakuramachi prepared letters asking for Ninomiya's return to service. *NSZ*, vol. 3, pp. 195-200.

Toyoda was sent back to Odawara in 1829, only one year after his appointment as a Sakuramachi project leader, when Ninomiya returned to the domain to resume the shiho programme. *Ibid.*, p.219. The so-called 'Toyoda rebellion' ended with the Sakuramachi peasants calling for Ninomiya's return to the domain and the resumption of his service.

29. Sasaki Junnosuke and Unno Fukuju, 'Ninomiya Sontoku to Bakumatsu no Nosei Kaikaku', *Bunka Hyoron* (March,

1978), p.122.

30. The details of the Hotoku loan system have been studied by Sasai Shintaro, and more recently, by economic historians Oto, Otsuka, and Niki. See Oto, 'Kanto Noson no Kohai to Sontoku Shuho', pp. 166-184; Otsuka, 'Kinsei Koki Kita-Kanto ni okeru Shono Saiken', pp. 44-50; and Niki, 'Odawarahan Kamado Shinden Mura', pp. 146-50.

31. *NSZ*, vol. 10, pp. 856-951. Also, *Yuzu Muri Toki Kashicho* recorded the system of interest-free loans. The records show that one household could borrow up to 1 ryo at any one time. Ninomiya Sontoku-O Zenshu Kankokai (ed.), *Kaisetsu Ninomiya Sontoku-O Zenshu*, vol. 4 (*Jissenhen*), Ninomiya Sontoku-O Zenshu Kankokai, Tokyo, 1937, pp.144-45. (abbreviated to '*KNSOZ*' hereafter) *Risoku Tsuki Kashikin Hikaecho* recorded the system of low-interest loans, mainly to aid low-income peasant households; it also assisted poor households who had used up their initial assistance. *Ibid.*, pp. 145-46.

32. *NSZ*, vol. 10, pp. 856-57.

33. The records show that all loans were made to the head of the household, except the loans to Enzo, Senji, and Heiji. *NSZ*, vol. 11, pp. 43-55. This fact is revealed through cross-reference of the list of the names of lessees in the records and the 'Shumon Aratamecho' of the domain. *Ibid.*, pp. 439-50. Moreover, while Enzo was not a household head, he was married, and had two daughters. He was the elder brother of Mataji, the head of a big household with nine menbers, and thus was like a leader of a quasi-family unit within Mataji's household. *Ibid.*, p. 442. In sum, according to the interest-free loan record of Bunsei 7, sixteen out of eighteen loans were offered to heads of production units in Tonuma village, most of them being heads of households.

34. *NSZ*, vol. 10, p. 810.

35. *Ibid.*, pp. 811-15. *NSZ*, vol. 12, pp. 372, 413, 451.

36. See note 28 of this chapter.

37. *NSZ*, vol. 10, p. 794.

38. *Ibid.*, pp. 794-96.

39. *NSZ*, vol. 13, p.14.

40. *NSZ,* vol. 6, p. 523.
41. *NSZ,* vol. 11, pp. 11-12.
42. *KNSOZ,* vol. 4, p. 140.
43. *NSZ,* vol. 11, pp. 292-300.
44. *NSZ,* vol. 12, p. 1,248.
45. *Ibid.,* p. 1,251.
46. *Ibid.,* p. 1,253.
47. See also Fukaya Katsumi, 'Hotoku Shiho', *Tochigikenshi: Tsushihen 5, Kinsei 2,* Tochigiken, Tochigi, 1984, pp. 910-11.
48. *NSZ,* vol. 10, pp. 1,023-77.
49. *Ibid.,* pp. 1,024-25.
50. *Ibid.,* p. 1,025.
51. *Ibid.,* p. 1,027.
52. Morita Shiro, *Ninomiya Sontoku,* p. 136.
53. Fukuzumi, 'Ninomiya-O Yawa vol. 2, No.25', *NSZ,* vol. 36, p. 691.
54. *Ibid.,* p. 694.
55. *NSZ,* vol. 6, pp. 240-41.
56. *NSZ,* vol. 3, p. 218. 1830 was the first year of Tenpo. But the letter was recorded to have been dispatched in 'Bunsei 13'.
57. *KNSOZ,* vol. 4, pp. 151, 153-57.
58. *NSZ,* vol. 10, p. 1,044.
59. *KNSOZ,* vol. 4, pp. 152-53.
60. *NSZ,* vol. 11, pp. 110-12.
61. *Ibid.,* pp. 113-24.
62. *NSZ,* vol. 10, p. 857. The amount spent in ryo was calculated by Sasai Shintaro.
63. Nakai Nobuhiko, *Ohara Yugaku* (Jinbutsu Sosho), Yoshikawa Kobunkan, Tokyo, 1963, pp. 152-8.
64. For Okura Nagatsune, see Smith, *Native Sources of Japanese Industrialization,* chapter 8.
65. *NSZ,* vol. 6, p. 10.
66. No record can be found of Ninomiya's direct contact with Ōkura. However, Ninomiya's enthusiasm regarding technological education is apparent from the 'Memoirs'. In No. 135 of the 'Memoirs', for instance, his detailed instructions for the timing of fertiliser application is

recorded. *NSZ,* vol. 36, p. 380.
67. *NSZ,* vol. 6, p. 14.
68. Nogyo Hattatsushi Chosakai (ed.), *Nihon Nogyo Hattatsushi: Supplementary, vol. 2,* Chuo Koronsha, Tokyo, 1981 (first published in 1959), pp. 233-49.
69. Sugano Noriko, 'Tenpoki Kaso Nomin no Sonzai Keitai', *Rekishigaku Kenkyu,* 365 (October, 1970), pp. 30-31.
70. Otsuka, 'Kinsei Koki Kita-Kanto ni okeru Shono Saiken', esp. pp. 47-49.
71. See, for instance, Nishikawa Shunsaku, 'The Economic Studies of Choshu on the eve of industrialization', *The Economic Studies Quarterly,* 38 (December, 1987), pp. 323-37, and T.C. Smith, *Native Sources of Japanese Industrialization.*
72. Oto Osamu's research, for instance, shows that the poorer peasants were actually favoured by the rice supply scheme. See Oto Osamu, 'Mura no Kohai to Sontoku Shuho', *Oyamachoshi, vol. 2, Kinsei Shiryohen 1,* Oyamacho, Shizuoka, 1991, pp. 930-35.
73. *NSZ,* vol. 12, pp. 169-94.
74. *Ibid.,* pp. 784.
75. *Ibid.,* pp. 185, 186.
76. Ninomiya also formulated plans for the pursuit of extra tasks. A plan for daily rope making was called *Hikake Nawanai Shudancho.* The S*hudancho* of 1838, introduced in *Sanshinden Shiho* in Kamonomiya, Odawara, estimated the annual earnings of the household from making rope. The *Shudancho* suggests that a household could earn 59 ryo per annum if it made five portions of rope a day. The formula showed a means of earning cash even for the elderly, the sick and the weak; through it they could stand on their own feet, and make a partial contribution to the restoration of the village economy. See Kodama Kota, 'Ningen to Daichi tono Taiwa', Kodama Kota (ed.), *Nihon no Meicho, vol. 26: Ninomiya Sontoku,* Chuo Koronsha, Tokyo, 1970, p. 538.
77. Morita, *Ninomiya Sontoku,* p. 13.
78. Fukaya, *Hyakusho Naritachi,* p. 129.
79. *NSZ,* vol. 6, p. 910.

80. Oto, 'Mura no Kohai to Sontoku Shuho'. Also, Kumakawa Yumiko, 'Ninomiya Kinjiro no Shiho ni Kansuru Ichi Kosatsu', *Jinbun Ronshu* (Shizuoka University), 25 (1974).
81. *NSZ*, vol. 10, pp. 1,021-23.
82. *NSZ*, vol. 12, pp. 346-55. The provision of rice assistance for the nourishment of children was also a common scheme in some *ryoshu shiho* programmes. See Nagano Hiroko, 'Kansei no Jidai', Hayashi Hideo (ed.), *Komonjo no Kataru Nihonshi, vol. 7: Edo Koki*, Chikuma Shobo, Tokyo, 1989, p. 159.
83. *NSZ*, vol. 6, p. 909. For Ninomiya's discourse of a similar tenor, see *NSZ*, vol. 12, p. 80.
84. *NSZ*, vol. 6, p. 187. Letters admiring the shiho programme could be found also in *Ibid.*, pp. 605, 607, 616, 770, 800, 822, 832, 843, and in *NSZ*, vol. 12, pp. 78-83.
85. *NSZ*, vol. 12, p. 371.
86. *NSZ*, vol. 10, p. 796.
87. *NSZ*, vol. 12, pp. 783-87.
88. The pace of population increase in Sakuramachi has been studied by Otsuka, 'Kinsei Koki Kita-Kanto ni okeru Shono Saiken', pp. 37-38.
89. *NSZ*, vol. 10, p. 810.
90. *NSZ*, vol. 6, p. 8.

Chapter 8

Ninomiya's work thought and the peasants' perception of work: An analysis

An inquiry was made in Chapter 6 into Ninomiya's philosophical writings through which his idea of work is expressed. In the last chapter, we investigated the *shiho* programme in an attempt to reveal how Ninomiya effected his thought on work and restored the agrarian economy. New economic measures were introduced under shiho, including the fiscal reform package, through which peasants were made economically competitive and their performance improved. The programme did not, however, involve any economic measures which were totally alien to the agrarian population, and thus the mode of production was not drastically changed. Shiho did not destroy the productive autonomy of the households, but preserved it; the programme facilitated the productive use of technology, labour, and time by the members of nuclear and stem families. Communal schemes regarding saving, development of public facilities, and the helping of the poor were preserved and promoted. Ideologically, the concept of *ie* appears central to Ninomiya's thought. It remained as the key factor through which incentives for work were given to peasants, and the transgenerational sense of cumulative betterment of the economy was enhanced.

The implications of all this are obvious: Ninomiya acted as a catalyst through which the prevalent mode of production and ideological constructs of the era were amalgamated, and a more active and structured mode of work produced. His frame of reference included ideology and economy, and through this and his familiarity with peasant producers, the meaning of work was identified. In turn, peasants were able to respond to Ninomiya's intentions, and his ideas on work spread rapidly among the agrarian population of the northern Kanto villages in the late Edo period.

This chapter seeks to articulate the contributions made by Ninomiya in structuralising and shaping agrarian work and the peasants' perception of it. In the next section, we discuss how managerial and technological elements of work came to be incorporated into the peasants' perception of work in shiho villages. It will be followed by a discussion on how these changes were incorporated into existing ideologies and social values. The last section attempts to identify the characteristic features of the idea of work developed by Ninomiya.

The scope of the perception of work
a) The introduction of the elements of management
Both Ninomiya's thought and his shiho programme helped develop the idea that work involved management of the process of work. This included financial planning and a modern formula for the control of production costs, effected mainly by the introduction of the concepts of *bundo* and *suijo*. Subsistence and surplus were distinguished one from the other in order to achieve a consistent supply of capital for

reproduction. Peasants were educated to develop time sense, capability in financial control, and the ability to make decisions concerning agricultural production, so that they could foresee and respond swiftly to events. As the following apologue by Ninomiya, collected in the 'Memoirs', puts it:

> On a voyage, you will not be able to get to the shore you intend to reach, if you simply follow the direction of the wind. If you want to reach there, you have to steer the helm [and control], and avoid drifting. One's life is just like this . . .[1]

Here, Ninomiya's apt use of the sailing metaphor effectively expresses his views on the need for management. The moral incentivising of work alone was not an adequate triggering device to develop necessary productive efficiency in nineteenth-century Tokugawa agriculture. Peasants had to be able to take managerial initiatives to organise production processes themselves. Ninomiya attempted to diffuse this idea of work, so that the elements of management were vividly recognised and the peasants' perception of work widened to accommodate it.

b) The introduction of the elements of technology

A similar enlargement in the scope of the perception of work occurred at the level of the actual production process. The technological evolution of Tokugawa agriculture followed a path that reinforced labour intensity. Wherever labour and capital were substitutable, the use of labour was opted for, and technology developed on that basis. A crucial element of this technology was, as conceived in the last chapter, the intensity of the 'care' involved[2]; it called for each worker's consistent exertion in close monitoring of plant growth processes, tight weed control, and the timely use of fertiliser and allocation of labour. In a technological environment of this kind, the actual putting into effect of acquired technology rested mainly in the hands of peasants; they were the subjects who responded to practical information, applied it to the production process, and circulated the information acquired during the process of its application that added practical information from the 'user-front'. Ninomiya was aware of this, and attempted to encourage peasants to become active participants in technological management.

The annual production schedule introduced in the *Kinmoroku* discussed in Chapter 6 contained detailed instructions on the specific timing of planting and harvesting, as well as that of seedbed preparation, fertiliser allocation, and so on. Instructions on fifteen different plants were listed as shown in the diagram.[3] But, crucially, Ninomiya not only presented the schedule in a diagrammatic form but also vigorously attempted to educate the peasants in its use.[4] Ninomiya lived in Sakuramachi, communicated constantly with local people, and watched the productive processes of peasant producers closely. The supervisory eyes of Ninomiya or a shiho leader were constantly monitoring peasants' work, and detailed instructions were given wherever necessary. This scheme of things was far removed from that of the so-called technologists, most of whom were more preoccupied with the diffusion of existing techniques than with practically applying and verifying the feasibility of technologies within the economic reality of the work place.[5] The eventual success of the shiho programme illustrates that the elements of technology were made central to peasants' work in the villages where the programme was introduced.

In an ultimate sense, Tokugawa peasants were indeed active participants in the improvement and reshaping of technology itself. T.C. Smith points out that there was a vast network of local agricultural experimental stations in rural Tokugawa Japan, where technologies were adapted to local conditions, information exchanged between stations, and applied advantageously elsewhere. He stated, albeit cautiously, that 'invention' was an outcome of successive discoveries of various sorts, and of the constant transmission of them.[6] In view of this, a recent discussion of how users of technology (those who put the technology into practice) contributed to technical development gives us a useful insight here. Scholars of the 'social constructivist' school have paid special attention to the forces that shaped technological change, and emphasised information networks and loops as decisive elements in the development of technology.[7] In their view, technological innovation is not achieved at the hands of particular individuals but through informational interaction. Moreover, the 'users' of technology are the crucial contributors to the 'informational loop', which gives feedback information for continuous technological development.[8]

The 'social constructivists' are mainly concerned with the development of industrial, not agricultural technology; nor have they referred to technological development in non-Western societies. Their findings nonetheless serve to reshape our view of the process of technological development in general. They are particularly significant when one considers the nature of Tokugawa agriculture, in which the heavy involvement of the users of technology was required in the process of technological application.

Nowhere does Ninomiya speak of the role of communication in technological advancement. Given the technological character of Tokugawa agriculture, however, the instruction he gave in technological management must have involved communicational elements that facilitated the informational loop. 'Initiative' was to be taken in establishing communication, in which peasant households participated as active co-generators of technological information, and, ultimately, as contributors to technological advancement itself.

The ideological interpretation and its impact
a) The idea of cumulative betterment
The 'perpetual continuation' (*eizoku*) of the household was

highly valued in Tokugawa society, and the meaning of work for the peasants evolved largely from it. Ninomiya spoke of this, and its cumulative betterment, on numerous occasions. He did not see work as a simple reproductive process; nor did he regard it as a means of acquiring material prosperity for one generation only. His idea of work was built around the value system associated with the household, and the village. In his philosophy, expressed in the diagram of *Hotokukun*, the household was regarded as a medium through which peasants could practise agricultural production for cumulative amelioration.

The integration of the ideology of 'succession' into the idea of production contributed to the enlargement of the scope of the perception of work. First, it released the view of work from the narrow focus of individual gain. A man could justify his work through his belief in cumulative betterment and the perpetual continuation of the household. Similarly, a wife could justify her work through her belief that it would improve the welfare of her descendants. Given that the focus of Tokugawa ideology lay around the concept of *ie*, it was essential for Ninomiya to go beyond economic individualism and create a concept of work within which the full benefit of 'self-exploitation' of the individual would be brought about. Second, once this was achieved, both managerial and technological concerns embodied in the perception of work would take on new meanings, and new dimensions: given that the importance of 'successive betterment' in the minds of peasants could be taken for granted, it was much easier for Ninomiya to make peasants understand the importance of economic calculations involving a time span of one generation or more. It was also much easier to make them grasp the importance of the long-term benefits of sharing technology and information. In fact, the whole concept of management and technology was built on the idea of progressive betterment as a goal.

b) Self-cultivation as work

In Ninomiya's concepts of *Tendō* and *Jindō*, agricultural work - the physical act of production - was elevated to the realm of metaphysics. Work became a process that activated the full potential of the creative force of nature, which, in turn, brought about prosperity and humane living. Man's active participation in the creative cycle of nature was encouraged, and was related to the cultivation of land and heart in Ninomiya's advocacy of *shinden kaihatsu*. On the other hand, an act of a non-productive sort, such as the practice of Neo-Confucian prescriptions for attainment, was dismissed.

So, having been engaged so whole-heartedly in the economic rehabilitation of deserted villages in northern Kanto, Ninomiya was anxious to embed economic rationale within the peasant *mentalite*. But his philosophies of work projected 'meanings' onto agricultural work in both a physical and a spiritual sense. Production was regarded as the fulfilment of virtue, and the cultivation of land acted as the medium for inner cultivation.

Significantly, this point reveals both a similarity with and a contrast to the thought of Ishida Baigan. Ishida argued that work was the process of the development of self. The language used might differ, but both Ishida and Ninomiya share a similar tenor in their thought here. The 'ingredients' of the means of cultivation in the thought of Ninomiya, however, differ considerably from that of Ishida. Ishida argued for the execution of managerial and inter-personal skills to secure the stable continuation of the household. In the thought of Ninomiya, the scope of that management was extended to embrace not only labour resource management but time, technology, capital, land, and other resources. The economic measures developed by Ninomiya were specific and production-oriented, and were accompanied by judicious planning and management. In Ishida's thought, retainers were not merely to be submissive in household business but to participate in its decision-making. But the informational infrastructure on which the decisions were to be made - information on resources, capital, and so on - was far more developed and structured in Ninomiya than in Ishida. Thus, both thinkers regarded work as the process of cultivation, but a far wider range of economic forms were identified as constituents of the perception of work in Ninomiya's thought. There is no doubt that one of his major contributions lay in the ideological underpinning of such a redefinition of self-cultivation.

Competitive cooperatism

Economic historians have focused largely on the communal schemes of the shiho programme - such as its financial schemes - that aided the hard-pressed peasants.[9] True, Ninomiya employed various schemes to assist these peasants, financially and otherwise, but most of these were launched with a view to activating labour service, not as 'charitable gifts' on which idling peasants could live. Moreover, the 'communal' approach detracted from the other important element of the shiho programme: the enhancement of internal competition within the village. Productivity increased with the use of an award system. This system, in conjunction with the predominant *ie* ideology and the values centred around that concept, promoted the psychological dynamism of competition between the households in the village, whereby a strong sense of achievement orientation was developed.

Certainly, *ie* ideology itself was particularistic, in so far as it referred to the succession of a particular household. Thus, it may not necessarily have been oriented to inter-household competition, but it was consistent with the *idea* of competition and occupied a central place, with a high moral value, in the life of ordinary peasants. When a peasant received an award, that peasant was honoured himself, but at the same time it was the honour of the household to which he belonged. A man without any awards might be 'ashamed' of himself. If so, it was the dishonour of his household as well. Because in many respects the household mattered more than the individual, this imposed a great psychological burden on each individual. The award system had so explicitly stratified the abilities of household members in terms of achievement - and thus the competitiveness and economic reputation of the households - that it encouraged the villagers to become competitive. It is thus possible to argue that performance value was brought about by 'generalised particularism'; the particularistic value system centred around *ie* ideology was 'generalised' by the award system, which had come to generate achievement orientation. The award system itself was a universalistic means which brought about performance values.[10] But it was this generalisation of particularistic values which contributed to the development of universalistic performance orientation. To some extent, these particularistic values referred to goals rather than means, while they did not only interfere with universalistic means, but actually promoted their introduction.

Ninomiya's education of peasants on time consciousness, work scheduling, and technological awareness all contributed to an improvement in performance. In fact, production increase was far more dramatic in the villages where Ninomiya's shiho programme was practised, than in the villages where *ryoshu shiho* was deployed.[11] It could be asserted that educational efforts made by Ninomiya culminated in the development of the norm of efficiency-driven industry.

The '*ie*-centred' explanation of the shiho programme, such as Fukaya's thesis, pays insufficient attention to its cooperative elements, namely, intra- and inter-village mutual assistance in the programme. Advanced technologies were not kept within one village but were shared by other villages where shiho was employed. Communally developed pool money (Hotoku Capital) was used to assist economically burdened households and villages. Labour forces were exchanged between shiho villages. Households that were about to be dissolved were incorporated into the economic fabric of the village. The shiho programme embraced cooperative elements that fostered mutual assistance, without losing sight of the elements of competition. There was a 'structural dualism' of the household and the village, and a sense of competition and cooperation in shiho villages. But the '*ie*-centred' thesis failed to recognise the cooperative element of the programme, while the 'communal' thesis overlooked the performance orientation inherent in it.

Ninomiya encouraged peasants to work for the benefit of the household and the village, while selfish acts of production were discouraged. His concepts of *Tendo* and *Jindo* encouraged man's initiative in production in accordance with the creative force of *Tendo*. Peasants were urged to work and to execute their managerial abilities, in order to improve economic conditions cumulatively for generations in the future. In other words, it was neither the subordination of individuals to collectivity nor the individualistic conduct of work *per se* that Ninomiya encouraged; it was one's subjective contribution to the initiation of organised and consolidated action comprising such abilities as calculation, anticipation, and coordination.

Thus, Ninomiya's idea of work may best be termed 'competitive cooperatism'. Improvements in the performance of peasant producers were sought through education, award systems and the integration of peasants into organised development projects; while finance, tasks, and technology were all shared in the village and the domain. The village was activated as the 'production support agency' of each household, which enhanced the competitiveness of the households. In turn, the competitive performance of each household made the communal functions of the village even more indispensable. In this way, the household and the village became interrelated entities which synergistically promoted economic dynamism within the village.

Notes
1. Saito Takayuki, 'Ninomiya Sensei Goroku vol. 2, No. 160', *NSZ*, vol. 36, p. 385.
2. Tanaka, 'Kinsei ni Okeru Shuyaku Inasaku no Keisei', p. 332. Akimoto, *Zen Kogyoka no Jidai*, Chapter 3.
3. See 'Diagram D: "*Ten*'s Order of Annual Yield" (annual production schedule)' introduced in Chapter 6.
4. See discussion in section 4-2 in Chapter 7.
5. Smith, *Native Sources of Japanese Industrialization*, p. 183. Sanpei Matazaemon, a leader of the Sakuramachi project, was an admirer of the agricultural technology of Okura Nagatsune. But even Sanpei sensed Okura's reluctance to focus on the actual process of application and the close monitoring of his technology to the locality. *IBZ*, vol. 6, p. 14.
6. *Ibid.*, p. 181.
7. A school that has recently emerged within the history of technology studies, termed 'social constructivist', has disassociated itself from the mainstream thesis of technological development, namely, 'technological heroism', which focuses on the individual innovator (or 'genius') as the central explanatory concept of technological development. See D. MacKenzie and J. Wajcman (eds.), *The Social Shaping of Technology*, Open University Press, Milton Keynes, 1985. W.E. Bijker, T.P. Hughes, and T. J. Pinch (eds.), *The Social Construction of Technological Systems*, MIT (Massachusetts Institute of Technology) Press, Cambridge (Massachusetts), 1987. N. Rosenberg, 'Technological Interdependence in the American Economy', *Technology and Culture*, 20-1 (January, 1979), esp., pp. 32-40. They also marginalised technological determinism. The scholars of this school concentrate on the social factors

that shaped technological change.
8. N. Rosenberg, *Inside the Black Box: Technology and Economics*, Cambridge University Press, Cambridge, 1982, esp., pp. 120-40.
9. See Otsuka, 'Kinsei Koki Kita-Kanto ni okeru Shono Saiken', and Niki, 'Odawarahan Kamado Shinden Mura'. For work in English emphasising the 'communal' element of the thought of Ninomiya, see Wm. T. de Bary, *et. al.* (eds.), *Sources of Japanese Tradition, vol. 1*, Columbia University Press, New York, 1958, p. 74.
10. As Morita Shiro argues, the system itself had the psychological effect on the villagers of motivating them to work. See the discussion in section 3-1 of the preceding chapter.
11. Otsuka, 'Kinsei Koki Kita-Kanto ni okeru Shono Saiken', p. 36.

Conclusion

I would like to make two or three qualifications which indicate the limit of this study, in order to define more precisely the scope of contribution to the study of work made by this book.

As discussed in Chapter 2, work was conceptually constructed in Tokugawa Japan as a 'role' to be played by people in each occupational group, behind which lay work stratification by the status grouping of *shi no ko sho*. The status groups had been politically constructed, and their enduring stability was ideologically endorsed by Neo-Confucianism, which provided society with a cosmology and a conception of order. Ishida never questioned the legitimacy of the Tokugawa social status groups. He regarded the assigned work of each occupational group (*shokubun*) as given, and took it for granted that individual workers had been given assigned tasks to pursue within that sphere. By doing so, he effectively endorsed such a status division. In contrast to Ando Shoeki (1703-1762), a thinker of the same era who spoke of radical social changes[1], Ishida supported the preservation of the existing social order.

Essentially the same observation applies to Ninomiya. He was not the kind of thinker who saw the causes of growing social distress as arising from the discrepancy between deteriorating polity and rising economy. In his view, the existing political and social frameworks were not the cause of economic difficulties. Unlike Kaiho Seiryo, who spoke approvingly of the emergence of the market system and pointed out its disparity with the static Tokugawa political and social system, thus hinting at the need of its reorganisation[2], Ninomiya attempted to establish a system for economic betterment that was workable within the existing political and social frameworks. Neither the thought of Ishida nor that of Ninomiya was designed to politically activate commoners to initiate changes in the socio-political environment from the root. Having focused arbitrarily on the two thinkers, therefore, an inquiry into the emergence of new thought on social and political reforms, such as that developed by Ando and Kaiho, has been excluded from this study.

Ishida does not seem to have been fully familiar with trading practices in areas outside Kyoto. In the trading houses of Edo, for instance, the casual, short-term employment of servants and shop assistants was more commonly practised than in Kyoto.[3] Work relations in Edo may have been more contractual than those in Kyoto for this reason. Such a difference in the form of employment might have brought about different ideas concerning work among the Edo merchants from those shared by Kyoto merchants. Ninomiya's thought does not represent the idea of work prevalent in the advanced areas such as the Kinai and western Japan - areas where such economic trends as the commercialisation of agriculture, large landholders' successful marketing of their surplus produce, and town merchants' investments in land were progressing with more rapidity than those in the Kanto region.

Given these factors, this study should not be taken to present a comprehensive picture of the idea of work in the mid-to-late Edo period. On the other hand, these factors do not detract from the fact that Ishida and Ninomiya were

Conclusion

among those thinkers closest to the life and work of the ordinary people. In spite of the reservations mentioned above, the two thinkers were able to pick up the undercurrents of the idea of work prevalent among the commoners of the era, undercurrents which developed as a result of common work experience, inherited or shared.

The idea of work as a force of socio-economic change

The two thinkers acted as key vehicles for the social construction of work in two respects: first, they acted as a medium through which ideology and economy were amalgamated, the meaning of work identified and intellectual expression given to it. Work is not an activity with solely economic purposes and meaning; it also embraces social and ideological meanings which reflect the ideas of society. On the other hand, the actual form of work is dictated by economic and technological factors. As we have seen, the thought of Ishida and Ninomiya represented both popular ideology and thought on work in the Tokugawa era, and the actual form of economic activities in commerce and agriculture based on their own work experience. The study of the two thinkers thus enables us to form a picture of the perception of work of Tokugawa commoners, without falling into the trap of politico-ideological determinism, of which some intellectual historians, particularly those who throw light on the linguistic and ritual features of work, appear to be the victims. Second, their own work experience, and the fact that they both had media for the diffusion of their thought - academic centres (*bosha*) and the family precepts for Ishida and the *shiho* programme for Ninomiya - suggest that they were in close contact with popular life and work, and were at the centre of the interactive process between commoners and thought. They were prompt to pick up the economic ideas in the popular work scene which usually existed in an intellectually unformed manner, and to articulate them as an *idea* of work which was then fed to commoners. Measured in terms of their contribution to the social construction of work, Ishida and Ninomiya are of more interest in the forming of an understanding of the Tokugawa perception of work than hitherto believed. Their contribution is certainly far more substantial in this respect than the image formed of them in the Meiji era would suggest.

Scholarship on Tokugawa history, particularly economic and intellectual studies, has consistently pointed to the development of the ethic of 'hard work' in Tokugawa society. R.N. Bellah's classic work apart, individual workers' pursuit of thrift, diligence and frugality for the sake of the collective interest were assessed by the scholars of Tokugawa history as the ideologically developed social norm, which compelled every member of society to work hard. Quite frequently, both Ishida and Ninomiya appear in these studies as chief figures who were responsible for the development of such a work ethic.[4] Some historians have even interpreted this as the 'origin' of the ethic of hard work prevalent among workers in the business enterprises of modern and contemporary Japan.

It must be noted, however, that the ethic of hard work alone would not have been adequate to meet the necessities in carrying out the ever more sophisticated and complicated economic activities of the mid-to-late Edo period. In agrarian settings, for instance, the successive evolution of a variety of labour-intensive technologies made peasants' understanding of organisation and management of work an increasingly important element of agriculture. Market forces penetrated into the life of the peasant population. Although village boundaries were strictly observed, and peasants were tied to the land, it was essential for peasant households to acquire fully the principle of economic rationale. Furthermore, prices tended to rise in the early nineteenth century, and the opportunity for savings and capital accumulation in the era became much greater than in the previous century. There was a need for the peasants to understand the meaning of these developments. Although Ninomiya was not fully responsive to commercialisation, he attempted to nurture peasants as able and efficient managers of their own production processes.

Neither Ninomiya nor Ishida advocated hard work pure and simple; nor did they merely teach the moral and ethical virtues of loyalty and submission to collectivities. They attempted to cultivate the attitude and capacity of common people toward work in the following way: first, both thinkers encouraged the active participation of each subject of work in the designing of his or her own household work. While work was recognised by the two thinkers as no more than an assigned role in a certain intrinsic context, role-play was taken to be neither a worker's passive adaptation to an assigned social role nor his submission to an order given by a superior, where individual workers existed purely as passive followers. Instead, the management of the production process by workers themselves was forcefully advocated. Second, their thought was marked by meritocracy; an incompetent leader was to be removed from his position in the thought of Ishida. Actual production increase was the primary concern of Ninomiya in both his thought and his shiho programme. For both Ishida and Ninomiya, efficiency accompanied by wit and judgment, not merely the exercise of hard work as an expression of loyalty, was an inherent element of the role-play. Third, the ideology of succession (and 'cumulative betterment' in the case of Ninomiya) was integrated into the scope of the perception of work. Work was recognised by the two thinkers as one's subjective participation in sustaining continuous prosperity for generations to come.

The interaction of ideology and socio-economic betterment
The degree of political influence cast by a thought system over society is not the sole criterion by which the value of that thought should be judged. One also needs to consider

the 'social group' over which that thought hold influence and in what way. There are interactions between ideology and society, in the spheres of less politicised, and more mundane aspects of economic and social life. Ishida and Ninomiya acted as key channels for this interactive process.

Ishida, by referring to both the Neo-Confucian concept of self-cultivation and the forms of work in trading houses, raised work within the merchant family business to the level of a process of cultivation. His thought provided merchants with a justification of trading and a meaning of work. A merchant's ability to organise the workgroup, manage the work process, and his participation in business decision-making were all identified as important aspects of work. The scope of work was thus enlarged so as to embrace inter-personal as well as managerial elements.

The physical act of agricultural production was related to human development in the thought of Ninomiya. His idea of work encompassed a fiscal reform package, daily and annual production schedules, formulas for extra cash earning, and economic measures which would enhance the competitiveness of peasants' work. These elements became integrated into agricultural production processes, and were recognised as a means of upholding the household and its successive betterment. In this way, the ideological constructs of Tokugawa society became inseparable from the economy for the two thinkers. The valuation of work was backed by a set of ideological principles, which, in turn, intensified the economic activity of the commoners. It was this interaction between ideology and forms of work that characterised the thought of Ishida and Ninomiya; the acceptance of such an idea of work by the commoners enlarged their perception of work.

True, even before Ishida, there existed ideologies in Tokugawa Japan, Confucianism among them, which encompassed universe, society, and human behaviour, and which also ideologised the everyday work of human beings.

Conclusion

One might argue that ideology and economy were inseparable from the beginning, and, as the economy began to become a dominant element of society, 'the frontiers of philosophical enquiry were broadened to include an increasing range of economic issues', and not vice versa.[5] But sublime ideologies remained for the most part the heritage of the intellectual few. Moreover, ideology was never as closely interlinked with the *details* of everyday work as in the thought of Ishida and Ninomiya. Thus, it was only after the emergence of the two thinkers that work was ideologised in depth, redefined and enriched with meaning; ideology belonging to the intelligentsia could not claim to have had a substantial impact on the everyday work of the populace for this reason.

The intellectual responses made by Ishida and Ninomiya were arguably more fundamental to economic and social change than political reforms, particularly when they penetrated the life and work of the ordinary people. 'Radical' political thought, such as that developed by Kaiho Seiryo, could not claim to bring any immediate benefit to the 'ordinary' life of the masses. Nor could it claim to encompass the need for economic betterment. By contrast, the thought of Ninomiya and Ishida can be viewed as an effective force which promoted economic and social change.

The Hotoku movement from Bakumatsu to Meiji

The immediate concern of this study is the idea of work developed in the thought of Ishida and Ninomiya and the perception of work among the Tokugawa commoners. Examination of the perception of work in Meiji society remains outside the scope of this study. However, the thought of Ishida survived in the Meiji period in the form of the family precepts of trading houses, despite the overall decline of the Shingaku movement from the beginning of the nineteenth century. The Hotoku movement spread in the Bakumatsu and Meiji periods with even more rapidity in terms of membership growth than in the late Edo. Thus, a brief sketch of the influences of Ishida and Ninomiya, and particularly that of the Hotoku movement, is given here to assess the significance of the idea of work shown in this study on the modern perception of work.

Ninomiya was successful in educating his disciples, and by the time of his death in 1856 some of them had already established themselves as agrarian leaders in their homelands. Tomita Kokei, who became Ninomiya's disciple in 1839, began his career as the leader of the shiho programme in his native domain of Soma (Fukushima Prefecture after 1871) in the Bakumatsu and early Meiji periods. He also compiled *Hotokuki,* which appeared in manuscript form in 1856 and was published in 1880, in which Ninomiya's deeds in the course of the village rehabilitation schemes were described. Fukuzumi Masae and Saito Takayuki came to serve Ninomiya in 1844. Both recorded Ninomiya's thoughts and deeds during his involvement in village rehabilitations, and later published *Ninomiya-O Yawa* (1884) and *Ninomiya Sensei Goroku* (1905) respectively. The most notable example of the Hotoku movement's practical influence was that of the village of Shimo-Ishida in the Province of Totomi, where the movement was introduced by Agoin Shoshichi, and its ideas subsequently diffused to other villages in the Province by such village leaders as Okada Saheiji and his son, Ryoichiro.

Agoin became a pupil of Ninomiya in 1842. He introduced Ninomiya's thought and the shiho programme to Shimo-Ishida in the mid-1840s. In 1847, Agoin and Kamiya Yoheiji, a headman of the village, founded a group to organise the Hotoku movement. The group was called *Hotoku Renju (Renchu),* a 'Party for the Repayment of Virtue'. The following is an extract from the Agreement concluded by the members of the group in 1848:

1. On this occasion we discussed and agreed on the

Conclusion

following: To be diligent in agricultural work from dawn to dusk; we devote ourselves to rope-making and other extra tasks ... we sincerely consent to these agreements ...

1. We consistently save for the help of the poor; we strictly observe the principle of Hotoku (*goho no suji*); and free interest loans will be offered to those peasants in economic difficulty upon consultation and selection by ballot system. Repayment of the loan is requested; in addition, the payment of an amount corresponding to one year's instalment, *reikin*, is also requested ...

1. On holidays, the members of the group will deal with road construction work from early morning; the members will have a rest in the afternoon.

1. One day in every month, we will organise meetings to discuss such agricultural issues as methods of land cultivation and the use of fertilisers. Other issues related to the benefit of the village are to be discussed on those occasions. We strictly observe the above.

March, Kaei 1 (1848) [6]

(signatures of the members)

In the second clause the observation of the 'principle of Hotoku' (*goho no suji*) is declared. Since the declaration is made in the context of a discussion on financial matters and the loan system, the observation of the 'principle' probably includes that of *bundo* and *suijo*, the fiscal reform package introduced in the shiho programme. The content of the Agreement ranges from admonitory words insisting on hard work to a brief description of the Hotoku loan system. It also refers to the general agreement on plans for infrastructure development, the implementation of extra tasks, and the exchange of technological information among the members.[7] The Agreement appears to be consistent with the content of the shiho programme discussed in Chapter 7.

Agoin met Okada Saheiji just after the pronouncement of the Agreement in Shimo-Ishida village in May, 1848.[8] As a result, Okada formed a group in his native village of Kurami with thirty other villagers and composed an agreement, virtually identical to that of Shimo-Ishida's, as the creed of the Hotoku movement in Kurami.[9] By the time Saheiji and company met Ninomiya in 1853, societies were founded in 32 villages with 419 participants.[10]

In the Meiji period, such a group was usually called *Hotokusha*, the 'Society for the Repayment of Virtue'.[11] The movement to form the Society spread throughout the villages in the Totomi and Suruga Provinces, which merged into the prefecture of Shizuoka after 1871. Some Societies were disbanded in the Bakumatsu and early Meiji periods, but the overall membership grew continuously in Shizuoka prefecture throughout the Meiji period. More than 300 Hotokusha had been founded in Shizuoka alone by the turn of the century.[12]

The agreement (or 'creed') of Hotokusha set out a system of economic activity similar to that provided by Ninomiya's shiho programme in the late Edo period: diligence was advocated, and this was backed up by economic plans to promote efficiency. Intra-village cooperation was encouraged, and peasants with economic difficulties were offered start-up capital. Strict observation of the 'principle of Hotoku', which included the observation of the fiscal reform package by every peasant producer, was declared. In this way, attempts were made to transplant Ninomiya's idea of work, the economic measures he devised, and the ideological discourses which underlined his economic ideas, to the peasants of the Meiji period. This strongly suggests the scope of influence that Ninomiya's thought had on the commoners' perception of work at the time.

Hotokusha also proved responsive to the changes caused by market price fluctuation. Shizuoka prefecture specialised

Conclusion

in tea production. The opening of ports to foreign trade in the years 1858 and 1859, and the rise in the price of tea in the external market during the subsequent two decades[13] provided tea producers with excellent export opportunities. But the producers were also hit by recessions between the boom years. Saito Osamu compares the timing of the recessions with the number of Hotokusha founded, and shows that more Hotokusha were established in the years of recession than in boom years. He concludes that the Society functioned as the 'shock-absorber' during the economic downturn in the early and mid Meiji period.[14]

In the first half of the nineteenth century, Ninomiya rescued peasants from economic disaster by providing them with workable measures for village rehabilitation. This time, Hotokusha provided commodity producers with a 'safety net' to counter the fluctuations in the economy. Whether or not the Society had by then become capable of making a more positive response to market changes has yet to be studied. For this reason, the impact made by Hotokusha upon the Meiji commoners in shaping their economic thinking, particularly their perception of commercial activities, cannot be ascertained. However, one can at least make the point that the Society had adapted itself to Meiji socio-economic circumstances, and had begun to play its role in an economic setting where the market system was becoming a far more dominant element.

So, it seems that Hotokusha transformed itself into a mainstream organisation which served the needs of the agrarian population of the Meiji period. True, the Society did not function as the chief agency in the transmission of mechanical and industrial technologies from the West. Nor did it foster 'Westernisation'. But it provided Meiji commoners with institutional devices backed by a set of ideological principles that encouraged the commoners' to look toward economic betterment.

The Hotoku movement from the 1890s onwards, however,

was gradually integrated into a strong sense of nation building, and its founder, Ninomiya, was used by the Government as a model to compel people to work hard[15]: Ninomiya was a common man who started out penniless and established himself as an agrarian leader. He was a familiar figure to the populace, and thus was ideal for the Meiji Government to use as a paragon of hard work. Ninomiya began to appear in the textbooks of elementary schools in 1893, and then in the textbooks of 1901, 1904, and 1910. He also appeared in revised versions of these texts. It has been said that Ninomiya and the Meiji Emperor were the most frequently mentioned figures in textbooks between 1910 and 1945.[16] His statue, invariably depicting him carrying fire wood home and studying his book on the way, stood in every elementary school play ground. It was his image as a hard worker that the Government attempted to diffuse. It attempted to encourage the commoners' hard work in support of the national policy of 'enrich the nation and strengthen the military' (*fukoku kyohei*).[17]

Ninomiya certainly valued hard graft. However, an important element of his thought had been overlooked in this Government propaganda: Ninomiya's emphasis on management was displaced by a mere ethic of hard work. It was production increase for the betterment of the economic conditions of the peasants themselves that was prioritised in Ninomiya's thought and his shihō programme, despite the fact that such production growth might well serve the national interest in an ultimate sense. Instead, the Government's use of Ninomiya only aimed to call for self-sacrifice for the strengthening of the state.[18]

Numerous Hotokusha were founded all over Japan by the turn of the century. *Chuo Hotokukai*, the 'Central Association of the Hotoku movement' was founded in 1906, and it functioned as the hub of informational exchange between the Societies. A nationwide periodical - *Shimin* - was published

Conclusion

by the Association.[19] It first appeared in 1906, and continued for forty years until 1946 (no publication in 1945). Although the periodical included admonitory articles on diligence and economy, pages were spared to introduce new machines and economic institutions, and to present successful examples of Hotoku members' deeds in agricultural and other activities.[20] Moreover, each number included at least one article related to topics from abroad: such subjects as agricultural and industrial technologies, cooperatives in Western nations, and their educational systems were discussed.[21]

The central Hotoku Association was founded by Meiji bureaucrats with the aim of integrating the Hotoku movement into the national movement for the strengthening of the nation. Some of the articles in *Shimin* apparently sounded like Government propaganda. While some Hotokusha at provincial level might have continued to serve the interests of the people, the movement seems to have broken ties with its original aims and function; which were, the provision of a workable economic system for the physical and spiritual enrichment of agrarian commoners.

Notes
1. Norman, E.H., *Ando Shoeki and the Anatomy of Japanese Feudalism*, University Publication of America Inc., Washington, D.C., 1979 (first published in 1949), chapters IV and VI. Matsumoto Sannosuke, 'Ando Shoeki', Sagara Toru, et. al. (eds.), *Edo no Shisoka Tachi, vol. 2*, Kenkyusha, Tokyo, 1979.
2. Kaiho Seiryo, 'Keikodan', Kuranami (ed.), *Kaiho Seiryo Zenshu*.
3. Saito Osamu, *Shoka no Sekai Uradana no Sekai*. Day labourers and other urban workers in the cities of

Tokugawa Japan have recently been studied in detail by G.P. Leupp, *Servants, Shophands, and Laborers in the Cities of Tokugawa Japan*, Princeton University Press, Princeton, 1992.

4. See, for instance, R.N. Bellah, *Tokugawa Religion*, Morris-Suzuki, T., *A History of Japanese Economic Thought*, Routledge, London, 1989, chapter 1.

5. Morris-Suzuki, *Ibid.*, p. 11.

6. Similar agreements were concluded in thirteen villages and towns of Totomi within five years from 1848. *NSZ*, vol. 27, pp. 728-37. The agreement in Shimo-Ishida village is not listed in *NSZ*. It is recorded, however, in Sagiyama Kyohei, *Hotoku Kaitaku-sha, Agoin Gido*, Dai Nihon Hotokusha, Kakegawa, 1963, pp. 31-32.

7. Unno Fukuju argues that Agoin was the first Hotoku member to attempt to transplant the advanced technology of the Kinai region. Unno Fukuju, 'Enshu Hotoku Shugi no Seiritsu', *Sundai Shigaku*, 37 (1975), p. 57. But, as we saw in section 4-2 of Chapter 7, there had already been communication between a Hotoku member and Okura Nagatsune, a foremost agricultural technologist with a good knowledge of the advanced technology of the Kinai, as early as 1829.

8. *NSZ*, vol. 27, p. 857.

9. *Ibid.*, pp. 817-18.

10. *Ibid.*, p. 726.

11. See note 1, Chapter 7.

12. Shizuokaken Nokai (ed.), *Shizuokaken Kangyo Tokei* (1915), Shizuokaken, Shizuoka, pp. 62-82.

13. Saito Osamu, 'Hotokusha Undo no Kuronorojii', *Mita Gakkai Zasshi*, 64-8 (A Supplement; 1971), p. 738.

14. *Ibid.*, pp. 734-41, 746.

15. Sugihara Shiro and Cho Yukio (eds.), *Nihon Keizai Shisoshi Dokuhon*, Toyo Keizai Shinposha, Tokyo, 1979, pp. 81-82.

16. Karasawa Tomitaro, *Kyokasho no Rekishi: Kyokasho to Nihonjin no Keisei*, Sobunsha, Tokyo, 1956, pp. 672-87.

17. Hiramatsu Nobuhisa, 'Tsukurareta Ninomiya Sontoku: Mohanteki Jinbutsuzo no Rufu ni Tsuite', Yoshida Mitsukuni

Conclusion

(ed.), *Jyukyuseiki Nihon no Joho to Shakai Hendo*, Kyoto Daigaku Jinbun Kagaku Kenkyusho, Kyoto, 1985.

18. Oto Osamu, 'Ishin, Bunmei Kaika to Okada Ryoichiro no Genron vol. 1', *Rekishi*, 66 (September, 1986), p. 2.

19. Chuo Hotokukai (ed.), *Shimin*, vols. 1-1 (1906) ~ 39-9 (1944); vols. 40-1 (1946) ~ 40-5 (1946).

20. The life and thought of Ninomiya and his educational efforts were discussed in the column '*shicho*'. The successful use of new technology and the adoption of new economic institutions were discussed in the columns '*setsuen*' and '*kowa*'.

21. For instance, a visit to vocational schools in Dresden by Hotoku members was reported in volumes 1-2 and 1-3 (both published in 1906) of *Shimin*.

Bibliography

Primary sources

Works by Ishida and his disciples:
Ishida Baigan
    'Tohi-Mondō', 'Seikaron', 'Ishida Sensei Goroku', 'Ishida Sensei Jiseki', Shibata Minoru (ed.), *Ishida Baigan Zenshu (IBZ)*, vols. 1 and 2, Sekimon Shingakukai, Tokyo, 1955.
Teshima Toan
    'Jijo Nemuri Samashi', 'Zenkun', 'Kaiyu Taishi', Meirinsha (ed.), *Teshima Toan Zenshu*, Meirinsha, Kyoto, 1931.
Nakazawa Doni
    'Doni-O Dowa', Shibata Minoru (ed.), *Iwanami Nihon Shiso Taikei, vol. 42: Sekimon Shingaku*, Iwanami Shoten, Tokyo, 1971.
Uekawa Kisui
    'Kyocho Gorakusha Shingaku Shoden no Zu', *Ibid.*, pp. 207-32.

Works by Ninomiya and his disciples:
Ninomiya Sontoku
    'Sansai Hotoku Kinmoroku', 'O'enkyo', 'Banbutsu Hatsugenshu', 'Hyakushu Rinnekyo', 'Tenmei Shichigenzu', 'Sansei Kantsu Gododen', Sasai Shintaro (ed.), *Ninomiya Sontoku Zenshu (NSZ)* vol. 1, Ninomiya Sontoku Igyo Senyokai, Shizuoka, 1927-1932.
Fukuzumi Masae
    'Ninomiya-O Yawa', *NSZ* vol. 36.

Bibliography

Saito Takayuki
'Ninomiya Sensei Goroku', *NSZ* vol. 36.
Documents regarding the *shihō* programme in Sakuramachi: *NSZ*, vols. 10-13.
Letters by Ninomiya, his disciples, and shihō leaders: *NSZ*, vols. 3-5.
Other correspondences by Ninomiya, his disciples, and shihō leaders: *NSZ*, vols. 6-9.
Chūō Hōtokukai (ed.), *Shimin*, vols. 1-1 (1906) ~ 39-9 (1944); vols. 40-1 (1946) ~ 40-5 (1946).

English translations of the works of Ishida, Ninomiya and their disciples:
Bellah, R.N., 'A Memoir of Our Teacher, Ishida ("Ishida Sensei Jiseki")', R.N. Bellah, *Tokugawa Religion*, The Free Press, New York, 1985 (first published in 1957).
Beonio-Brocchieri, P., 'Ishida Baigan: Seiri Mondo ("Seiri Mondo no Dan" in Ishida's Tohi-Mondo) - Dialogues on Human Nature and Natural Order', V.S. Agrawala, *et. al.* (eds.), *Orientalia Romana 2*, Instituto Italiano Per Il Medio Ed Estremo Oriente, Roma, 1967.
Yamagata Isoh, *Sage Ninomiya's Evening Talks* ("Ninomiya-O Yawa"), Tokuno Kyokai, Tokyo, 1937.
Yoshimoto Tadasu, *A Peasant Sage of Japan: The Life and Work of Sontoku Ninomiya* ("Hotokuki"), Longmans, Green & Co., London, 1912.

Other primary sources:
Kaiho Seiryo, 'Keikodan' and 'Goshudan', Kuranami Shoji (ed.), *Kaiho Seiryo Zenshu*, Yachiyo Shuppan, Tokyo, 1976.
Kawachiya Yoshimasa, 'Kawachiya Yoshimasa Kyūki', Nomura Yutaka and Yui Kitaro (eds.), *Kawachiya Yoshimasa Kyuki*, Seibundo Shuppan, Osaka, 1970 (first published in 1955).
Miura Baien, 'Jihi Mujin Ko', (Copyright by the Center for East Asian Studies, University of Chicago) *Readings in Tokugawa Thought: Selected Papers, vol. 9*, The Center for East Asian Studies, University of Chicago, 1993. Translations by T. Najita, *et. al.*
Muro Kyuso, 'Fubosho', Takimoto Seiichi (ed.), *Nihon Keizai*

Bibliography

Taiten, vol. 6, Keimeisha, Tokyo, 1928-1930.
Ogyu Sorai, 'Seidan, vol. 2' and 'Taiheisaku', Nishida Taichiro, Maruyama Masao, et. al. (eds.), *Iwanami Nihon Shiso Taikei vol. 36: Ogyu Sorai*, Iwanami Shoten, Tokyo, 1973.
Tamura Yoshishige, 'Yoshishige Ikun', Iinuma Jiro, et. al. (eds.), *Nihon Nosho Zenshu vol. 21*, Nosangyoson Bunka Kyokai, Tokyo, 1981.

Secondary sources (Japanese literature)

Adachi Seiko, *Yamazaki Enkichi*, Riburo Pooto, Tokyo, 1992.
Akimoto Hiroya, *Zen Kogyoka Jidai no Keizai*, Mineruva Shobo, Kyoto, 1987.
Aoki Masahiko, *Information, Incentives, and Bargaining in the Japanese Economy*, Cambridge University Press, Cambridge, 1988 (printed in the U.S.).
Aoki Michio, 'Kinjiro to Sontoku' in Aoki, *Bunka Bunseiki no Minshu to Bunka*, Bunka Shobo Hakubunsha, Tokyo, 1985.
Asao Naohiro, 'Kogi to Bakuhan Ryoshusei', Rekishigaku Kenkyukai and Nihonshi Kenkyukai (eds.), *Koza Nihon Rekishi, vol. 5 (Kinsei 1)*, Tokyo Daigaku Shuppankai, Tokyo, 1985.
Bito Masahide, "Tokugawa Jidai no Shakai to Seiji Shiso no Tokushitsu', *Shiso*, 685 (July, 1981).
Denda Isao, *Gono* (Kyoikusha Rekishi Shinsho), Kyoikusha, Tokyo, 1978.
Dore, R.P., Iwata Ryushi, Morikawa Hidemasa, et. al., 'Tokushu: Nihonteki Keieiron no Saikento', *Keizai Hyoron*, 30-7 (July, 1981).
Fukawa Seiji (ed.), *Kinsei Shomin no Ishiki to Seikatsu*, Nosangyoson Bunka Kyokai, Tokyo, 1984.
Fukaya Katsumi, 'Hyakusho Denki ni arawareta Kinseiteki Hyakusho Jinkaku', *Sodai Daigakuin Bungaku Kenkyuka Kiyo*, 2 (March, 1980).
_____, 'Hotoku Shiho', *Tochigikenshi: Tsushihen 5, Kinsei 2*, Tochigiken, Tochigi, 1984.
_____, 'Kinsei Kazoku to Kyodotai', *Rekishi Hyoron*, 441 (January, 1987).
_____, *Hyakusho Naritachi*, Hanawa Shobo, Tokyo, 1993.
_____, and Matsumoto Shiro (eds.), *Koza Nihon Kinseishi*

vol. 3, Yuhikaku, Tokyo, 1980.
Fukuda Ajio, *Kanosei to shite no Mura Shakai: Rodo to Joho no Minzokugaku*, Seikyūsha, Tokyo, 1990.
Furushima Toshio, *Kyodotai no Kenkyu* (Furushima Toshio Chosakushu 7), Tokyo Daigaku Shuppankai, Tokyo, 1983.
_____, *Nosho no Jidai*, Nosangyoson Bunka Kyokai, Tokyo, 1980.
Haga Noboru, *Bakumatsu Kokugaku no Tenkai*, Hanawa Shobo, Tokyo, 1963.
_____, 'Nihon no Nohon Shugi', *Shigaku Sosho, vol. 1*, Tokyo Kyoiku Shuppan Sentaa, Tokyo, 1982.
Hasegawa Shinzo, 'Bunseiki Shimodatecho ni okeru Sekimon Shingaku no Seinen Kyoka no Jissai', *Ibarakiken-shi Kenkyu*, 16 (1970).
_____, 'Kita-Kanto Noson no Kohai to Nominso', Murakami Tadashi (ed.), *Ronshu Kanto Kinseishi no Kenkyu*, Meicho Shuppan, Tokyo, 1984.
Hasekura Tamotsu, 'Karasuyamahan ni okeru Bunsei, Tenpo Kaikaku to Hotoku Shiho no Ichi', *Nihon Rekishi*, 338 (July, 1976).
_____, 'Odawarahan ni okeru Hotoku Shiho ni tsuite', Kitajima Masamoto (ed.), *Bakuhansei Kokka Kaitai Katei no Kenkyu*, Yoshikawa Kobunkan, Tokyo, 1978.
Hayami Akira and Miyamoto Matao (eds.), *Iwanami Nihon Keizaishi, vol. 1 (Keizai Shakai no Seiritsu)*, Iwanami Shoten, Tokyo, 1988.
Hayashi Reiko, 'Shimodatehan ni okeru Sontoku Shuho no Haikei', *Ibarakiken-shi Kenkyu*, 6 (November, 1966).
Hazama Hiroshi, *Nihon Romu Kanrishi Kenkyu*, Ochanomizu Shobo, Tokyo, 1978 (first published in 1964).
Hiraishi Naoaki, 'Kinsei Nihon no "Shokugyo"kan', Tokyo Daigaku Shakai Kagaku Kenkyusho (ed.), *Gendai Nihon Shakai, vol. 4 (Rekishiteki Zentei)*, Tokyo Daigaku Shuppankai, Tokyo, 1991.
Hiramatsu Nobuhisa, 'Tsukurareta Ninomiya Sontoku: Mohanteki Jinbutsuzo no Rufu ni Tsuite', Yoshida Mitsukuni (ed.), *Jyukyuseiki Nihon no Joho to Shakai Hendo*, Kyoto Daigaku Jinbun Kagaku Kenkyusho, Kyoto, 1985.
_____, 'Hotoku Shiso no Tenkai to Kessha Undo', *Noringyo Mondai Kenkyu*, 74 (20-1; March, 1984).

Bibliography

Ichimura Yuichi, 'Shingaku Dowa to Komyunikeishon', Bito Masahide Sensei Kanreki Kinenkai (ed.), *Nihon Kinseishi Ronso*, vol. 2, Yoshikawa Kobunkan, Tokyo, 1984.

Iinuma Jiro, *Sekai Nogyo Bunkashi*, Yasaka Shobo, Kyoto, 1983.

―――――, 'Igirisu Jyuhasseiki ni okeru Sonraku Kozo', Iinuma Jiro, *Nogyo Kakumei no Kenkyu*, Nosangyoson Bunka Kyokai, Tokyo, 1985.

Imai Atsushi and Furuta Shokin (eds.), *Ishida Baigan no Shiso*, Perikansha, Tokyo, 1979.

Imamura Hitoshi, *Rodo no Ontorogii*, Keiso Shobo, Tokyo, 1981.

Ishikawa Ken, *Sekimon Shingakushi no Kenkyu*, Iwanami Shoten, Tokyo, 1938.

―――――, *Ishida Baigan* (Nihon Kyoiku Sentetsu Sosho), Bunkyo Shoin, Tokyo, 1943.

―――――, *Ishida Baigan to Tohi-Mondo* (Iwanami Shinsho), Iwanami Shoten, Tokyo, 1968.

―――――, *Shingaku Kyoka no Honshitsu narabi ni Hattatsu*, Seishisha, Tokyo, 1982 (first published in 1931 by Shokasha, Tokyo).

Ishikawa Matsutaro, *Hanko to Terakoya* (Kyoikusha Rekishi Shinsho), Kyoikusha, Tokyo, 1978.

Iwashiro Takuji, Mizumoto Kunihiko, Morishita Toru, et. al., 'Sho Tokushu: Kinsei no 'Yaku' to Minshu', *Nihonshi Kenkyu*, 324 (August, 1989).

Kamata Satoru (ed.), *Nihonjin no Shigoto*, Heibonsha, Tokyo, 1986.

Karasawa Tomitaro, *Kyokasho no Rekishi: Kyokasyo to Nihonjin no Keisei*, Sobunsha, Tokyo, 1956.

Kataoka Nobuyuki, 'Edoki no Shogyo, Shonin Kyoiku, Shoningaku', *Keizai Keiei Ronshu* (Ryukoku University), 23-3 (December, 1983).

Kimura Motoi, *Nihon Sonrakushi*, Kobundo, Tokyo, 1978.

――――― (ed.), *Ohara Yugaku to sono Shuhen*, Yagi Shoten, Tokyo, 1986.

Kodama Kota, 'Ningen to Daichi tono Taiwa', Kodama Kota (ed.), *Nihon no Meicho: Ninomiya Sontoku*, Chuo Koronsha, Tokyo, 1970.

Kouchi Hachiro, 'Hanada Mura no Sontoku Shiho' 1~8, Sekijochoshi Hensan Iinkai (ed.), *Sekijocho no Rekishi*, 1 (March, 1981)

Bibliography

~ 8 (March, 1988).

_____ and Mori Yutaka, 'Nikko Jinryo no Hotoku Shiho Kaishi', *Imaichishi-shi vol. 1, Tsushihen, Beppen I*, Imaichishi, Tochigi, 1980.

Kumakawa Yumiko, 'Ninomiya Kinjiro no Shiho ni Kansuru Ichi Kosatsu', *Jinbun Ronshu* (Shizuoka University), 25 (1974).

Maruyama Masao, *Nihon Seiji Shisoshi Kenkyu*, Tokyo Daigaku Shuppankai, Tokyo, 1952.

Matsumoto Sannosuke, 'Ando Shoeki', Sagara Toru, *et. al.* (eds.), *Edo no Shisoka Tachi, vol. 2*, Kenkyusha, Tokyo, 1979.

Minamoto Ryoen, *Kinsei Shoki Jitsugaku Shisō no Kenkyu*, Sobunsha, Tokyo, 1980.

_____ (ed.), *Kata to Nihon Bunka*, Sobunsha, Tokyo, 1992.

Minegishi Kentaro, *Kinsei Mibunron*, Azekura Shobo, Tokyo, 1989.

Miyamoto Mataji, 'Sekimon Shingaku to Shonin Ishiki', *Shingaku* (a periodical of Sekimon Shingakukai), 2 (1942). This article has been reprinted in Miyamoto Mataji, *Kinsei Nihon Keieishi Ronko* published in 1979.

_____, *Kinsei Shonin Ishiki no Kenkyū: Kakun Oyobi Tensoku to Nihon Shonindo*, Yuhikaku, Tokyo, 1942.

_____, *Kamigata no Kenkyu*, Seibundo, Osaka, 1977.

_____, *Kinsei Nihon Keieishi Ronko*, Toyo Bunkasha, Kyoto, 1979.

_____ and Sakudo Yotaro (eds.), *Sumitomo no Keieishi-teki Kenkyu*, Jikkyo Shuppan, Tokyo, 1979.

Mizumachi Kiyoshi, *Ninomiya Sontoku-Ō no Dotoku Keizai Shiso*, Meirosha, Tokyo, 1937.

Mizumoto Kunihiko, 'Mura Kyodotai to Mura Shihai', Rekishi-gaku Kenkyukai and Nihonshi Kenkyukai (eds.), *Koza Nihon Rekishi, vol. 5 (Kinsei 1)*, Tokyo Daigaku Shuppankai, Tokyo, 1985.

Morishita Toru, 'Kinsei no Fusei ni okeru 'Yaku' Hensei to Rodo Katei', *Shakai Keizai Shigaku*, 58-2 (June, July, 1992).

Morita Shiro, *Nihon no Mura* (Asahi Sensho), Asahi Shinbunsha, Tokyo, 1978.

_____, *Ninomiya Sontoku* (Asahi Sensho), Asahi Shinbunsha, Tokyo, 1989 (first published in 1975).

Nagano Hiroko, 'Kansei no Jidai', Hayashi Hideo (ed.), *Komonjo no Kataru Nihonshi, vol. 7: Edo Koki*, Chikuma Shobo, Tokyo,

Bibliography

1989.

Nakai Nobuhiko, *Ohara Yugaku* (Jinbutsu Sosho), Yoshikawa Kobunkan, Tokyo, 1989 (first published in 1963).

─────── and Naramoto Tatsuya (eds.), *Iwanami Nihon Shiso Taikei, vol. 52: Ninomiya Sontoku, Ohara Yugaku*, Iwanami Shoten, Tokyo, 1973.

Nakamura Hajime, 'Suzuki Shosan, 1579-1655, and the Spirit of Capitalism in Japanese Buddhism', *Monumenta Nipponica*, 22,1-2 (1967).

Nakamura Yujiro and Kimura Motoi (eds.), *Sonraku Hotoku Jinushisei*, Toyo Keizai Shinposha, Tokyo, 1976.

Nakane Chie, *Tate Shakai no Ningen Kankei*, Kodansha, Tokyo, 1967.

Naramoto Tatsuya, *Ninomiya Sontoku* (Iwanami Shinsho), Iwanami Shoten, Tokyo, 1959.

─────── , 'Ninomiya Sontoku: Sansai Hotoku Kinmoroku wo chushin to shite', *Shiso*, 548 (February, 1970).

Niki Yoshikazu, 'Noson Fukkou no Seisan Rinri: Ninomiya Sontoku, Ohara Yugaku', Sugihara Shiro, Sakasai Takahito, et. al., (eds.), *Nihon no Keizai Shiso Yonhyakunen*, Nihon Keizai Hyoronsha, Tokyo, 1991.

─────── , 'Odawarahan Kamado Shinden Mura no Hotoku Shiho ni Tsuite', *Rikkyo Keizaigaku Kenkyu*, 45-3 (January, 1992).

─────── , 'Hotoku Shiso no Jyuyo ni tsuite - Kobayashi Heibei wo Jirei to shite', *Rikkyo Keizaigaku Kenkyu*, 47-2 (October, 1993).

Ninomiya Sontoku-O Zenshu Kankokai (ed.), *Kaisetsu Ninomiya Sontoku-O Zenshu*, vol.4 (*Jissenhen*), Ninomiya Sontoku-O Zenshu Kankokai, Tokyo, 1937.

Ninomiya Sontoku Seitan Nihyakunen Kinen Jigyokai and Hotoku Jikko Iinkai (eds.), *Sontoku Kaiken*, Yurindo, Yokohama, 1987.

Nogyo Hattatsushi Chosakai (ed.), *Nihon Nogyo Hattatsushi: Supplementary, vol. 2*, Chuo Koronsha, Tokyo, 1981 (first published in 1959).

Nojiri Shigeo, *Nomin Rison no Jisshoteki Kenkyu*, Iwanami Shoten, Tokyo, 1942.

Odaka Kunio, *Nihonteki Keiei: Sono Shinwa to Genjitsu* (Chuko Shinsho), Chuo Koronsha, Tokyo, 1984.

Bibliography

Oishi Shinzaburo, *Kinsei Sonraku no Kozo to Ie Seido*, Ochanomizu Shobo, Tokyo, 1968.

Oka Mitsuo, *Nihon Nogyo Gijutsushi: Kinsei kara Kindai e*, Mineruva Shobo, Kyoto, 1988.

Okutani Matsuji, *Ninomiya Sontoku to Hotokusha Undo*, Koyo Shoin, Tokyo, 1936.

Orihara Hiroshi, 'Edoki ni okeru Shori Koteiron no Keisei: Ishida Baigan to Yamagata Banto', *Keiai Daigaku Kenkyu Ronshu*, 42 (September, 1992).

Oshima Mario, 'Kinsei Nomin Shihai to Kazoku, Kyodotai', *Nihonshi Kenkyu*, 308 (1988).

Oto Osamu, 'Mibun to Ie', Fukaya Katsumi and Matsumoto Shiro (eds.), *Koza Nihon Kinseishi*, vol. 3, Yuhikaku, Tokyo, 1980.

_____, 'Kanto Noson no Kohai to Sontoku Shiho', *Shiryokan Kenkyu Kiyo*, 14 (supplement volume; September, 1982).

_____, 'Ishin, Bunmei Kaika to Okada Ryoichiro no Genron 1', *Rekishi*, 66 (September, 1986).

_____, 'Mura no Kohai to Sontoku Shuho', *Oyamachoshi*, vol. 2 (Kinsei Shiryohen 1), Oyamacho, Shizuoka, 1991.

Otsuka Eiji, 'Kinsei Koki Kita-Kanto ni okeru Shono Saiken to Hotoku Kinyu no Tokushitsu', *Nihonshi Kenkyu*, 263 (July, 1984).

_____, 'Hotoku Shiho Seiritsuki ni okeru Shomondai', *Jinbun Kagaku Kenkyu* (Nagoya University), 15 (March, 1986).

Pak, T., 'Richo Koki ni okeru Seiji Shiso no Tenkai', *Kokka Gakkai Zasshi*, 88-11, 12 (1975).

Rekishigaku Kenkyukai and Nihonshi Kenkyukai (eds.), *Koza Nihon Rekishi*, vol. 5 (Kinsei 1), Tokyo Daigaku Shuppankai, Tokyo, 1985.

Sagara Toru, et. al. (eds.), *Edo no Shisoka Tachi*, vols. 1, 2, Kenkyusha, Tokyo, 1979.

Sagiyama Kyohei, *Hotoku Kaitakusha, Agoin Gido*, Dai Nihon Hotokusha, Kakegawa, 1963.

Saito Osamu, 'Hotokusha Undo no Kuronorojii', *Mita Gakkai Zasshi*, 64-8 (1971: A Supplement).

_____, *Puroto Kogyoka no Jidai*, Nihon Hyoronsha, Tokyo, 1985.

_____, *Shoka no Sekai, Uradana no Sekai*, Riburo Pooto, Tokyo, 1987.

Bibliography

_____, 'Jukuren, Kunren, Rodo Shijo', Kawakita Minoru (ed.), *Shiriizu Sekaishi eno Toi, vol. 2: Seikatsu no Gijutsu, Seisan no Gijutsu*, Iwanami Shoten, Tokyo, 1990.

Saito Yasuhiko, 'Noson Kohaiki no Han Kokin Kashitsuke Seisaku no Tenkai', *Nihon Rekishi*, 424 (September, 1983).

Sakasai Takahito, 'Sekimon Shingaku ni okeru Jissen Tetsugaku no Tenkai - Ishida Baigan to Teshima Toan', *Rikkyō Keizaigaku Kenkyu*, 34-3 (December, 1980).

Sasai Shintaro, *Ninomiya Sontoku Kenkyu*, Iwanami Shoten, Tokyo, 1927.

_____, *Ninomiya Sontokuden*, Nihon Hyoronsha, Tokyo, 1935.

Sasaki Junnosuke and Unno Fukuju, 'Ninomiya Sontoku to Bakumatsu no Nosei Kaikaku', *Bunka Hyōron* (March, 1978).

Sekiyama Naotaro, *Kinsei Nihon no Jinko Kozo*, Yoshikawa Kobunkan, Tokyo, 1958.

Shibata Minoru, *Shingaku* (Nihon Rekishi Shinsho), Shibundo, Tokyo, 1967.

_____, *Baigan to sono Monryu*, Mineruva Shobo, Kyoto, 1977.

Shinbo Hiroshi and Saito Osamu (eds.), *Iwanami Nihon Keizaishi, vol. 2 (Kindai Seicho no Taido)*, Iwanami Shoten, Tokyo, 1989.

Shitahodo Yukichi, *Tendo to Jindo: Ninomiya Sontoku no Tetsugaku*, Iwanami Shoten, Tokyo, 1942.

Sugano Noriko, 'Tenpoki Kaso Nomin no Sonzai Keitai', *Rekishigaku Kenkyu*, 365 (October, 1970).

Sugihara Shiro and Cho Yukio (eds.), *Nihon Keizai Shisoshi Dokuhon*, Toyo Keizai Shinposha, Tokyo, 1979.

Sugihara Shiro, Sakasai Takahito, et. al. (eds.), *Nihon no Keizai Shiso Yonhyakunen*, Nihon Keizai Hyoronsha, Tokyo, 1991.

Sugimura Yoshimi, *Datsu Kindai no Rodokan*, Mineruva Shobo, Kyoto, 1990.

Takagi Shosaku, 'Bakuhan Shoki no Mibun to Kuniyaku', *Rekishigaku Kenkyu*, special edition (November, 1976).

Takebayashi Shotaro, 'Baigan to Banto no Shogyoron', *Kansai Daigaku Shogaku Ronshu*, 19-3, 4 (October, 1974).

Takenaka Yasukazu, 'Ishida Baigan no Shiso ni tsuite', Horie Yasuzo (ed.), *Kinsei Nihon no Keizai to Shakai*, Yuhikaku, Tokyo, 1958.

Bibliography

_____, 'Teshima Toan no Chonin Tetsugaku', *Shokei Gakuso* (Kinki University), 7-1, 2 (1961).
_____, *Sekimon Shingaku no Keizai Shiso*, Mineruva Shobo, Kyoto, 1962.
_____, 'Robaato Beraa (Robert N. Bellah) no Shingakukan', Miyamoto Mataji (ed.), *Amerika no Nihon Kenkyu*, Toyo Keizai Shinposha, Tokyo, 1970.
_____, 'Ishida Baigan no Keiei Rinen', Keiei Shigakukai (ed.), *Keiei Shigaku, vol. 4 No. 3*, Tokyo Daigaku Shuppankai, Tokyo, 1970.
_____, *Nihonteki Keiei no Genryu*, Mineruva Shobo, Kyoto, 1977.
Tanaka Koji, 'Kinsei ni okeru Shuyaku Inasaku no Keisei', Watanabe Tadayo (ed.), *Ine no Ajiashi, vol. 3*, Shogakukan, Tokyo, 1987.
Tokyo Daigaku Shakai Kagaku Kenkyusho (ed.), *Gendai Nihon Shakai, vol. 4 (Rekishiteki Zentei)*, Tokyo Daigaku Shuppankai, Tokyo, 1991.
Tsuda Hideo, 'Kyoiku no Fukyu to Shingaku', Asao Naohiro, Ishii Susumu, *et. al.* (eds.), *Iwanami Koza Nihon Rekishi, vol. 12 (Kinsei 4)*, Iwanami Shoten, Tokyo, 1976.
Tsukuba Tsuneharu, 'Nihon Nohonshugi Jyosetsu', *Shiso no Kagaku*, 18 (June, 1960).
_____, 'Okura Nagatsune to Ninomiya Sontoku', *Shiso no Kagaku*, 35 (November, 1961).
_____, *Nihon no Nosho*, Chuo Koronsha, Tokyo, 1987.
Tsunasawa Mitsuaki, *Nihon no Nohon Shugi*, Kinokuniya Shoten, Tokyo, 1980.
Uesugi Mitsuhiko, 'Hotokusha Undo no Genten: Soshu Kataoka Mura no Shiho wo Chushin to shite', *Shakai Kagaku Tokyu*, 22-3 (January, 1977).
_____, 'Bakuseiki no Hotoku Shiho: Ohnogo Mura no Shiho wo Chushin to shite', *Rissho Shigaku*, 43 (February, 1978).
Unno Fukuju, 'Enshu Hotoku Shugi no Seiritsu', *Sundai Shigaku*, 37 (1975).
_____ and Kato Takashi (eds.), *Shokusan Kogyo to Hotoku Undo*, Toyo Keizai Shinposha, Tokyo, 1978.
Utsuki Saburo, 'Ninomiya Sontoku no Shiso no Tokushitsu to

Shiho', *Kaibyaku*, 27-6, 1978. This article was first published in *Rekishi Dojin Koyozaka*, 4 (1977).

Watanabe Hiroshi, 'Tokugawa Zenki Jugakushi no Ichi Joken', *Kokka Gakkai Zasshi*, 94-1,2 (1981).

Weber, M., *Purotesutantizumu no Rinri to Shihon Shugi no Seishin*, Iwanami Shoten, Tokyo, 1991. Translated by Otsuka Hisao from *Die protestantische Ethik und Der Geist des Kapitalismus, Gesammelte Aufsatze zur Religionssoziologie*, Bd. 1, 1920, SS. 17-206.

Yanabu Akira, *Hon'yakugo Seiritsu Jijo* (Iwanami Shinsho), Iwanami Shoten, Tokyo, 1982.

Yasumaru Yoshio, *Nihon no Kindaika to Minshu Shiso*, Aoki Shoten, Tokyo, 1974.

――――――, 'Minshu Shisoshi no Tachiba', *Hitotsubashi Ronso*, 78-5 (445; November, 1977).

Yoshinaga Akira, 'Tokusan Shorei to Hansei Kaikaku', Asao Naohiro, Ishii Susumu, et. al. (eds.), *Iwanami Koza Nihon Rekishi, vol. 11 (Kinsei 3)*, Iwanami Shoten, Tokyo, 1976.

Yu, Ying-shi, *Chugoku Kinsei no Shukyo Rinri to Shonin Seishin*, Heibonsha, Tokyo, 1991.

Secondary sources (English literature)

Anderson Sawada, J., *Confucian Values and Popular Zen: Sekimon Shingaku in the Eighteenth Century*, University of Hawaii Press, Honolulu, 1993.

Aoki Masahiko, *Information, Incentives, and Bargaining in the Japanese Economy*, Cambridge University Press, Cambridge (printed in the U.S.), 1988.

Applebaum, H. (ed.), *WORK in Non-market and Transitional Societies*, SUNY (State University of New York) Press, Buffalo, 1984.

――――――, *Concept of Work: Ancient, Medieval, and Modern*, SUNY (State University of New York) Press, Buffalo, 1992.

Armstrong, R.C., *Just Before the Dawn; the Life and Work of Ninomiya Sontoku*, Macmillan, New York, 1912.

Asao Naohiro, 'The Sixteenth-Century Unification', John W. Hall, et. al. (eds.), *The Cambridge History of Japan vol. 4*, Cambridge University Press, Cambridge, 1991.

Bibliography

Bellah, R.N., *Tokugawa Religion*, The Free Press, New York, 1985 (first published in 1957).

Berg, M., 'Women's Work, Mechanization and the Early Phases of Industrialization in England', R.E. Pahl (ed.), *On Work: Historical, Comparative & Theoretical Approaches*, Basil Blackwell, Oxford, 1988. Reprinted from Joyce (ed.), *The Historical Meanings of Work*.

Bijker, W.E., T.P. Hughes, and T. J. Pinch (eds.), *The Social Construction of Technological Systems*, MIT (Massachusetts Institute of Technology) Press, Cambridge (Massachusetts), 1987.

Braverman, H., *Labor and Monopoly Capital: The Degradation of Work in the Twentieth Century*, Monthly Review Press, New York, 1974 (first published in 1957).

Briggs, A., 'Review of Thompson, *The Making of the English Working Class*' in *Labour History*, 6 (1965).

Chan, Wing-tsit (ed.), *Chu Hsi and Neo-Confucianism*, University of Hawaii Press, Hawaii, 1986.

_____, *Neo-Confucian Terms Explained*, Columbia University Press, New York, 1986.

de Bary, Wm. T., *Neo-Confucian Orthodoxy and the Learning of the Mind-and-Heart*, Columbia University Press, New York, 1981.

_____, et. al. (eds.), *Sources of Japanese Tradition* vol. 2, Columbia University Press, New York, 1958.

_____ and I. Bloom (eds.), *Principle and Practicality: Essays in Neo-Confucianism and Practical Learning*, Columbia University Press, New York, 1979.

Dore, R.P., *Education in Tokugawa Japan*, Athlone Press Ltd., London, 1984 (first published in 1965).

_____, *Flexible Rigidities*, Stanford University Press, Stanford, 1986.

Droppers, G., 'A Japanese Credit Association and Its Founder', *Transactions of the Asiatic Society of Japan*, 22, 1894.

Firth, R., 'Work and Value: Reflections on Ideas of Karl Marx', S. Wallman (ed.), *Social Anthropology of Work*, Academic Press, London, 1979.

Fung, Yu-lan, 'The Philosophy of Chu Hsi', *Harvard Journal of Asiatic Studies*, 7 (1942-1943). Translated by D. Bodde.

Bibliography

Garon, S., *The State and Labor in Modern Japan*, University of California Press, Berkeley, 1987.

Gluck, C., 'The People in History: Recent Trends in Japanese Historiography', *Journal of Asian Studies*, 38-4 (November, 1978).

_____, *Japan's Modern Myths: Ideology in the Late Meiji Period*, Princeton University Press, Princeton, 1985.

Gordon, A., *The Evolution of Labor Relations in Japan: Heavy Industry, 1853-1955*, Council on East Asian Studies/Harvard University Press, Cambridge (Massachusetts), 1985.

Gutman, H.G., 'Work, Culture and Society in Industrializing America, 1815-1919', Pahl (ed.), *On Work: Historical, Comparative & Theoretical Approaches*.

Hall, J.H., et. al. (eds.), *The Cambridge History of Japan*, vol. 4, Cambridge University Press, Cambridge, 1991.

Hardacre, H., *Kurozumikyo and the New Religions of Japan*, Princeton University Press, Princeton, 1986.

Harootunian, H.D., *Things Seen and Unseen: Discourse and Ideology in Tokugawa Nativism*, University of Chicago Press, Chicago, 1988.

_____, 'Metzger's Predicament' in the 'Review Symposium: Thomas A. Metzger's Escape from Predicament', *Journal of Asian Studies*, 34-2 (February, 1980).

Johnson, D., et. al. (eds.), *Popular Culture in Late Imperial China*, University of California Press, Berkeley, 1985.

Joyce, P. (ed.), *The Historical Meanings of Work*, Cambridge University Press, Cambridge, 1987.

Le Goff, J., *Time, Work, and Culture in the Middle Ages*, University of Chicago Press, Chicago, 1980. Translated by A. Goldhammer.

Leupp, G.P., *Servants, Shophands, and Laborers in the Cities of Tokugawa Japan*, Princeton University Press, Princeton, 1992.

MacKenzie, D. and J. Wajcman (eds.), *The Social Shaping of Technology*, Open University Press, Milton Keynes, 1985.

Malcolmson, R.W., 'Ways of Getting a Living in Eighteenth-Century England', Pahl (ed.), *On Work: Historical, Comparative & Theoretical Approaches*.

Marx, K., *Capital*, vol. 1, Lawrence and Wishart, London, 1983 (L&W version first published in 1954). *Das Kapital* was first

Bibliography

published in German in 1867. English edition first published in 1887.

———— and F. Engels, 'The German Ideology', J. Cohen, E.J. Hobsbawm, *et. al.* (eds.), *Collected Works,* 5, Lawrence and Wishart, London, 1976. 'The German Ideology' was first published in German in 1845.

Middleton, C., 'The Familiar Fate of the *Famulae*: Gender Divisions in the History of Wage Labour', Pahl (ed.), *On Work: Historical, Comparative & Theoretical Approaches.*

Mitchell, B.R. and P. Deane, *Abstract of British Historical Statistics*, Cambridge University Press, Cambridge, 1971.

More, C., *Skill and the English Working Class, 1870-1914*, Croom Helm Ltd., London, 1980.

————, 'Skill and the Survival of Apprenticeship', S. Wood (ed.), *The degradation of work?: Skill, De-skilling and the Labour Process*, Hutchinson, London, 1982.

Morris-Suzuki, T., *A History of Japanese Economic Thought*, Routledge, London, 1989.

Najita, T., *Visions of Virtue in Tokugawa Japan*, University of Chicago Press, Chicago, 1987.

———— and I. Scheiner (eds.), *Japanese Thought in the Tokugawa Period*, University of Chicago Press, Chicago, 1978.

Nakane Chie, *Kinship and Economic Organisation in Rural Japan*, London School of Economics/Athlone Press, London, 1967.

————, *Japanese Society*, University of California Press, Berkeley, 1970.

Norman, E.H., *Ando Shoeki and the Anatomy of Japanese Feudalism*, University Publication of America Inc., Washington, D.C., 1979 (first published in 1949).

Nosco, P. (ed.), *Confucianism and Tokugawa Culture*, Princeton University Press, Princeton, 1984.

Pahl, R.E. (ed.), *On Work: Historical, Comparative & Theoretical Approaches*, Basil Blackwell, Oxford, 1988.

Roberts, B., R. Finnegan, and D. Gallie (eds.), *New Approaches to Economic Life*, Manchester University Press, Manchester, 1985.

Roberts, J.G., *Mitsui: Three Centuries of Japanese Business*, Weatherhill, New York, 1973.

Robertson, J., 'Rooting the Pine: Shingaku Methods of Organization', *Monumenta Nipponica*, 34-3 (Autumn, 1979).

Rosenberg, N., 'Technological Interdependence in the American Economy', *Technology and Culture*, 20-1 (January, 1979).

_____, *Inside the Black Box: Technology and Economics*, Cambridge University Press, Cambridge, 1982.

Rosenberger, N.R. (ed.), *Japanese Sense of Self*, Cambridge University Press, Cambridge, 1992.

Rule, J., 'The Property of Skill in the Period of Manufacture', Joyce (ed.), *The Historical Meanings of Work*.

Schwarz, L.D., 'Income Distribution and Social Structure in London in the Late Eighteenth Century', *Economic History Review*, 32 (1979).

Smith, T.C., *The Agrarian Origins of Modern Japan*, Stanford University Press, Stanford, 1959.

_____, *Native Sources of Japanese Industrialization, 1750-1920*, University of California Press, Berkeley, 1988.

Thompson, E.P., *Customs in Common*, Merlin Press, London, 1991.

Thompson, P., 'Playing at Being Skilled Men: Factory Culture and Pride in Work Skills among Coventry Car Workers', *Social History*, 13 (1988).

_____, *The Nature of Work*, Macmillan, London, 1989 (first published in 1983).

Tucker, M.E., *Moral and Spiritual Cultivation in Japanese Neo-Confucianism: The Life and Thought of Kaibara Ekken (1630-1714)*, SUNY (State University of New York) Press, Buffalo, 1990.

Turner, H.A., *Trade Union Growth: Structure and Policy*, George Allen and Unwin, London, 1962.

Vlastos, S., *Peasant Protests and Uprisings in Tokugawa Japan*, University of California Press, Berkeley, 1986.

Wagatsuma Hiroshi, 'Status and Role Behavior in Changing Japan: Psychocultural Continuities', G.A. De Vos, *Socialization for Achievement: Essays on the Cultural Psychology of the Japanese*, University of California Press, Berkeley, 1973.

Wall, R. and Saito Osamu (eds.), *The Economic and Social Aspects of the Family Life-cycle: Europe and Japan, Traditional and Modern*, Cambridge University Press, Cambridge, forthcoming.

Wallman, S. (ed.), *Social Anthropology of Work*, Academic Press, London, 1979.

Walthall, A. (ed. & tr.), *Peasant Uprisings in Japan*, University of Chicago Press, Chicago, 1991.
Weber, M., 'The Religions of Asia', W.G. Runciman (ed.), *Weber: Selections in translation*, Cambridge University Press, Cambridge, 1978. The article was translated from *Gesammelte Aufsatze zur Religionssoziologie*, 2nd edn, Tubingen, 1923, II, s. 363-78.
Wood, S. (ed.), *The degradation of work?: Skill, De-skilling and the Labour Process*, Hutchinson, London, 1982.
Yasunaga Toshinobu, *Ando Shoeki: Social and Ecological Philosopher of Eighteenth-Century Japan*, Weatherhill, New York, 1992.

Encyclopedias, dictionaries

Aoki Kazuo, et. al. (eds.), *Nihonshi Daijiten*, Heibonsha, Tokyo, 1992-1994.
Hepburn, J.C., *Waei Gorin Shusei*, American Presbyterian Mission Press, Shanghai, 1867, 1872.
Kindaichi Kyosuke, et. al. (eds.), *Nihon Kokugo Daijiten*, Shogakukan, Tokyo, 1972-1976.
Kokushi Daijiten Henshu Iinkai (ed.), *Kokushi Daijiten*, Yoshikawa Kobunkan, Tokyo, 1972-1994.
Maeda Isamu (ed.), *Edogo no Jiten* (Kodansha Gakujutsu Bunko), Kodansha, Tokyo, 1991 (first published in 1979).
Morrison, R., *A Dictionary of Chinese Language*, Black, Parbury, and Allen, London, 1822.
Niimura Izuru (ed.), *Kojien* third and revised edition, Iwanami Shoten, Tokyo, 1983.
Takenaka Yasukazu, 'Sengo ni okeru Sekimon Shingaku no Bunken to Kenkyu', Takenaka, *Sekimon Shingaku no Keizai Shiso*, A Supplementary.
Tsuchiya Tadao, et. al. (eds.), *Nippo Jisho* (Japanese-Portuguese Dictionary - translated into contemporary Japanese language from Vocabvlario Da Lingoa De Iapam: com a declaracao em Portugues of 1603), Iwanami Shoten, Tokyo, 1980.
Yagi Shigeki, 'Ninomiya Sontoku Kankei Shuyo Bunken', Nagasawa Motoo (ed.), *Ninomiya Sontoku no Subete*, Shin Jinbutsu Oraisha, 1993.

Bibliography

Archives consulted
Hotoku Hakubutsukan, Odawara
Keio Gijuku Daigaku, Tokyo
Keizai Kenkyusho, Hitotsubashi Daigaku, Tokyo
Kokuritsu Kokkai Toshokan, Tokyo
Meirinsha (Shingaku), Kyoto
Sekimon Shingakukai, Tokyo

INDEX

Agoin Gidō-Shōshichi, 164-65, 200, 202
Analects, the, 51, 53, 96
Andō Shōeki, 193, 194
Applebaum, Herbert, 37, 39
Asao Naohiro, 29

Bakumatsu period, 6, 14, 39, 109, 199, 202
Bellah, R.N., 7-8, 58, 196
Bitō Masahide, 28-29
Braverman, H., 76
Buddhist, 53-54; see also Zen

Calvinist, 86
Ch'eng-Chu, 58
Chou Tun-yi, 54-55
Chu Hsi, 54-55
Chuang tzu, 51
Classical School, 61
'Code on the Way of the Family', 102
'Collection of Ninomiya's Words On Things', 124, 126
Confucian, 5, 40, 51, 53-54, 60, 122-23, 128, 198

de Bary, William T., 58, 62

economic development, 23, 34-36; compared to England, 35, 77-78, 79-80; population decline, 141; villages in 19th century, 139-41; see also shihō programme, village economy

Fukaya Katsumi, 9
Fukuzumi Masae, 122, 200

Great Learning, the, 51, 53

Harootunian, H.D., 13-14, 57
Heaven, 27, 55-56, 84, 112; in thought of Ninomiya, 124-30
Hiraishi Naoaki, 31
Historical Meanings of Work, The, 24
Hodō Tsūkan, 26
Hōtoku movement, 6, 9, 19n6, 96, 99, 110, 199-205

Hōtoku Museum, Odawara, 9
Hōtokuki, 200
Hyakushō Denki, 119
ie (household), see Ishida Baigan, Ninomiya Sontoku
Ishida Baigan, 5, 15-18; Buddhism and, 53-54; career, 49-52; Confucianism and, 53; contrasted with Ninomiya Sontoku, 187-88; disciples, 52, 94-98; endorses social order, 193; experiences enlightenment, 59; exploited in government ideology, 6-7, 204; falsely stereotyped, 196-97; force for social change, 197-99; on household work, 11, 85-88; lectures, 51-52; Neo-Confucianism and, 54-61; on self-cultivation, 55-63, 66, 68, 87; on skill acquisition, 82-84; Shintō and, 53, 54; on trading, 64-68; see also Shingaku
Ishida Baigan Zenshū, 7
Ishida Sensei Goroku (Memoirs), 52, 82-83 (*cit.*), 100, 101, 183 (*cit.*)
Ishida Sensei Jiseki, 54
Ishikawa Ken, 7, 10, 19n9, 59, 93, Ito Jinsai, 61

jitsugaku, see practical learning school
Jōruri, 26
Joyce, Patrick, 3, 24

kachō, (household head), 32-33
Kafū Shikimoku, 102
kagyō (household work), 31-32, 36, 98
Kaibara Gakken, 26
Kaihō Seiryō, 194
Kaitokudō scholars, 13-14
Kaiyū Taishi, 97-98
Kamada Ryūō, 93
Kamiya Yoheiji, 200
Kinmōroku, 112-13, 120-21 (*cit.*), 131 (*cit.*), 184
Kojima Yasunori, 61
kokugaku (nativist school), 13
Kokura Masatsune, 103
Korea, 62

INDEX

Labor and Monopoly Capital, 76
Lao tzu, 51

Maruyama Masao, 128
Marx, K., 76
Mean, the, 51, 53
Meiji period, 6, 14, 103, 199-205; government ideology in, 6-7, 204-205
'Memorandum for the Well-Being of the Household', 82-83, 100, 101
Mencius, 51, 53, 54, 60, 65, 96, 98
Minamoto Ryōen, 62
minshūshi studies (*see* popular consciousness)
Miyamoto Mataji, 93, 100, 102-103
Miyauchi Yoshinaga, 27
More, Charles, 76
Muro Kyūsō, 26

Najita Tetsuo, 13-14, 61
Nakai Nobuhiko, 13, 163
Nakane Chie, 30-31
Nakazawa Dōni, 95, 97, 98-99
Nansō Satomi Hakkenden, 26
Naramoto Tatsuya, 9
Neo-Confucian, 5, 15, 26, 51, 54-62 *passim*, 83, 104n22, 111, 123, 187, 193, 198
Ninomiya Sensei Goroku, 200
Ninomiya Sontoku Zenshū, 9
Ninomiya Sontoku, 5-6, 16-18, 99; appointed to village restoration project, 143-44; career, 109-12; contrasted with Ishida Baigan, 187-88; disciples, 200; educates villagers, 159-61, 184; encourages immigration, 161-62; encourages industry and planning, 112-24, 182-83; endorses social order, 194-95; establishes rehabilitation, 149-56; exploited in government ideology, 6-7, 204; faces opposition, 147, 174n28; falsely stereotyped, 196-97, 204; force for social change, 197-99; household (*ie*) in thought of, 11, 120-22, 182, 185-86; humans and nature in thought of, 122, 124-30; links activity with spiritual affairs, 130-33; opposes intellectualism, 122-24, 187; 'virtue' in thought of, 112-13, 131-33; *see also* Hōtoku movement, shihō programme
Ninomiya-Ō Yawa, 200
Nōkaeki, 164

Ogyū Sorai, 28, 63-64, 65
Ōhara Yūgaku, 163
Okada Saheiji, 202
Okite, 102
Ōkura Nagatsune, 79, 164
Ōtō Osamu, 9
Ōtsuka Eiji, 9, 165-66

Pak, T., 62
popular consciousness, 13-15
practical learning school (*jitsugaku*), 61-63
'Provision of Household Business, A', 101
'Provisions', 102

religion, 7-8; *see also* Buddhism, Heaven, Shintō, Zen
Robertson, J., 93-94

'Sage Ninomiya's Evening Talks', 122
Saitō Masakado, 100-101, 102, 103
Saitō Osamu, 31
Saitō Takayuki, 200
Sakasai Takahito, 10
Sanpei Matazaemon, 164
Sasai Shintarō, 9
Sawada, Anderson, 93, 104n22
scholarship, *see* Shingaku, work
Seigaku movement, 163
Seikaron, 52, 54, 67
Sekimon Shingaku Association, 103
Sekimon Shingakushi no Kenkyū, 7, 93
Shibata Minoru, 7, 19n9, 52, 93
shihō programme, 6, 11, 17, 96, 99, 112; administration of, 172n1; aims of, 144; capital accumulation in, 145-47; competitive cooperatism, 188-91; credit facilities, 9, 147-49, 166; education, 159-61, 167; infrastructure development, 154-56; ini-

-228-

INDEX

tial survey, 144-45; investment plan, 149-52; labour incentives, 156-59, 188-89; land reclamation, 152-54; opposition to, 147, 174n28; settlement policy, 161-62; social welfare, 165-67, 178n76; success of, 138-39; 168-71; summary, 137-39; technology, 162-65, 183-85; types of, 171n1; *see also* village economy, Ninomiya Sontoku

Shingaku Kyōka no Honshitsu Narabini Hattatsu, 93

Shingaku, 5, 16, 51, 52, 55, 58, 59, 68n2, 70n11, 85; *bōsha* (academic centres), 94-6; decline, 98-99, 103; influence in trading houses, 99-103; in modern scholarship, 93-94; spread of, 94-96; survives into modern era, 103; teaching strategy, 96-8; *see also* Ishida Baigan

Shintō, 53, 54

Shoku Nihongi, 31

skill: in thought of Ishida, 82-84; linguistic terms, 78, 84; trading houses and, 80-82; Western valuation of, 76-80

Smith, T.C., 119, 184

Sugano Noriko, 165-66

Sugawara family, 26

Sugiura Munenaka, 101, 102

Sugiura Muneyuki, 94

Sugiura Shisai, 94

Sumitomo family, 103

Suzuki Shōsan, 53, 75

Takenaka Yasukazu, 102

Takizawa Bakin, 26

Tenmei Shichigenzu, (*cit.*), 113-33

Teshima Toan, 93, 94, 96

Teshima Wa'an, 95

Thompson, E.P., 78

Thompson, Paul, 76

Todoya Shōsaku, 174n28

Tohi-Mondō, 49, 52-53, 54, 55, 56, 60, 67, 83, 101, 105n22

Tokugawa Religion, 7

Tomita Kōkei, 200

trading houses, 50-51, 63-68, 72n41, 80-82, 99-103, 194

Turner, H.A., 77

Uekawa Kisui, 55, 93, 95

village economy: apathy in, 142-43; devastated by famine, 141, 142; financial insecurity, 140-41; growth of, 139-40; labour intensity, 142, 173n6; technology improvements, 163-65; *see also* shihō programme

Visions of Virtue in Tokugawa Japan, 13

Wang Yang-ming, 54, 61-62, 69n9

Watanabe Hiroshi, 56

Weber, M., 8, 20n11

work: ethic, 8, 196-97; in government ideology, 6-7, 204-205; household, 30-33; in modern scholarship, 6-15, 24, 85, 93-94, 185, 188, 195, 196; linguistic terms, 25-30, 31-33; multi-task concept of, 34-46; as self-cultivation, 10-12, 15, 16-17, 55-63, 66, 68, 87, 187-88; as social construct, 3-4, 195-96; social roles, 26-30; time-orientation, 119-120; *see also* Ishida Baigan, Ninomiya Sontoku, skill

yaku (service), 28-30

Yamaga Sokō, 61

Yasumaru Yoshio, 10

yogyō (additional tasks), 34-35, 38

Yu Ying-Shi, 61-62

Yura Hisahide, 102

Yura Shichihei, 102

Zen, 53, 88, 104n22

Zenkun (provisional training), 97